RECIPROCITY
1911

A STUDY IN
CANADIAN-AMERICAN RELATIONS

BY

L. ETHAN ELLIS
ASSISTANT PROFESSOR OF HISTORY IN RUTGERS UNIVERSITY

GREENWOOD PRESS, PUBLISHERS
NEW YORK

First Greenwood Reprinting, 1968

Library of Congress Catalogue Card Number: 68-57601

PRINTED IN THE UNITED STATES OF AMERICA

TO

MY WIFE

FOREWORD

THIS book is one more proof, if proof were needed, that the history of tariffs is much more than the register of the business interests of the nations concerned. The economic arguments advanced by the advocates of either protection or greater freedom of trade may quickly lose their allurements if other national interests are thought to be involved. Then politics takes command of the situation and public opinion swings away from problems of welfare to enlist in mass mobilization under the banners of nationalism. However much economic causation may operate in the relatively simplified field of domestic affairs, it is checked and modified in the dealings of countries with each other by influences which spring from circumstances of a totally different kind. Historical memories, friendships or hostilities in the past, a sense of neighborliness on the one hand or distrust and suspicion on the other may determine the course of international trade fully as much if not more than the opening of advantageous markets for either producer or consumer.

Nowhere else have these effects been more in evidence than in the history of customs tariffs between the United States and Canada. While there has been and still is a wide difference of opinion as to the effect of the various tariffs which both governments have either imposed or negotiated, there is no room for doubt as to their political implications. The history is one rich in incidents especially in Canadian politics. Its importance for the United States has been gaining recently owing to the new situation in which both the United States and the British Commonwealth of Nations have found themselves with reference to other nations, especially Germany and Japan. Statesmanship has found the way to use obstacles as stepping stones, until on both sides it is recognized that the patient insistence of Secretary Hull upon the moral values in fair and generous dealings between nations is good business as well as sound policy. In 1911 the theatre of action was not world wide, but the reaction to what was done or not done was none the less intense.

This volume, with its careful and detailed analysis of what happened in 1911, is a welcome addition to this series of studies on Canadian-American relations. Other studies in tariff history are planned and under way, but the subject is also one which enters into other studies in history and economics, both because of its own importance and because of the effect which it has had upon industry and commerce of both countries and upon the political fortunes of those who have taken sides in the major issues of the past. But while Professor Ellis' history of the episode of 1911 gains in interest with the exploration of the wider field, it is a story of dramatic interest in itself, and the author presents it, not in the abstract terms of political argument, but as a vital human document.

J.T.S.

AUTHOR'S PREFACE

THIS study presents the results of an investigation into the forces underlying and conditioning an experiment in the field of international trade. It attempts to indicate the setting of uneasiness and multiple dissatisfactions on both sides of the Canadian-American border out of which came William Howard Taft's offer and Sir Wilfrid Laurier's acceptance of a reciprocity which as negotiated carried large possibilities of mutual advantage. It surveys the development of opinion and of legislative discussion and action on both sides of the border, culminating in success to the south and in an appeal to the country and failure to the north. An effort is made to clarify the activities of interested parties, political and economic, and to show their influence, through skillful manipulation of the organs of propaganda and public opinion, upon the issue in each country.

As the story proceeds it becomes increasingly apparent that on neither side of the frontier was the question wholly decided upon its merits. To the south reciprocity became a battleground whereon was fought a skirmish in the background of the 1912 presidential campaign and whereon was won a battle for the advancement of the economic interests of the newspaper press; this in addition to whatever benefits the agreement might have brought the country at large. To the north its obvious economic advantages to the producing classes were obscured by a smoke screen of national and Imperial patriotism designed to induce repudiation of the agreement. Behind the scenes the discerning reader will discover at work protected interests and their allies, direfully fearful of any slightest breach in the tariff wall behind which they had grown strong. The whole story gives evidence that the "undefended frontier," of which so much has been written loosely, was in reality defended by something stronger for the moment than bullets, bayonets, and battleships—an aroused desire for self-sufficiency adroitly fostered by those who could profit by such self-sufficiency.

Acknowledgments may be briefly if sincerely rendered. First place should be given the author's wife, Elizabeth Breckenridge Ellis, who has patiently lived with both reciprocity and one of its students during the four years of this study's progress. To the Carnegie Endowment for International Peace goes the author's gratitude for making possible the study's publication. If reader and reviewer find merit in its pages, much credit will be due to the following who have read and criticized either all or part of the manuscript: J. Bartlet Brebner, Edward McNall Burns, Whidden Graham, Harold A. Innis, Alexander Johnston, Clara Marburg Kirk, Joseph E. Ridder, and James T. Shotwell. The author's files contain many letters from contemporaries and participants from which have been drawn fact and interpretation to verify or modify his own findings; that their writers prefer to remain anonymous should not detract from the value of their contribution. Particular mention should be made of permission to use the papers of William Howard Taft, not generally accessible at the time the study was undertaken.

L. E. E.

New Brunswick, New Jersey
May, 1939

CONTENTS

RECIPROCITY, 1911

CHAPTER I

TARIFF BACKGROUND OF RECIPROCITY

THE year 1911 contributed a significant chapter in the long history of Canadian-American tariff relations. Since 1866, when the United States abrogated the Elgin-Marcy Treaty of 1854, tariff reciprocity had never been far from Canadian minds and had been of at least intermittent interest to Americans. This agreement had given United States fishermen privileges in Canadian waters and had established free trade between the two parties in a considerable number of articles. Its abrogation by the United States, because of a complex of local, national, and international frictions and antagonisms, sharply curtailed the volume of cross-border trade and deprived Canada of a principal market. In the United States it was the symbol of triumphant protectiveness; in Canada it was an irritant to both pride and pocket.[1]

The cavalier treatment by her southern neighbor helped to launch Canada upon a tariff history at first concerned in considerable part with regaining lost advantages. These overtures proving fruitless, Canada explored other avenues of economic self-sufficiency and inaugurated, with bipartisan support, a "National Policy" designed to render her independent of the United States. This independence established, the Dominion entered a period of outward indifference to the issue of closer trade relations with the Republic which lasted until complex circumstances caused the responsible heads of each to seek in a renewal of reciprocity the solution of pressing personal, party, and national problems.

Beginning in 1866, there followed an era of Canadian efforts to secure restoration of reciprocity by negotiation and by retaliation. Thrice between 1866 and 1874 were attempts made at renewal, twice by concurrent legislation and once by treaty in the latter year.[2] Meantime the Anglo-American Treaty of Washington in

1. Keenleyside, H. L., *Canada and the United States: Some Aspects of the History of the Republic and the Dominion*, New York, 1929, pp. 299–302.
2. Porritt, E., *Sixty Years of Protection in Canada, 1846–1907: Where*

1871 had carried among its numerous provisions one reopening the Canadian fisheries, at a price, to the United States. This disappointed those Canadians who had desired to make the fisheries a means of prying trade concessions from their reluctant neighbor.[3] After the United States abrogated this part of the treaty in 1885 the Dominion attempted to use the fisheries as a makeweight in this direction. In the same year a Canadian law authorized the Governor General to lighten or remit duties on fish and fish products whenever the United States should reduce her levies on imports from Canada. With minor modifications this offer remained open until 1907.[4]

The Canadian Liberal government in 1874 carried negotiation to the point of a formal treaty proposal through the agency of George Brown and Hamilton Fish. This treaty, drafted with one eye on American manufacturers, disgruntled because the Elgin-Marcy agreement failed to give them desired access to Canadian markets, dropped all trade barriers on a list of sixty natural products, forty agricultural implements, and thirty-seven other manufactured articles. Conversely, it was not particularly kind to budding Canadian manufactures, already seeking benefits of tariff protection. Brown was willing to tie Canada to this broad offer for twenty-one years, after which either party might abrogate upon three years' notice. It was not accepted by the United States Senate.[5]

The Conservative government elected in 1891 fulfilled an election pledge by sending a delegation to Washington in 1892. This was met with James G. Blaine's refusal to deal on any basis short of free trade in manufactures and natural products and a united tariff front against other countries. Protectionist sentiments had by this time so taken possession of Conservative party doctrine that the Canadian negotiators refused concessions on other than natural

Industry Leans on the Politicians, London, 1908, pp. 161–173. This work, allowing for the author's antiprotectionist bias, serves as a useful outline of the period covered.

3. United States Tariff Commission, Reciprocity with Canada: A Study of the Arrangement of 1911 (pamphlet), Washington, 1920, p. 28.

4. Rutter, F. R., Tariff Relations of Canada (pamphlet), Washington, 1911, p. 11. Department of Commerce and Labor, Bureau of Manufactures, Tariff Series, No. 26.

5. Porritt, Sixty Years, pp. 165–174.

products, and the conference terminated unsuccessfully.⁶ Thus, so far as actual negotiations went, no headway was made down to 1896, when Wilfrid Laurier began his long career as head of a Liberal government; the Canadian official position had tended to change from one favoring broad reciprocity to one limited to reciprocity in natural products. This change and its relationship to the reciprocity problem can perhaps be better understood by a brief survey of Dominion tariff legislation. Such a survey will show that Canadian tariff policy was for some years compounded of a growing protectionism, eventually taking possession of both parties, and of a desire to leave the door open to reciprocity with the United States.

As early as 1870 a Canadian tariff (which contained an offer of reciprocity) taxed many articles previously admitted free, on the basis of Sir John A. Macdonald's dictum that Canada's hope of regaining reciprocity lay in making Canadian restrictions burdensome to the United States. This act, an early example of Conservative protectionism, was mainly retaliatory in character and directed toward forcing American concessions, and was unsuccessful.⁷ Its passage and repeal in 1871 mark a step in the advance of the Conservative party to its ultimate stand as the champion of protection. This Conservative progression involved some years of tariff agitation in the course of which the protected interests appealed more and more successfully to Conservative leaders, who leaned more and more toward the American policy of a tariff wall designed to safeguard industry.

This trend, patterned after the American model and developed in part in reply to American indifference to Canada, came to be called the National Policy and was formally embodied in a resolution offered by Macdonald to Parliament on March 12, 1878:

This House is of opinion that the welfare of Canada requires the adoption of a National Policy, which by a judicious readjustment of the tariff will benefit and foster the agricultural, the mining, the manufacturing, and other interests of the Dominion; that such a policy will retain in Canada thousands of our fellow-countrymen who are now obliged to expatriate themselves in search of the employment denied them at home; will restore prosperity to our struggling industries now

6. *Ibid.*, pp. 177–178.   7. *Ibid.*, pp. 165, 266–267.

so sadly depressed; will prevent Canada from being made a sacrifice
market; will encourage and develop an active inter-provincial trade;
and moving, as it ought to do, in the direction of a reciprocity of tariffs
with our neighbours, so far as the varied interests of Canada may demand, will greatly tend to procure for this country eventually a reciprocity of trade.

Here, evidently, protection has become an end in itself; however, its
use as a means conducing to reciprocity is still prominent, as evidenced in the resolution and in Macdonald's remarks supporting it.
The resolution was defeated but later in the same year Macdonald
and his party returned to power. His government formally launched
Canada upon the National Policy, which had as one objective the
regaining of reciprocity and which presently became thoroughly
protectionist through an alliance with the manufacturing interests.
As has been seen above, these developments had been paralleled in
time by a series of efforts to negotiate reciprocity—efforts which
were repeatedly discouraged by the United States until it became
fairly evident that success was unlikely.[8]

However hopelessly, Canadian tariff laws through 1894 carried
formal offers of reciprocity in some products. The Conservative
tariff of 1879 permitted the Governor General to admit animals,
some minerals, and several agricultural products, upon adoption of
a similar policy by the United States. This, amended in 1888, was
replaced in 1894 by a series of separate articles angling for reciprocal concessions on such commodities as hay, barley, apples, shingles,
wood pulp, and eggs. Meeting no encouragement, these provisions
were repealed in the Tariff Act of 1897. Thus Canada, in a series of
negotiations and legislative enactments, gave repeated evidence of
her desire to open United States markets to the products of her
farms and fisheries.[9] Meanwhile, the protective policy had produced
in the Dominion a situation comparable to that in the United States
after the Civil War: the emergence of a tariff-fed group of industrialists with connections interweaving the fabric of Canadian economic life.[10]

8. *Ibid.*, pp. 282–325; U.S. Tar. Comm., *Rec. with Can.*, pp. 27–28.
9. U.S. Tar. Comm., *Rec. with Can.*, p. 28; Rutter, *Tar. Rel. of Can.*,
pp. 11–12.
10. Porritt, *Sixty Years*, p. 384.

Thus it was that when Laurier and the Liberals came to power in 1896 it was easy to forget the low-tariff and proreciprocity planks which had largely aided their election, and to slip into a relationship with the protected interests not unlike that of their Conservative predecessors. There is evidence, however, that this forgetfulness, so generously spread upon the record by Laurier's opponents in 1910–11, was not entirely premeditated nor, indeed, altogether his fault. Rather, it was largely the realization of the finality of American lack of interest which drove the Liberal government to adopt a Conservative type of economic nationalism which had already gained a considerable hold upon the Canadian people. Laurier early put out a reciprocity feeler toward the United States. Rebuffed, he replied with a public statement which was to plague him in 1911: "There will be no more pilgrimages to Washington. We are turning our hopes to the old motherland."[11] The Dingley Tariff of 1897 struck a further blow at waning Canadian hopes. Laurier's final effort to secure concessions came in connection with the meeting of the Joint High Commission, charged in 1898–99 with consideration of all outstanding Canadian-American problems. Again tariff adjustment was discussed but the American delegates held out no hope and the matter was dropped.[12]

11. U.S. Tar. Comm., *Rec. with Can.*, p. 28; Harpell, J. J., *Canadian National Economy: The Cause of High Prices and Their Effect upon the Country*, Toronto, 1911, pp. 157–158. In the *Philander C. Knox Papers* in the Library of Congress is a memorandum drawn up by Charles M. Pepper for the use of President William H. Taft in July, 1909, entitled "The Open Door to Canada," which contains the following: "When Major McKinley was elected President in 1896 Sir Wilfrid Laurier and the Liberals were in power and it was their decision to make a final effort for permanent reciprocal trade relations on a broad basis. Mr. Laurier went to Cleveland early in 1907 [1897] and had an interview with Major McKinley at Myron Herrick's home. He proposed to wipe out all the custom houses on the boundary and was confident his government was strong enough to carry such a policy. Major McKinley said that it would be impossible to secure concurrent action in the United States but he thought material concessions might be made and a reciprocal tariff be established."

It should be noted further that the famous "no more pilgrimages" statement did not preclude adoption of a receptive attitude toward any desirable moves which might be made by the United States.

12. Pepper, "The Open Door to Canada." A somewhat different view of

Thus a combination of domestic protectionism and American rebuffs fostered in Canada Liberal adoption of the National Policy
originated by their opponents. The result was that the Dominion
tariff of 1897, sponsored by William H. Fielding, increased many
duties. It also contained an innovation—a tariff preference for the
products of the United Kingdom, an adroit device enabling Canada
to retaliate against the American Dingley rates without raising the
general tariff level.[13] So the turn of the twentieth century saw the
situation at a stalemate, with the United States indifferent to Canada's overtures and the latter resisting American coldness by building an insulating wall of protection behind which the warmth of the
British preference had begun to dispel the earlier frigidity.

The new cycle opened with nearly a decade of political indifference to reciprocity, combined with persistent efforts of Canadian
protected interests, largely unscathed by the Dingley Tariff, to secure retaliatory measures against the United States. General elections were held in 1900, 1904, and 1908, in none of which was reciprocity an issue.[14] When in 1905–6 the Laurier government prepared
to revise the tariff, a commission held sixty-seven public hearings
preparatory to the legislation. Edward Porritt, an English journalist, traveled seven weeks with this group in Ontario, Quebec, New
Brunswick, and Nova Scotia, following which he wrote that "the
reciprocity movement is dead beyond all possibility of early resur-
rection."[15] Beneath this seeming indifference, however, agrarian dissatisfaction with high protection in Ontario and the Prairie Prov-

the prospects in 1898 is given by John Ball Osborne, chief of the Bureau of
Trade Relations of the Department of State. Writing in *The Annals of the
American Academy of Political and Social Science,* 32:342 (September,
1908), he says that the Commission had made "substantial progress toward
an agreement on the subject of commercial reciprocity . . . when the sessions came to an abrupt termination as the result of a disagreement respecting the settlement of the Alaskan boundary dispute. There is every reason to
believe that a satisfactory treaty of reciprocity could have been arranged had
the Canadian commissioners been willing to conclude independently of the
Alaskan boundary."

13. U.S. Tar. Comm., *Rec. with Can.,* p. 28.

14. Foster, G. E., "Canadian Autonomy and American Reciprocity," *The
Nineteenth Century and After,* 69:965 (June, 1911).

15. "Canada's Tariff Mood Towards the United States," *The North American Review,* 182:577 (April, 1906). *Cf.* also his *Sixty Years,* pp. 425–435.

inces awaited only a proper combination of circumstances to flare into a demand for reciprocity with the United States as a means to the larger end of tariff reduction. The year 1907 saw the next step in the crystallization of Canadian tariff policy relative to the United States with the establishment of a triple-schedule tariff; at the top were the maximum rates of the general schedule; at the bottom, about a third lower, were the British preferential rates; and intermediate between these a bargaining schedule which an Order in Council might bestow upon countries according trade favors to Canada.[16] These last were not intended to apply to the United States, but to open to Canada other markets which would render her increasingly independent of American products.

Despite these brave assertions of indifference, born of necessity, and these policies of national and Imperial self-defense, Canada never abandoned hope of better trade relations.[17] Indeed, a representative of some Minnesota business interests, investigating in the winter of 1902–3 the possibility of reconvening the High Commission for a consideration of reciprocity, derived from his interviews with Laurier and other members of the government conclusions which he presented to Taft in 1910 as still valid. He wrote the President that

the Government as then constituted . . . was far more desirous of a reciprocity agreement with this country than they are willing to intimate or wanted any one to know, but that, thoroughly understanding the political situation in our country, they meant to take at all times full advantage of it, both in securing all they could for their own country, and in guarding themselves against such rebuffs and failures as their previous efforts had met with.

It seemed to this investigator that the principal reason for Canadian hesitancy at this time was fear of the United States Senate, and that "if the Canadian government could be convinced that the Senate of the United States would ratify a treaty, they would be eager for it and would make very substantial concessions in it."[18]

16. U.S. Tar. Comm., *Rec. with Can.*, p. 29.
17. Patton, H. S., "Reciprocity with Canada. The Canadian Viewpoint," *The Quarterly Journal of Economics*, 35:575 (August, 1921).
18. Eugene G. Hay to Taft, March 29, 1910. *Eugene G. Hay Papers*, Library of Congress.

South of the border the situation which had conduced to Canadian disappointment and subsequent outward indifference was one of long standing. Like all long-standing situations it had bred both general and particular dissatisfactions. Essentially a protectionist country since the Civil War regardless of party changes, the United States had in two successive revisions, the McKinley Tariff of 1890 and the Dingley Tariff of 1897, raised the principle of protection to the status of a fetish.[19] After the latter revision a burgeoning imperialism, combined with issues of pressing domestic importance and Theodore Roosevelt's canny sense of the explosive qualities of the tariff, kept that question in the background for several years. Early in the century, however, a bogey called the "High Cost of Living" appeared and there were those who suggested that the tariff might have raised the specter. This conviction gathered headway until in his message of December 2, 1907, Roosevelt prepared the deluge by saying: "In a country . . . such . . . as ours it is probably well that every dozen years or so the tariff laws should be carefully scrutinized. . . . In my judgment the wise time to deal with the matter is immediately after such [Presidential] election."[20] Thus adjured, the Republican platform of 1908 advocated a special session of Congress to revise the rates immediately after the inauguration of the new President.

Together with this general dissatisfaction with the tariff, a number of American interests, several of them beneficiaries of protection, shared Canada's chagrin at the repulse of reciprocity. In addition to those academic advocates of low tariffs or free trade who viewed reciprocity as a move in this direction, the movement attracted many who envisioned in reciprocity political or economic advantage and whose motives were far from altruistic. Together they created a

19. It should be noted that the McKinley Tariff contained a provision designed to secure reciprocity in noncompeting products such as sugar, coffee, tea, and uncured hides. It allowed the President to suspend the provisions of the act allowing these commodities free entry into the United States if at any time he became convinced that the exporting nation was placing discriminatory duties on imports of American agricultural commodities. *Statutes of the United States of America, Passed at the First Session of the Fifty-first Congress, 1889–1890, and Recent Treaties and Executive Proclamations*, Washington, 1890, p. 612 (cited subsequently as *U.S. Stat. at Large*).

20. *The Congressional Record, Washington*, 1874 ff., 60th Cong., 1st Sess., p. 71 (cited subsequently as *Record*).

situation favorable to the development of reciprocity sentiment. In 1901, for example, there was held at Washington a National Reciprocity Convention under the auspices of the National Association of Manufacturers.[21] A National Reciprocity League functioning from Chicago in 1902–3 had on its board of directors G. Watson French, chairman of the executive committee of the Republic Steel and Iron Works of Chicago, James Deering of the Deering Harvester Company, C. B. Hoffman, a miller of Enterprise, Kansas, A. Karpen of Chicago, president of the Karpen Furniture Company, and S. R. Calloway of New York, president of the American Locomotive Company. This group was expanding, as evidenced by the formation of a branch in Minneapolis in January, 1903.[22] A New England Reciprocity League was at work in that industrial section and its enthusiastic secretary insisted that "the reciprocity movement is beginning to sweep the state."[23] And as early as 1906 James J. Hill, the railroad potentate of the Northwest, had begun to advocate reciprocity so volubly and so cogently that in the Senate debate of 1911 William E. Borah could refer to him as "the real author of reciprocity in this country of late years" and could say of him that "he has furnished all the arguments I have ever, as yet, heard advanced in its behalf."[24] A map of the Northwestern railroads clarifies his interest—numerous branches of the Hill system running fanwise north to the Canadian border and eager to serve as arteries of the increased commerce which reciprocity might bring.

Thus the developments of years had produced on each side of the border a general situation in which there were factors of uncertainty. To the north repeated rebuffs, a new tariff orientation, and prosperity fathered an outward indifference which was tempered by a

21. November 19–20. Its proceedings were reported in *Circular of Information of the National Association of Manufacturers of the United States of America* (pamphlet), Philadelphia, 1911, No. 43.

22. Hay, E. G., *Reciprocity with Canada: Report of Eugene G. Hay, to the Advisory Board of the Minnesota Branch of the National Reciprocity League, upon the Present Attitude of United States and Canada and the Prospects for Reciprocity between the two Countries* (pamphlet), Minneapolis, n.d., p. 2.

23. W. E. Brigham to Eugene G. Hay, March 17, 1904. *Hay Papers.*

24. Pyle, J. G., *The Life of James J. Hill*, 2 vols., Garden City, New York, 1917, II, 287–288; *Record*, 62d Cong., 1st Sess., p. 2576.

feeling in high quarters that good commercial relations with the United States, on self-respecting terms, were desirable. To the south the blessings of a decade of high protection were being increasingly called in question and interested groups were actively at work to break down the tariff wall to the north. The Payne-Aldrich Tariff revision of 1909 furnished the catalysis which precipitated the elements of this unstable equilibrium into the economic and political life of both Canada and the United States.

CHAPTER II

TWO ANXIOUS MEN

As the year 1909 wore on into 1910 two chiefs of state faced an immediate future which was to bring to each disappointment, disillusionment, and defeat. In the nation served by each a complex of circumstances was preparing for public attention an old issue long politically quiescent; an issue on the one hand ignored and on the other forsworn. To the south reciprocity was to become the focus of a growing impatience with things as they were and the vehicle of uncertain gropings toward a better order. To the north it was to register disapproval of affairs as they had been conducted and to transfer the management of affairs to those who would continue the former pattern. To the individuals involved it offered on one side of the border an opportunity to assert a leadership hitherto lacking in a cause which it was hoped would serve many and antagonize few; on the other a chance to gain a new lease on a long life by renewing the quest for a long-sought goal. The leadership came too late and the lease had no renewal clause.

In Washington, William Howard Taft, heir to "My Policies," was finding his heritage a burden. Coming home to him, too, were the fruits of his own alliance with the standpat elements of his party and of their victory in legislation. Answering the popular cry for relief from the high cost of living, the party had placed in the platform on which Taft was elected a plank echoing Roosevelt's call to tariff reform. Convoked in special session, March 15, 1909, Congress proceeded to organize. Immediately there appeared an omen evil for the future: thirty-one members of the President's party joined the opposition to defeat a routine motion adopting the rules of the previous House of Representatives. This marked the appearance of a fairly cohesive group, mainly from midwestern farm states, which lost no opportunity to daub dark colors on party tariff policy. Its members, indeed, demanded tariff reform so lustily that later, when offered reduction in the unpalatable form of reciprocity, they were forced into some elaborate gymnastics to explain their divergent positions.[1]

1. U.S. Tar. Comm., *Rec. with Can.,* pp. 29–31.

Presently Sereno E. Payne of New York introduced the bill that was to fulfill Republican promises. It bade fair to do so, ran the gauntlet of attacks by Democrats and midwestern Republicans, and went to the Senate. Here most of the 847 amendments tended upward, and the Conference Committee generally sustained the raises.[2] Standpattism, under the lead of hard-bitten Nelson W. Aldrich of Rhode Island, had blasted the hopes of millions who had vaguely expected Taft to call down the manna of relief from high prices. More articulate than the disappointed millions were the newspaper publishers, thwarted by the act's provisions in their bitter fight with the American manufacturers of newsprint paper. This commodity had paid $6.00 per ton under the existing schedules. The Payne bill carried a duty of $2.00 per ton, pursuant to the recommendation of a special committee appointed in 1908 under the chairmanship of James R. Mann of Illinois, which had spent ten months in a thorough study of the newsprint situation in the United States and Canada. This committee was appointed at the instigation of the publishers and its findings, as written into the Payne bill, were presumably acceptable to them.[3] In the Senate this favorable action was reversed and a rate of $4.00 per ton, subsequently reduced in the Conference Committee and the final act to $3.75, was substituted. The publishers blamed Taft for this blow at their pocketbooks, asserting that the conferees had substantially agreed upon a compromise rate of $3.00 per ton,

when President Taft announced to Congressional callers on or about Saturday, July 24th, that a $4 rate was necessary for the application of the protection principle to print paper. The President made this *ex parte* decision without that full and impartial ascertainment of cost to which the consumers were entitled, and in disregard of numerous assur-

2. *Ibid.*, pp. 31–32.

3. *Reciprocity with Canada: Hearings before the Committee on Finance of the United States Senate Sixty-Second Congress on H.R. 4412 An Act to Promote Reciprocal Trade Relations with the Dominion of Canada and for Other Purposes, Senate Document 56,* 62d Cong., 1st Sess., Washington, 1911, p. 1234 (cited subsequently as *Sen. Doc. 56*). Reprint of a report of John Norris to the American Newspaper Publishers Association, April 26, 1910. Payne himself considered that this rate was unfair to the American manufacturer. W. H. Taft to Horace Taft, June 27, 1909. *William Howard Taft Papers* (Library of Congress).

ances volunteered by him in favor of the lower rate. In accordance with that intimation from the President, the conferees reported $3.75 per ton.[4]

The results were a hostile press, largely irrespective of party affiliations, directed against the legislation as a whole, and a feeling of frustration on the part of the press which was to result in renewed efforts to influence the administration in favor of lower rates on newsprint.[5]

Having thus incurred the enmity of the press, Taft blundered still further by defending his handiwork. In a speech which was to be meat and drink to his enemies, he defended the act at Winona, Minnesota, on September 17 as "the best tariff measure ever passed by a Republican Congress, and hence the best tariff bill the people have ever known."[6] This aligned him in the minds of most observers with the Aldrich-Cannon standpatters, an impression which he was later to seek means of correcting.

In the summer of 1909 the Roosevelt heritage still further burdened the Taft administration. As part of his much-touted conservation policy Roosevelt had ordered withdrawn from private entry large tracts of valuable land, but was unable to secure Congressional confirmation of his action. Taft's Secretary of the Interior, R. A. Ballinger (originally a Roosevelt appointee), was convinced that these withdrawals were illegal and restored a number of areas to private operation. Attention was called to this action by Gifford Pinchot, head of the National Conservation Commission (also a Roosevelt appointee), who alleged that Ballinger was knifing con-

4. *Bulletins of the American Newspaper Publishers Association,* No. 2037, "B" Special, August 3, 1909, p. 545.

5. Porritt, E., "The Value of Political Editorials," *The Atlantic Monthly,* 105:65 (January, 1910): "Condemnation by the press was almost universal, without regard to party lines." Taft wrote Theodore Roosevelt some months later that the act "did not cut low enough the rate on print paper and so we have had a hostile press, and this whether Republican or Democrat." May 26, 1910. *Taft Papers.*

6. *New York Tribune,* September 18, 1909. No general list of newspapers and periodicals has been appended to this volume, but in course of its preparation some forty American and twenty-seven Canadian newspapers, and forty-nine periodicals from both sides of the border have been examined for all or part of the period covered by the narrative.

servation. Ballinger was also accused by L. R. Glavis of the Public Land Office of conniving at the too hasty exploitation of Alaskan coal lands by the Guggenheim-Morgan interests. Forced by his sense of the legal proprieties to back Ballinger, Taft removed Pinchot and allowed the dismissal of Glavis. The storm engendered by these incidents resulted in a Congressional investigation exonerating Ballinger and in the latter's ultimate resignation under fire in March, 1911. It also indicated to many liberals that Taft was no longer on the side of the angels.[7]

In 1909 occurred also what to many was a misstep in foreign policy, almost resulting in coöperation in the international exploitation of China. In November the Knox-Taft "Dollar Diplomacy" proposed that the United States join several other powers in lending China funds to enable her to take over immediately several Manchurian railroads which existing treaties permitted her to purchase at a later date. This move, though intended to aid China to preserve her national integrity, was viewed in many quarters as involving the United States in dangerous entanglements. Paralleling these neutralization negotiations came an American proposal to participate in a four-power consortium to finance the Hukuang Railway in the Yangtze Valley. During the discussions Taft took the unusual step of communicating directly with the head of the Chinese government to urge American entry into the affair. As the administration carefully explained through a public statement of Secretary of State Philander C. Knox, in January, 1910, the United States was concerned largely with aiding China in both these moves. Nevertheless, "Dollar Diplomacy" got a bad name and some of the odium adhered to the Chief Executive.[8]

In March of 1910 began the famous emasculation of the Speakership. Aroused Insurgents led a move to strip Joseph G. Cannon, heir and efficient wielder of the scepter bequeathed by "Czar" Reed, of part of his prerogatives. This cost him his membership on and right to appoint the all-powerful Committee on Rules, which largely controlled the course of legislation. It had been packed, as had other

7. Hacker, L. M., and Kendrick, B. B., *The United States Since 1865*, New York, 1932, pp. 410–412.

8. Bemis, S. F. (ed.), *The American Secretaries of State and Their Diplomacy*, 10 vols., New York, 1927 ff., IX, 327–333.

committees (also chosen by the Speaker), with leaders of the stand-pat, conservative type. Its reorganization meant that no longer could Cannon keep the Insurgent-Democratic opposition quiet.[9] It meant, too, that the thunder of the opposition would boom louder in the ears of the man in the White House. And in November a new Congress was to be elected.

Shortly after the Cannon episode Eugene N. Foss was elected to Congress as a Democrat in the strongly Republican fourteenth Massachusetts district, and the problem of November had become an acute one. In what the *Boston Daily Advertiser* called "the first test of public opinion regarding the first year's record of the Republican administration" Foss launched his by-election campaign on a platform containing a variety of national issues, including anti-Cannonism, free raw materials, and reciprocity with Canada.[10] When the excitement had died down somewhat it was discovered that a number of local factors had rendered the issue less clear-cut than at first it had appeared. Foss, originally a Republican, was running against a former Democrat, whose efforts to secure the nomination were of questionable honesty. Foss promised not to run for the regular term in the autumn and it was alleged that many voted for him because of this, as a protest against his opponent.[11] The fact remained, however, that he had won as a Democrat in a Republican district and that he had talked better trade relations with Canada. Well might the President send an Iowa correspondent a labored explanation of these complications; November was not far off.[12]

All in all the times were troubled for Mr. Taft. Tariff reform a boomerang, the powerful press hostile, foreign policy under attack, Congress in a turmoil, and the country showing signs of revolt, small wonder that he sought a way out of the woods. A path must if possible be opened to the clearing before a November storm closed the way. Meantime the tariff act had created an emergency which, aggravating in itself, brought the two governments into negotiation and seemed in its aftermath to offer a way of escape. This was the controversy over the maximum and minimum provisions of the Payne-Aldrich Act.

9. Hacker and Kendrick, *The U.S. Since 1865*, pp. 392–395.
10. March 14, 1910.   11. *Ibid.*, March 23, 1910.
12. To J. L. Waite, Burlington, March 24, 1910. *Taft Papers.*

If all was not quiet on the Potomac, neither was all serenity on the heights above the Ottawa. Sir Wilfrid Laurier and the Liberal party which he had long led were feeling the combined influences of fourteen years in office, a series of embarrassing incidents spreading wide over the Dominion, an increasingly vocal Western demand for tariff revision, and the approach of a general election. These factors caused the wily leader to turn to the political breezes a nose keen to discover some program which would insure himself and his party another term in office. Presently his questing brought downwind a once-familiar scent—reciprocity with the United States.

The Liberal machine, long in service, was beginning to develop creaks and signs of obsolescence. These were more apparent in the machine than in its guide, whose erect carriage and robust activity belied his years. He realized the facts, however, and faced them frankly. Many of the leaders with whom he had risen to power had passed off the scene; he remained as head of a group composed partly of oldsters and partly of those who had come forward under his own leadership. Part of his energies had been perforce devoted to preserving harmony between the old and the new groups in his party and its leadership. Inevitably, furthermore, long tenure brought the increasing burdens of continued incumbency; burdens due to errors both of omission and commission. Good fortune, prosperity, a comfortable alliance with Canadian business interests, and the lack of an effective opposition had long minimized these burdens. But by 1910 he realized that, lacking a real issue on which to revive his party's fortunes, he must eventually follow it into oblivion. A year earlier, indeed, he had written in condolence to a defeated candidate for a local nomination: "What has happened to you in your county will happen to me before long in Canada. Let us submit with good grace to the inevitable."[13] An editorial written in the Toronto *News* viewed him in October, 1910, as being, for the first time since assuming power, on the defensive in Quebec, Saskatchewan, Alberta, and British Columbia, and not gaining ground in Ontario or the Maritimes, concluding: "After fourteen years of office nothing else should be expected."[14]

13. Quoted in Dafoe, J. W., *Laurier: A Study in Canadian Politics*, Toronto, 1922, p. 124.

14. *The News* (Toronto), October 10, 1910. A similar opinion from be-

In addition to the general burdens of the long-in-office, the party had accumulated an administrative record which, while probably no worse than the Conservatives would have acquired under similar circumstances, offered a broad target for opposition shafts. Department after department and individual after individual had incurred charges of extravagance, inefficiency, and actual graft. Relatively little formal criticism had been leveled at this situation prior to 1910, but a feeling of restiveness had reached a point where any untoward incident would bring hostility to the surface. Two such incidents offered themselves. In May of 1910 the Prime Minister was questioned in the Commons concerning a testimonial gift of $120,000 with which an anonymous group of donors had honored his Minister of Finance, William H. Fielding. The matter had been undertaken some months earlier with Laurier's consent in order to assure Mr. Fielding a competence in his declining years after a long career in the public service. Reaction to the episode was divided. Part of the Conservative press commended the action. Other journals made insinuations as to the contributors and Laurier felt impelled to declare that neither the Bank of Montreal nor other such organizations had participated. The sniping had begun.[15] The same session focused public attention upon a problem which was to be freighted with important consequences: the Canadian navy became a parliamentary issue which passed on to the country and furnished Laurier, in the autumn of 1910, with considerable food for thought.

The German saber-rattling in 1909 actuated the delicate mechanism which registers British concern for the adequacy of the fleet. Debates in the homeland brought Canadians to consider Dominion obligations in time of Imperial crisis, and in March Parliament adopted a resolution, supported by the leader of the Opposition, Mr.

low the boundary is found in *The Nation,* 91:258 (September 22, 1910): "Never since Laurier came into office fourteen years ago was there more discontent with his Administration . . . than on the eve of the assembling of the Dominion Parliament for the session of 1910–11."

15. Hopkins, J. C. (comp.), *The Canadian Annual Review of Public Affairs,* Toronto, 1901 ff., 1910, pp. 222–223. This useful annual compendium has been drawn upon by the author for accounts of several episodes not essential to the development of the reciprocity story and in some instances for quotations from newspapers to which he has not had access. Cited subsequently as *Can. Ann. Rev.*

Robert L. Borden, favoring a Canadian navy. January 12, 1910, Laurier introduced the Government's plan to implement the resolution proposing the construction, at Canadian charges of over eleven millions, of eleven vessels to be manned by a volunteer force. By this time Conservative opinion had veered a bit and Borden advocated contributing to the British Admiralty a sum sufficient to pay for two dreadnoughts. He opposed committing Canada to a permanent naval policy without a plebiscite. A third point of view was presented by F. D. Monk, a French-Canadian Conservative from Quebec, who voiced the growing nationalism of his people by opposing either navy or contribution until after an election. Around these viewpoints raged a long and bitter Parliamentary debate which canvassed the problem of national integrity and imperial obligations from all angles.[16]

Monk's opposition was abetted by the powerful French journal, *Le Devoir*, published under the aegis of Henri Bourassa, a Liberal of somewhat mercurial temperament. These and other leaders launched an attack on the naval program and all who condoned it, Governor General Earl Grey, Laurier, and Borden alike being used as stalking-horses for a fiery appeal to the nationalist sentiments never far beneath the surface in French Canada. The whole episode, indeed, called forth a display of feeling not equaled since Canadian military participation in the Boer War had evoked similar attacks. Feeling remained at a high pitch all summer and the stage was well set for an event of early November which was to give Laurier to think almost as seriously as his fellow chief-of-state was given to think by the Congressional elections—the by-election in the Quebec constituency of Drummond-Arthabaska.

On October 19, 1910, was announced the appointment to the Senate of Louis Lavergne, a Liberal Member of Parliament. This vacated the riding in Laurier's home county which he had first represented at Ottawa. It was soon apparent that the immediate issue would be Laurier *versus* the navy, and the larger one, his hold upon his Province and upon the whole Dominion. Drummond-Arthabaska

16. *Ibid.*, 1910, pp. 139–208, covers the development of opinion and policy in Parliament and the country. The same author reviews the situation briefly in an article, "Canada's Conservative Policies," in *The North American Review*, 194:818–825 (December, 1911).

had been Liberal since 1887 and the least majority any candidate had received was 834. Quebec was also Liberal, but presently the Government found its candidate fighting for his life against a determined onslaught by the combined forces of Monk and Bourassa, aided by many Ultramontanists and ultraconservative Bleus. The crisis in Government fortunes was apparent, as defeat in this normally Liberal constituency, hedged about by all its associations with the Premier, would brand party and leader with shame. The party candidate, Mr. J. E. Perrault, defined the issue in his acceptance speech, October 18:

The Nationalists want to fight us. Let them come on, then. They have boasted that the people of the Province are behind them, but I call on you to aid in proving that the Province of Quebec is behind Sir Wilfrid Laurier and that it desires that victory rest with the Liberal party. I appeal to all moderate men to vote for a policy that has contributed so much to make the Dominion of Canada what it is to-day. We must demonstrate that in the Counties of Drummond and Arthabaska we recognize what Sir Wilfrid Laurier has done and that the Naval Bill enjoys the confidence of the people.

Sir Wilfrid appeared personally to support the candidate and plead their joint cause. Seventy Liberal speakers, the Opposition press asserted, were decanted into the district in an effort to swing the issue.

Monk and Bourassa spoke jointly in a vitriolic denunciation of the navy, of the Imperial connection, of Laurier and of all his works, with particular emphasis on the pet Nationalist bogey, the argument that the navy would lead inevitably to conscription: " 'A day will come,' said Bourassa, 'when draught officers will be scouring the country and compelling young men to enlist either in the Navy or the Army, to go to foreign lands and fight the battles of Great Britain, to co-operate with Downing Street in the oppression of weak countries, and to maintain, at the price of their blood, the supremacy of the British flag in Asia or Africa.' "[17] The Nationalist spellbinders injected further appeals to race, religion, and prejudice into the campaign. Their candidate won by 207, a result viewed by the Nationalist press with jubilation and by the Liberal and Conservative journals of the Dominion with mingled sentiments. All agreed

17. Quoted in *Can. Ann. Rev.*, 1910, p. 196.

upon the seriousness of the portent; many Liberal sheets took it as an omen of future danger, evidencing the party's loosened hold on Quebec and the urgency of renewed activity in a cause not yet lost; Conservative papers saw in the result a threat to the Government not confined to Quebec but Dominion-wide. And none of this was lost upon Sir Wilfrid himself who meantime had faced a further breath of discontent blowing across the Prairie Provinces, whither he had betaken himself during the summer preceding the Drummond-Arthabaska election.[18]

While Eastern industrial interests enjoyed the benefits of their alliance with the Liberal party the Canadian Middle West had been less fortunate. Peopled largely by migrants from Ontario and immigrants from Britain and the United States, primarily devoted to large-scale staple-crop agriculture, the West had certain inevitable needs and felt the pull of former ties. The Laurier ministry had not met these needs, including transportation, control of grain elevators and the chilled-meat industry, and cheaper agricultural implements, to their satisfaction. Their memories of British free trade and of cheaper agricultural implements in the United States made many of them desire lower tariffs. For some years Western interests had been forwarded by active farmer organizations which may for present purposes be included under the term "Grain Growers." These groups voiced increasing dissatisfaction with the shortcomings of the Ottawa government. All in all, the West was in a touchy frame of mind on several important matters and had been irritated by several factors of more strictly local application. The Premier had not visited that section since his accession to power. A general election could not, in the nature of things, be far off in the year 1910. The new census, to be taken in the summer of 1911, would call for a redistribution which would considerably increase the twenty-seven Commons seats filled from the Prairie Provinces. When, therefore, Sir Wilfrid announced in April a summer tour of the West, the farmers began whetting their axes on the rough edges of long-deferred hopes. The Western summer was to be warm for Laurier in more ways than one.[19]

18. *Ibid.*, pp. 192–211; Toronto *News,* October 24, 28; November 3, 4, 1910.

19. April 20 he promised a delegation of Western Liberals that he would

Shortly after the Premier's announcement the wheels of agitation started turning. The influential *Grain Growers' Guide*, organ of the prairie farmers, suggested as early as May 18 that the tour would offer a good opportunity "to bring before Sir Wilfrid an idea of what the western farmers think of the tariff." Its editorial platform as outlined May 25 included government ownership of terminal elevators, abolition of the protective tariff, construction of a railroad linking the West with salt water through Hudson Bay, and federal control of the chilled-meat industry. In the same issue Roderick McKenzie, secretary of the Manitoba Grain Growers' Association, urged his adherents to formulate their desires for presentation to the Premier. The Manitoba Executive (committee charged with interim management of the association's affairs) on June 3 reiterated the problems at issue and first mentioned reciprocity specifically, "emphasizing specially the importance of the Dominion government taking advantage of the offer of the United States government for a Reciprocity Treaty and the accepting of the offer of the United States government for reciprocal Free Trade in agricultural implements."[20] As soon as Laurier promised to meet the Manitoba farmers at Brandon it was proposed to impress upon him the desirability of tariff reduction and "the advisability of the government accepting the offer of the United States government to enter into negotiations for a reciprocity treaty."[21] The foregoing seems a fair picture of the farmers' feelings at the time: the tariff was one of a number of general grievances, probably second to the terminal-elevator and Hudson Bay Railroad questions in importance; reciprocity in agricultural implements met a pressing need and offered an entry to the larger problem of tariff reduction; and before long the question of general reciprocity was brought forward. It was, however, at this stage only one of a number of points of attack and by no means the primary consideration in the farmers' minds; it was more or less an afterthought and decidedly a means to an end.

Laurier's Western tour opened at Fort William, Ontario, on July

spend two months in the West, taking with him other leaders of the party. *The Globe* (Toronto), April 21, 1910.

20. *The Grain Growers' Guide* (Winnipeg), June 8, 1910.

21. *Ibid.*, June 22.

10, continued through Manitoba, Saskatchewan, and Alberta to British Columbia, with a return swing into Alberta, ending at Medicine Hat, September 2. The Premier addressed fifty-seven meetings and delivered an equal number of car-platform talks. More to the point, he was made the recipient—perhaps target would be a better word—of numerous and pointed suggestions as to his duty. What started out as a "promising campaign," concerned largely with discussions of the transportation situation, presently found Laurier facing large numbers of determined farmers who wanted to know about the tariff.[22] At Brandon he was met on July 18 by a large delegation from the Manitoba Grain Growers' Association and interrogated sharply on the general question. Reciprocity was here first openly discussed. Laurier evidently dodged the issue thus raised, declaring himself in sympathy with much of their program, but insisting that he was at present seeking information. The *Guide* asserted that he "did not answer a single argument that the Grain Growers put to him at Brandon."[23] At Melville, Saskatchewan, July 22, the farmers again demanded reciprocity, and in reply he asserted: "I am in favor of reciprocity if the United States gives us a fair deal. At no time have our relations been so cordial and friendly as at present, but human nature—and the United States has much human nature—prompts man to reciprocate with the man who is himself prepared to reciprocate."[24]

Numerous demands along other lines were presented and were generally met with a statement to the effect that he was willing to consider reciprocity, but the tariff was a complicated subject upon which haste must be made slowly and that the Government would try to act for the best interests of the entire country.[25] Several times

22. *Can. Ann. Rev.*, 1910, pp. 265–286, outlines the principal meetings with issues discussed at each. The *Grain Growers' Guide* gives the part played by that organization. The author has relied here, as all through the study, primarily upon two daily papers for his narrative of *facts:* the Toronto *Globe,* staunch supporter of the Laurier regime, for the Canadian side, and the New York *Tribune,* semiofficial spokesman for the administration, for the story in the United States. Subsequent footnotes will, of course, give evidence that matters of opinion and interpretation have been drawn from widely variant sources.

23. July 27, 1910. *Cf.* also Toronto *Globe,* July 19.

24. Toronto *Globe,* July 23, 1910.   25. *Ibid.,* August 4, 5, 12, 1910.

he proposed the establishment of a tariff commission to investigate the whole Canadian tariff structure—a device not unknown to statesmen in the United States when the question has threatened to become a live political issue. Thus he completed his tour with the tariff, among other matters, very much to the fore (and it must be clearly remembered that this discussion has borne upon only one of a number of important, controversial, and pressing issues which were discussed by press and Premier during the journey), and left the fiscal issue "hung up between the announced Royal Commission of Inquiry into the Tariff and the promised Reciprocity negotiations with the United States. The Premier, therefore, returned without having refused anything of importance for which he was asked by the West and with the one new and most difficult proposition held over for other and later developments."[26] The West had placed him definitely on the defensive on the tariff and reciprocity questions, had convinced him of the sincerity of its demands for remedies along both lines, and had given clear evidence of dissatisfaction with his promises.[27] For even before his caravan had wheeled eastward from British Columbia the *Grain Growers' Guide* had begun an agitation that was to take hundreds of farmers to Ottawa in December to urge more specific promises from the Premier who had, somehow, failed to promise very much in July and August.[28] And may not Sir Wilfrid, during the long train journey from Medicine Hat to Ottawa, have bethought him of the possibilities of a limited reciprocity with the United States, as a palliative for Western low-tariff demands which might be administered without seriously upsetting his comfortable relations with the Eastern manufacturers?[29] At any rate, he had been given cause to think.

26. *Can. Ann. Rev.,* 1910, p. 285.

27. The *Guide* for August 10 commented on his suggested tariff commission: "There is no need of any commission. Sir Wilfrid knows exactly what the farmers meant." And September 7: "There has been no honest and sincere attempt to secure better trade relations with United States [*sic*]. . . . The Western farmers want tariff reduction and better relations with United States." And the friendly *Globe* commented that he would "not soon forget the protests of the western people against being taxed first under a protective tariff and then by excessive freight rates."

28. This idea appears in the issue of August 17 and those succeeding.

29. Dafoe, J. W., *Clifford Sifton in Relation to His Times,* Toronto, 1931, p. 360.

An organization for registering Canadian rather than merely Western agrarian discontent had existed for some months. The Canadian Council of Agriculture had been set up as a result of prolonged correspondence between several farmers' groups. The names of its officers and their other farmer affiliations will indicate the scope of the group which sponsored the most formidable demonstration so far staged to influence a Canadian Government: president, D. W. McCuaig (also president of the Manitoba Grain Growers' Association); vice-president, James Bower (president of the United Farmers of Alberta); secretary-treasurer, E. C. Drury (Master of the Dominion Grange). Management of details was entrusted to Roderick McKenzie of the Manitoba Grain Growers' Association.[30] A proposed delegation to make representations to the Premier relative to terminal elevators was held back and merged with the larger group. On September 22 Drury requested an audience for the organized farmers of Canada "in regard to the tariff and other matters." It was desired to hold the interview following the meeting of the Dominion Grange, after Parliament was in session, prior to the budget speech and late enough to enable the Westerners to secure the advantage of winter excursion rates on the railroads. This careful setting of the stage was urged in order to insure the farmers an opportunity to influence any tariff discussions the session might bring forth. December 16 was chosen as fulfilling all these requirements.[31]

It was proposed to hold a meeting of the delegates in Ottawa shortly before the interview to formulate demands, which Drury indicated on October 17 would be somewhat as follows:

It is probable that the delegation will ask for the best reciprocal terms that can be arranged with the United States on agricultural products and agricultural implements, as well as certain things that are commonly used on farms, as cement, drain tile, and a few other articles. A commission, to make thorough inquiry into the working of the tariff,

30. *Grain Growers' Guide*, February 23, November 16, 1910; Dafoe, *Sifton*, p. 361.

31. *Report of Proceedings in the Hearings by Members of the Government of the Farmers' Delegation, December 16, 1910, With Correspondence Preliminary to the Hearing*, Ottawa, 1911, pp. 3–7. (I Geo. V. Sessional Papers No. 113.)

would be asked for. . . . It is likely that a substantial increase in the British Preference will be asked for.[32]

Pursuant to this proposal, the National Council of Agriculture assembled on December 15, numbering according to different accounts from 800 to 1,000. Every Province was represented, but 500 of those present were from the West, 250 from Ontario, and the rest mainly from Quebec, with a scattering few from the Maritimes. The press was excluded from the morning session because of fear that the Eastern farmers might object to Western radicalism. Little bickering developed, however, and four hours of discussion produced a series of resolutions to be presented to the Prime Minister and his Cabinet for submission to Parliament. The first of these urged reciprocal free trade in all horticultural, agricultural, and animal products, spraying materials, fertilizer, fuel, illuminating and lubricating oils, cement, fish, and lumber. The second advocated reciprocity in all agricultural machinery, implements, vehicles, and parts thereof. The third and fourth proposed immediate increase of the British preference to 50 per cent and gradual lowering of this rate to provide for free trade with the mother country after ten years. Finally, the group declared that the farmers were willing to face the prospect of direct taxation to make up any loss of revenue resultant from this new fiscal orientation.[33] A new tone pervaded the resolutions. Whereas in the summer Laurier had faced a number of issues, with reciprocity not the most important, here were but two—reciprocity and a stronger Imperial preference. Granting that the resolutions represented the Council's considered opinion, and that the Council represented the farmers of the Dominion (which Conservative journals were not slow to deny), a new force was to be dealt with.

The following day witnessed a remarkable scene in the House of

32. *Ibid.*, p. 8. George F. Chipman of the *Grain Growers' Guide*, who was influential in organizing the "Siege of Ottawa," wrote the author, May 8, 1935, that he was in close touch with Dr. J. E. Jones, American Consul at Winnipeg, during the preparations. Jones in turn was in contact with Washington and was in a position to know what concessions the administration would make in a possible negotiation. The result was that "we framed our demands upon the government all in accord with the Washington suggestion."

33. Toronto *Globe*, New York *Tribune*, December 16, 1910.

Commons, which filled to overflowing with farmers come to state their demands, for such was their tone, rather than one of petition. They spoke through McCuaig and J. W. Scallion and registered their program in a series of resolutions more inclusive than those of the previous day but with reciprocity still the dominant factor. As in the summer, terminal elevators, chilled meat, and the Hudson Bay Railroad occupied considerable space. The tariff came last and according to both leading speakers was most important of all.[34] Faced by this challenge—but perhaps mindful that the Canadian Manufacturers' Association had a delegation in the city to watch proceedings as well as to invite the farmers on a tour of the Eastern industries as an antidote for their low-tariff sentiments—the Premier spoke warily. While sympathizing with their desires for lower rates on natural products, he carefully guarded his language respecting manufactured articles and referred specifically to pending negotiations which should not be disturbed. He reiterated that nothing would be done to impair the British preference.[35]

The farmers were disappointed, though their spokesmen expressed understanding of the "reasonableness" of Laurier's reply to their requests.[36] Nevertheless the press contained rumors of complaint and plain statements that he had not gone far enough.[37] And the *Grain Growers' Guide* felt that "there is little that may be expected from the government" and that the Premier had shown himself an Easterner against the West.[38] It was plain that a new issue had

34. *Report of Proceedings,* pp. 9 ff.

35. Toronto *Globe,* December 17, 1910. As reported, his remarks were: "There are difficulties in this which no Government can ignore, and we are not ignoring them. But at all events we see our goal, and in this our goal is very much in your own direction. But you go farther, and say that in this particular session we should commence to amend the tariff also. I suggest to you that as practical legislators it would be hardly advisable for the Parliament of Canada to undertake this session to revise the tariff while our negotiations are pending with our neighbors. Upon this I will say no more."

36. McKenzie spoke for them: "We recognize the reasonableness of Sir Wilfrid's public statement on the tariff, that so long as negotiations were pending with reference to reciprocity no action would be taken on the tariff." *Globe,* December 21, 1910.

37. New York *Tribune,* December 17; Toronto *News,* December 23, 1910.

38. December 21, 1910.

arisen in the land and that in addition to rising Nationalism in Quebec, Laurier had an aroused agrarianism to deal with.

Thus by the end of 1910 domestic factors had placed both Taft and Laurier on the defensive. Each had met economic criticism from widespread areas and had received political warnings: Taft in Western Insurgency and the choice of a hostile Congress; Laurier in the Grain Growers' revolt and Drummond-Arthabaska. Against this background of rising disturbance on both sides of the border the two governments had been negotiating for some months. These parleys, starting as an adjustment of a specific problem growing out of the Payne-Aldrich Act, seemed first to Taft and then to the Canadian Premier to offer hope of solving larger problems by reverting to a reciprocity which, as the negotiations proceeded, grew to proportions surpassing in economic and political importance the expectations of either party to the arrangement.

CHAPTER III

PUBLISHERS AND PAPERMAKERS

ALLUSION has already been made to the controversy between the makers and users of newsprint paper.[1] The American Newspaper Publishers Association, representing the latter interest, played no slight part in the story leading up to reciprocity. Furthermore, the press of the United States largely reflected Association policy during the discussion and passage of the agreement. An outline of the controversy prior to the Canadian-American negotiations of March, 1910, over the maximum provisions of the Payne-Aldrich Tariff has therefore seemed desirable. Thereafter an effort will be made to include in the regular narrative the respective roles played by the protagonists of publisher and manufacturer. The reader should note that the following chronicle is a chapter in a conflict still current, enacted by men whose acts and opinions are reflected by those with whom the author has had contact through interview and correspondence. The publishers were to win, in the reciprocity fight, one round in a long battle which ultimately discomfited and nearly ruined the manufacturers. The evidence available on both sides is extremely partisan. If the following discussion leans, in fact and in interpretation, toward the publishers' contentions it may be partially due to the greater volume of information preserved in the press and in Association files and partly to the Association's greater willingness to permit the exploitation of this information. Finally, it should be noted that the following story does not propose to parade all the battalions that waged the struggle, but merely to recount such skirmishes as have some bearing on the main subject under consideration.

The publishers' story is one of repeated and strenuous attacks upon alleged high prices and monopolistic control. The manufacturers vainly fought to maintain, behind the wall of tariff protection, the right to supply the American market under conditions which they themselves would lay down. In this battle both parties sought and at various times secured the support of the federal government.

1. *Cf.* above, p. 12.

The story opens with the government siding with the manufacturers; as it progresses these win another partial victory in the Payne-Aldrich Act of 1909, only to lose, as a result of reciprocity, in 1911. All of this to an obbligato of crimination and recrimination.

The Dingley Tariff of 1897 laid duties of $1.67 per ton on mechanically ground wood pulp and $6.00 per ton on the cheapest grades of newsprint, with countervailing duties against pulp and paper coming from areas which taxed exports of pulpwood.[2] These duties were imposed at a time when improving machinery and methods had driven down the price of newsprint in the United States, endangering the domestic manufacturer whose machinery was not of recent installation. In the light of these developments the International Paper Company was formed in January, 1898, by the consolidation of twenty-four mills, absorbing about 80 per cent of newsprint production and including nearly every important Northeastern mill.[3] After some years of sparring during which the International allegedly burdened the publishers with obnoxious conditions and increased prices, hostilities began in earnest in 1907 and 1908, following a threatened further price increase.[4] In the summer of 1907 Herman Ridder of the New York *Staats-Zeitung*, president of the A.N.P.A., was forced to make his paper contract for the following year at an advanced rate, following which, in September, he called his organization into special session and launched a fight to reduce prices. After this, in season and out of season, he belabored

2. U.S. Tar. Comm., *Rec. with Can.*, p. 47.

3. Palmer, L. B., *Light on the Print Paper Situation* (pamphlet), New York, 1917, p. 4; *Sen. Doc.* 56, 62d Cong., 1st Sess., pp. 1155–1161. It was the contention of the publishers, represented by John Norris from whose testimony the above facts are in part taken, that the mills of its constituent firms were largely obsolescent, that they could not compete with those having more modern machines, and that the early effect of the organization was to curtail production and raise prices to the consumer through monopoly control.

4. The A.N.P.A. convention of 1900 urged Congress to investigate the price of newsprint, which it was alleged had increased from 60 to 100 per cent. The Association also urged the prosecution under the Sherman Anti-Trust Act of the General Paper Company, a combination of Wisconsin and Minnesota manufacturers. It was dissolved by the courts in 1906. Palmer, *Light on Print Paper*, pp. 4–5; *Sen. Doc.* 56, 62d Cong., 1st Sess., pp. 1157–1158.

Congress, the President, and the public with blasts against the "trust" and demands for relief of his special interest.[5] Two others ably seconded his labors: Don C. Seitz, publisher of *The New York World*, and John Norris. Seitz, whose name appears less frequently in the press accounts, was an able journalist who appears to have functioned effectively behind the scenes with counsel and advice. Norris, with Ridder, formed the spearhead of the publishers' drive. By his own boast a contender for cheaper newsprint since 1896, he had been connected with the *World* and was in 1907 business manager of *The New York Times*. When the fight grew warm he was brought from that journal to become chairman of the A.N.P.A.'s "Committee on Paper," which in normal times furnishes the trade with information on supplies, prices, and general market conditions, and which on occasion becomes a lobbying agency to prevent adverse tariff legislation. His connection with the committee and with the fight lasted until the Underwood Tariff of 1913 registered complete victory. The campaign was financed by the Association, in 1911 comprising slightly over three hundred of the country's two thousand dailies, through an assessment of five cents per ton of newsprint consumed. With this war chest Norris went to work collecting data which he, like Ridder, used to belabor anyone considered influential; and as a result he became the bête noire of the manufacturers and a powerful factor in the ultimate attainment of free newsprint.[6]

The first tangible result of publishers' pressure was the Mann Committee's investigation into the newsprint industry, already mentioned.[7] Appointed in April, 1908, the committee worked ten months and recommended free ground wood and a duty of $2.00 per ton on newsprint.[8] This proposal seemingly suited the publishers and was

5. Palmer, *Light on Print Paper*, pp. 5–6; *Sen. Doc.* 56, 62d Cong., 1st Sess., pp. 1261, 1279. After reading this chapter, Mr. Joseph E. Ridder, son of Herman Ridder and familiar with the circumstances herein described, suggested to the author that his father, Norris, and Seitz were all interested in reciprocity from the standpoint of a general lowering of tariff barriers, which they favored, as well as because of their pecuniary interest in free newsprint.

6. *Sen. Doc.* 56, 62d Cong., 1st Sess., pp. 1137–1145, 1302–1318; interview with Lincoln B. Palmer, general manager of the A.N.P.A.

7. *Cf.* above, p. 12.

8. *Report on Pulp and Paper Investigation, House Report* 2206, 60th

included in the Payne bill as it left the House. It was also framed with an eye to soothing northern susceptibilities, Canadians having made the point that in order to secure Canadian pulpwood free of export charges, papermakers below the line ought to permit reduction of the rate on Canadian-made newsprint to a reasonable level. As has been seen, the Senate raised the rate on newsprint to $4.00 per ton and the final act set it at $3.75. The publishers laid the blame for this failure of their aims at the door of everyone whom they wished to make uncomfortable: Senator Aldrich, activated by the International Paper Company, President Taft, Senator Robert M. LaFollette, and Senator Eugene Hale were variously charged with responsibility.[9] Furthermore, the act "retained the previous rates and the countervailing duties on pulp, with the provision that ground pulp should be free when sent from a Province which imposed no restrictions, contractual or otherwise, upon the export of any of its paper, pulp, or mechanically ground pulp wood." As has been seen, the rate on newsprint was reduced from $6.00 to $3.75 per ton, but the manufacturers were solaced for this slight reduction by "a provision for the levy of a surtax of one-tenth of a cent per pound, in addition to the countervailing duty, upon paper from any Province restricting exports of printing paper, wood pulp, or pulp wood."[10] These retaliatory measures applied to Ontario, which had already prohibited exportation of pulpwood cut from Crown lands, and to Quebec, which it was feared might do likewise.

The situation thus created offered considerable possibilities of friction. The International had extensive timber rights in Quebec

Cong., 2d Sess., Washington, 1909; *Record,* 60th Cong., 2d Sess., pp. 2700–2702.

9. Norris advanced the LaFollette theory in a statement to the Associated Ohio Dailies, February 2, 1910. *Reciprocity with Canada: Hearings before the Committee on Finance of the United States Senate on H.R. 32216 An Act to Promote Reciprocal Trade Relations with the Dominion of Canada and for Other Purposes,* Senate Document 834, 61st Cong., 3d Sess., p. 175. April 26 the Committee on Paper reported to the A.N.P.A. that Aldrich had insisted on the $3.75 rate. *Sen. Doc.* 56, 62d Cong., 1st Sess., p. 1234. In September, 1909, the A.N.P.A. had asserted that the Senate had inserted the raise to please Senator Hale. A.N.P.A. *Bulletin,* No. 2066, "B" Special, September 27, 1909, p. 721.

10. U.S. Tar. Comm., *Rec. with Can.,* p. 47.

Crown lands, obtained largely on the strength of a promise made by the Provincial Premier in September, 1900, that the stumpage rate of sixty-five cents per cord levied on such timber would not be raised for ten years. Quebec had not yet prohibited exportation of Crown land pulpwood, but enforcement of the Payne-Aldrich retaliatory measures might induce such action, either in September, 1910, or earlier. This might force the removal of the papermaking industry to Canada, a consummation not entirely objectionable to Canadian interests. The tariff act, however, contained a club which might be wielded against anyone attempting such action: this was a provision allowing the imposition, after March 31, 1910, of maximum duties of 25 per cent ad valorem, in addition to the regular rates, against any country or province thereof which discriminated against the United States.[11] The publishers charged that both the retaliatory and maximum rate provisions had been inserted at the behest of the papermakers, with the object of bullying Canada into providing the United States with a steady supply of pulpwood; and that this was done in contrast to their own conciliatory policy as proposed by the Mann Committee and embodied in the Payne bill which had passed the House. Their contention is given some color by a statement of C. W. Lyman, connected with the International Paper Company, late in 1909. Referring to the maximum provision of the tariff he is reported to have said: "It would be an unfortunate thing to have to invoke the application of this provision against any of the provinces of Canada on account of their attitude in this matter of pulp wood exportation, but this provision was incorporated into the law for just such a purpose and was so drawn as to exactly cover this particular situation."[12] Thus it would appear that the Payne-Aldrich Tariff gave some comfort to the manufacturers, who were still protected at a reduced rate which was potentially enhanced by the retaliatory and maximum provisions of the act.[13]

A far-reaching train of consequences was launched by a Treasury

11. *U.S. Stat. at Large, 1909,* p. 82.

12. Quoted in A.N.P.A. *Bulletin,* "B" Special, No. 2099, December 4, 1909, p. 859.

13. *Sen. Doc. 56, 62d Cong.,* 1st Sess., p. 1234; A.N.P.A. *Bulletin,* "B" Special, No. 2057, September 14, 1909, p. 609; No. 2169, April 7, 1910, p. 284.

Department circular of August 26, 1909, imposing the retaliatory duty of $2.00 per ton on print paper made from wood cut from Crown lands in Ontario and Quebec.[14] This raised the total duty to $5.75. On September 6 Premier Lomer Gouin of Quebec announced that the Province, at a date yet to be decided, would join Ontario in prohibiting the exportation of unmanufactured wood cut from Crown lands.[15] This left impending the possibility of the imposition, March 31, 1910, under the maximum provisions of the Payne-Aldrich Act, of an additional 25 per cent levy on Canadian newsprint, computed at about $8.75 per ton, bringing the total possible duties to the prohibitive figure of $14.50. The likelihood that the Dominion might be subjected to the maximum rates was enhanced by the fact that Canada had negotiated a treaty with France whereby the latter received preferential rates which might be interpreted as discrimination against the United States, thus subjecting not only newsprint but all Canadian goods imported into the States to the 25 per cent additional rate.[16] Thus a long-standing controversy over the price of newsprint and the control of the market had insinuated itself first into the enactment of tariff legislation in the United States and then into the relations between that nation and her northern neighbor.

That the President was at least partly responsible for this state of affairs was brought home by a sharp letter addressed to him by Ridder, October 18, 1909, with which this pulp-and-paper background of our story may well be concluded. It closes on a minatory note which was practically a demand for remedial action. Referring to the presidential remarks on the newsprint clause of the Payne-Aldrich Act in his ill-starred Winona speech, Ridder said:

With the utmost respect, we submit that your statement respecting the paper schedule shows that you could not have correctly read or

14. A.N.P.A. *Bulletin,* "B" Special, No. 2066, September 27, 1909, p. 719. The actual duty on paper coming from Quebec was $2.35, due to a countervailing duty imposed to offset the Quebec export tax of twenty-five cents per cord on pulpwood cut from Crown lands. It takes 1.4 cords of wood to make a ton of print paper. *Ibid.,* No. 2053, September 3, 1909; New York *Tribune,* August 28, 1909.

15. A.N.P.A. *Bulletin,* "B" Special, No. 2066, September 27, 1909, p. 719.

16. *Ibid. Cf.* also No. 2037, August 3, 1909, p. 546.

understood what the print paper paragraph contained, as it passed the House of Representatives.

You were apparently misled by designing men into a serious blunder when, in the closing days of the tariff conference, they induced you to reverse your previous attitude on print paper, and changed your notions of what the Mann Committee recommended and of what the House of Representatives had approved. The Mann Committee . . . reported that a rate of $2.00 would cover the difference in cost of production at home and abroad. The draft proposed absolutely safeguarded American paper mills against the serious Canadian tangle which your advice to the tariff conferees has since precipitated.

The fixing of the rate on print paper at $3.75 per ton, which you advised, has decided the Province of Quebec to prohibit the exportation of its pulp wood, and many American paper mills must close or move to Canada to obtain their supplies of raw materials. The country is now in a fair way for a trade war with Canada because of your apparent failure to read carefully the Mann Committee's recommendations. We are threatened with an industrial disturbance which will involve business interchanges with Canada amounting to $285,000,000 per annum.

We trust that you can find some method of rectifying the mistake into which you were led. We fully appreciate the difficulties and responsibilities of your exalted office, and we believe you are trying to do the best you can. We know that you must rely upon others for your information. We feel that every citizen is under obligation to help you. Therefore we write this letter to you.[17]

17. *Taft Papers.*

CHAPTER IV

RECIPROCITY PROPOSED

As has been seen in a previous chapter, the winter and spring of 1910 brought Taft's embarrassments to a focus. The Insurgent defection was under way. Cannon was unhorsed in March and with his fall went effective control over the House. Others in the party resented the Payne-Aldrich Tariff and the press was vocal because of the act's failure to provide more favorable terms for newsprint. An election loomed in November—an election which Taft frankly feared.[1] The month of March also witnessed a minor crisis in Canadian-American relations, resulting from the maximum provisions of the Act of 1909—a crisis in which, as the result of a timely personal intervention in diplomacy and with Canadian coöperation, the President was able to avert a threatened trade war and to lay firm the foundations of wider negotiations looking specifically to reciprocity.

February saw both governments preparing for the discussions necessarily arising from the prospective application to imports from Canada of the maximum rates levied by the Payne-Aldrich Act against countries or dominions discriminating against the United States.[2] The question of discrimination resulted from the intermediate schedule of the Canadian tariff of 1906, a scale below the general level, to be extended by order in council to nations according return favors to Canada. Under this bargaining arrangement a treaty had been negotiated whereby France granted Canada her

1. He wrote H. H. Kohlsaat, March 14, 1910: "I have not been familiar myself with any situation politically where there has been so much hypocrisy, so much hysteria, so much misrepresentation by the press growing out of their own personal interest in legislation as within the last year. . . . I am quite willing to admit that this endangers the success of the Republicans in the next House." *Taft Papers.*

2. Indicated by an exchange of letters between Taft and H. C. Emery of the Tariff Commission, February 19, *Taft Papers;* and by a confidential memorandum of the twenty-second addressed by Fielding to Earl Grey, Governor General of Canada. *Tariff Relations between the United States and the Dominion of Canada: Correspondence Concerning Negotiations 1910* (pamphlet), Ottawa, 1910, p. 4 (cited subsequently as *Tar. Rel.*).

minimum rates on numerous Canadian commodities and in return received the Canadian intermediate levies on certain French exports to Canada. The problem facing the tariff officers of the United States was: Did the Canadian concessions to France constitute a discrimination against the United States and so force the imposition of the maximum rates of the Payne-Aldrich Act against the Dominion after March 31, 1910? After careful study it was decided that exports from the United States to Canada valued at about twenty millions of dollars, as of the fiscal year 1909, were placed at a disadvantage in the Canadian market by the favorable terms of the Franco-Canadian agreement. It would therefore be impossible to waive the maximum provisions of the Payne-Aldrich Act respecting Canada unless the Dominion conceded to the United States treatment similar to that accorded France.[3] In view of these circumstances the Department of State, mindful of the diplomatic proprieties but anxious to open discussion, approached the British Embassy with a request for negotiation.[4] Taft was represented as, in prospect, feeling "keen regret if, merely for the lack of opportunity for sympathetic and frank negotiation, the maximum tariff of the United States should automatically become operative upon Canadian products imported into the United States after March 31." The American Consul General at Ottawa, J. G. Foster, was summoned to supply any needed information, and it was announced that Knox was considering sending experts to Ottawa to seek further facts. It was intimated that "by the force both of logic and of precedent" negotiations should take place at Washington, either through the

3. *Canadian Tariff Negotiations,* pp. 1–2. This pamphlet, marked EX-CEPTIONALLY CONFIDENTIAL. TO BE FILED AS A CONFIDENTIAL DOCUMENT AND ISSUED ONLY UPON THE WRITTEN ORDER OF THE SECRETARY OF STATE, is in the *Knox Papers.* It contains an invaluable compilation of correspondence and memoranda covering the negotiations through November 18, 1910, and data bearing upon the general background of reciprocity, much of which is in manuscript form in the Archives of the Department of State. It was evidently compiled by Charles M. Pepper. Cited subsequently as *Can. Tar. Negot.* The March negotiations are covered in a memorandum drawn up by Pepper and dated April 19, 1910, in which numerous letters are cited.

4. A memorandum of Huntington Wilson, Assistant Secretary of State, to Mitchell Innes, Chargé d'Affaires of the British Embassy, February 16, 1910, formed the avenue of formal approach. Quoted, *Can. Tar. Negot.,* p. 3.

British Embassy or otherwise. The State Department, however, made plain that it desired to consult, as far as possible, "the preferences of Canada, even if this should involve departure from the established mode of procedure."[5] Ambassador James Bryce submitted these facts to the Canadian authorities. Fielding, carefully assuming a waiting attitude, informed the Governor General on the twenty-second that his government, while ready to discuss, preferred Ottawa or some intermediate point for the purpose.[6] On the twenty-eighth Knox, pursuant to the Canadian intimation, informed Bryce that he had appointed delegates to proceed to Ottawa to open negotiations which he hoped would enable him to inform the President that Canada was entitled to the minimum tariff.[7]

American interests were represented by Consul General Foster, Charles M. Pepper—a former newspaper man who had since 1909 been connected with the Bureau of Trade Relations of the Department of State and who plays a major part in the subsequent story—and Henry C. Emery of the Tariff Commission.[8] Foster was titular head of the group, which from the beginning was divided as to the proper policy to be followed, though this difference does not appear to have affected the course of the negotiations. Emery believed that immediate granting of the American minimum to Canadian imports would be more likely to induce Canada to accord the United States her own intermediate rates. Pepper, who represented the views of the State Department, shared by the President, insisted upon an effort to secure concessions from Canada by threatening to apply the American maximum rates.[9] The Department's instructions contemplated the possibility of ultimate compromise on something short of the full American demands. The delegates were authorized to lay

5. *Ibid.*, p. 4.   6. *Tar. Rel.*, p. 4.
7. *Ibid.*, pp. 6–7.

8. This group was not particularly acceptable to the protected interests, Pepper being characterized as a writer on "general topics" but without pretense to special knowledge of the tariff, and Emery, formerly of the Yale faculty, being damned as the possessor of the "usual knowledge of the Tariff acquired by professors who oppose the Protection policy." *American Economist*, March 11, 1910, p. 115.

9. An exchange of letters between Taft and Emery, February 19, and a letter of Pepper to Henry M. Hoyt, Counselor of the State Department, March 5, 1910, in the *Taft Papers*, make clear this difference of opinion.

down the general outlines of what the administration was likely to accept.[10] Laurier and Fielding spoke for the Canadian government.

The delegation arrived on March 3, remained a week and held four conferences, the course and results of which were outlined to the President in a memorandum prepared by Pepper and concurred in by Emery.[11] The discussions were watched with interest by the Canadian press which, while deprecating a tariff war, felt that Canada was in the right and should stand pat, and furthermore minimized the likelihood of American imposition of the maximum rates.[12] It was apparent from the first that both parties envisaged the larger question of reciprocity as well as the immediate difficulty, a fact which undoubtedly contributed to the final compromise. At the opening conference the United States' representatives rather pointedly suggested that Canada ought not to jeopardize the improvement of existing good feeling by unwise action in the immediate juncture.[13] It was further stated that the United States felt that the Franco-Canadian treaty gave France and twelve other countries included by the favored-nation clause preferential treatment denied the United States. This, it was argued, was "denial of the equality of opportunity for the products of the United States in competition with other countries which was sought to be secured under the Payne law." A formal request was made for the Canadian intermediate rates "or compensatory concessions." The Canadians, as in duty bound, denied the American contentions, asserting that the French bargain intended no undue discrimination. Moreover, they refused to "buy" the American minimum rates by allowing the United States the French or intermediate tariff.[14] This, they asserted (and it was

10. *Can. Tar. Negot.*, pp. 7–8.

11. *Ibid.*, pp. 8–12. Quotations, unless otherwise indicated, are from this memorandum.

12. *The Halifax* (N.S.) *Chronicle*, March 7; *Winnipeg* (Man.) *Free Press*, March 5, Toronto *News*, March 7; Toronto *Globe*, March 4, 5; *The Daily Telegraph* (St. John, N.B.), March 4, 1910.

13. "It was stated a feeling existed that perhaps in the past Canada had not received proper recognition in its efforts to obtain reciprocity . . . and the hope was expressed that the current of favorable sentiment which had now set in would not be interrupted by the failure to adjust trade relations under the existing conditions."

14. It would seem that here the Canadians had their adversaries in an em-

their principal contention throughout the conferences), would be to surrender their tariff autonomy by subjecting all future Canadian trade treaties to the veto of the United States. In the same breath, however, they rose to the American bait by declaring "their readiness to negotiate for reciprocal trade concessions with the minimum tariff as a basis."

Thus balked in their direct request for the intermediate schedule by the Canadian statement of principle, the Americans sought to maneuver themselves into a more favorable position by shifting the discussion to the relative level of the actual levies of each country on imports from the other. Here, by presenting tables prepared by the Bureau of Trade Relations, it was possible to show that the Payne-Aldrich rates involved a reduction of a million dollars in duty on Canadian exports to the United States for 1909, as compared with the Dingley rates. It was also maintained that the average American ad valorem duty, both on total imports and on dutiable imports from Canada, was considerably lower than the Canadian levels on similar imports from the States.[15] Both Laurier and Fielding accepted the facts as stated and "agreed that it put the situation as to reciprocity and tariff in a somewhat different light."

Returning to the charge, in the conference of March 7, the Americans again requested the intermediate rates and cited several instances where failure to receive them would be a discrimination against manufacturers in the United States. Canadian determination seemed to be weakening somewhat, as at this conference a request was made for a list of intermediate rates considered essential by the United States. This was furnished, but to no avail, for at the final conference the Canadians reverted to their original refusal to

barrassing position, for the United States' request was a reversal of that nation's traditional and peculiar interpretation of the favored-nation idea; they were, in effect, asking Canada to grant the United States for nothing (i.e., the minimum schedule, enjoyed by every other nation under the Payne-Aldrich Act) a favor (the Canadian intermediate rates) which Canada had granted France for a consideration—an interpretation which under ordinary circumstances would have been scorned by the United States.

15. The figures were: Average ad valorem rate on total Canadian imports into the United States, 11.2 per cent; on American imports into Canada, over 12½ per cent. On dutiable imports the rates were respectively 19.4 per cent and 24 per cent. *Can. Tar. Negot.*, p. 10.

admit the American contentions. While reiterating their position in the immediate situation, the Canadian representatives declared

that they would welcome any arrangement which would enable the trade relations of the two countries to be readjusted, and they expressed the hope that the representatives of the United States would return to Ottawa for such negotiations. This declaration opened the way for the representatives of the United States to ask the direct question whether, if a foundation for such negotiations could be laid, Canada would not be willing to send representatives to Washington. Mr. Laurier replied with much earnestness that while he had once thought he never would go to Washington again, yet if a means of readjusting the tariff relations on the lines indicated could be found he would be willing to go himself.

Thus the conference left the immediate problem unsettled. However, it brought to the fore as a by-product the larger problem of the whole future trade relations of the two countries. In summarizing his report to the President, Pepper indicated that Canada was satisfied with the reductions secured under the Payne-Aldrich Act, was convinced that the maximum would not be enforced, and insistent that the United States must pay in the form of concessions for the Canadian intermediate rates. He felt that the Canadian nibble at the bait of a general understanding might be turned into a strike should "some temporary arrangement be effected by which the United States would receive a selected list of intermediate rates." Events were to prove that this was the actual way in which the path to reciprocity was to be made smooth.

The American delegates had also found occasion to press the pulpwood question at all the conferences, emphasizing the dangers facing American vested interests should the threatened Quebec export restrictions become operative. Laurier said that he had advised Gouin against the proposal and had himself resisted pressure to put a Dominion export duty on pulpwood. Under the circumstances, however, it was unlikely that a formal veto of the Quebec proposal would issue from Ottawa. Following an American suggestion, a messenger was sent to talk further with Gouin. He returned to inquire whether a suspension of the proposed restrictions would induce the United States to reduce duties on print paper and cardboard. A disposition to bargain was evidenced and Pepper hinted to the President that lower rates on print paper would be a great help in the larger negotiations which seemed to wait only upon a successful solution of the immediate difficulty over the maximum.

The scene shifted southward when Taft learned the results of the Canadian conferences on March 12. As before, he received conflicting advice. The Tariff Commission contended that, all proper means to secure the intermediate schedule having been exhausted, the United States should concede Canada the minimum tariff. The State Department, in a view shared by the President, held that undue discrimination did exist on some American commodities competing in the Canadian market with similar French goods.[16] There is evidence, however, that while Taft shared the legal view of the State Department, he was personally anxious to avert a tariff war and willing to grasp at any straw which would avert the consequences which that view might impose upon him—namely, application of the maximum rates to Canada. On February 19 he had written Emery that "while I am willing to 'eat dirt,' it sometimes comes to such a situation that nations have to forego what is profitable in order to meet the demands of dignity and self-respect." On March 19, at the height of the crisis, he wrote Mrs. Taft: "I am very anxious not to have a trade war with Canada, and am willing to go a long way to prevent it. If they will only give me something upon which I can hang a decision, I will be glad to seize an excuse and make the announcement required." And to Eugene G. Hay, March 30, after the danger had passed: "It is a great deal better not to have a tariff war with Canada, and but for the imposition of the statutory duty on me, I should have been willing to accept the Canadian tariff as it is."[17]

On March 14 the President focused public attention by allowing the newspapers to announce that the situation was "very critical."[18] At this point, with the Canadians standing fast and Taft outwardly unyielding, an unofficial negotiator appeared to help bridge the gap between success and failure. Dr. James A. Macdonald, a minister turned newspaperman, a free trader, a confidant of Laurier, and managing editor of the Toronto Globe, arrived in Washington and took a hand in the proceedings. The evidence available does not warrant a categorical statement as to who or what was behind his visit.

16. *Ibid.*, p. 12.   17. *Taft Papers.*
18. Toronto *Globe*, March 15, 1910.

Sam Hughes, an ebullient Member of Parliament, later charged that
he had been sent to Washington to open up the question of reciprocity, inferentially as the paid agent of a Boston advocate of
peace and free trade.[19] His indignant reply was that "reciprocity
had absolutely nothing to do with my going to Washington a year
ago." He explained that he had "dropped off at Washington" on his
way from Canada to Atlantic City, New Jersey, for a rest after
strenuous litigation, and insisted that he would have been unrecog-
nized had not members of his craft "dragged" him into the discussion.[20] Pepper considered him "to some extent an unofficial envoy of
the Laurier Government," though he himself insisted that Laurier
knew nothing of his journey at first.[21] Whatever the auspices under
which he traveled, his "rest" must have been postponed, for the next
days were among his busiest. In frequent consultation with Washington officials, he journeyed thence to Ottawa as an intermediary
through whom was arranged the meeting which led to the final settlement of the maximum-tariff problem.

Macdonald saw the President briefly on Saturday, March 12, evidently before the Ottawa commissioners made their visit to report,
and had a longer discussion with Senator Aldrich the same day.[22]
Over the week end, while the President attended a funeral in Pittsburgh, he reviewed the situation at length with Pepper, after which
the latter reported to Taft that Macdonald "was properly impressed
with the suggestion of my personal disappointment that the moderate list of intermediate rates was not accepted as a basis for adjustment by the Laurier Government and expressed his own belief that
some such adjustment might yet be made."[23] That evening Macdonald gave an interview to *The Washington Herald* in which he
was hopeful that the United States would not interpret discrimination too literally.[24] On Monday the fourteenth Taft held long conferences with Knox, Aldrich, the Ottawa commissioners, and tariff

19. In a speech at St. Catharines, Ont., in January, 1911. *The Daily
Herald* (Stratford, Ont.), January 24, 1911.

20. To the editor of the Stratford *Herald;* issue of February 21, 1911.

21. Pepper to Taft, March 14, 1910. *Taft Papers.*

22. *The Washington* (D.C.) *Herald,* March 14, 1910.

23. March 14. *Taft Papers.*

24. Washington *Herald,* March 14, 1910.

advisers, after which he saw Macdonald, who had meantime seen Knox and Senator Henry Cabot Lodge. After this Taft issued his "situation is critical" statement. Macdonald reported to his paper that all hands in the Republican command deprecated a tariff war, but that the law left the President no discretion if undue discrimination were discovered. He stated that Taft's advisers held that the only possible way to avoid imposition of the maximum was for Canada to offer "even a short list of articles on the intermediate schedule now given other countries, excluding articles specially important to Canadian protected industries."[25]

Tuesday the fifteenth witnessed a parade of dignitaries past the President. Ambassador Jules Jusserand called to confer about the Franco-American tariff situation, somewhat similar to the Canadian-American problem, and also at an acute stage of negotiation. He was followed by Macdonald, who was succeeded by Knox and members of the Tariff Commission. Macdonald also talked with Knox; he was reported in the press as having suggested that the Dominion authorities avert further trouble by granting intermediate rates on a short list of commodities.[26] At one of the meetings with Macdonald, Taft expressed the wish to talk matters over with Sir Wilfrid Laurier or some other member of the Canadian government, and asked Macdonald to make the necessary overtures for a meeting at Albany, New York, where the President had some months before arranged to go.[27] Meantime, perhaps to gain time for further maneuver, the press announced that no decision would be made for some days.[28] The Canadian left forthwith for Ottawa and sounded the government, discovering that illness would prevent Laurier from making the journey, but that Fielding, "with full official powers," would go.[29] On Friday, February 18, Taft formally invited Fielding to Albany where, over the week end, the essentials of the ultimate settlement were worked out between the two, with Pepper standing by to advise the President.

The Taft-Fielding conferences of March 20, lasting nearly all

25. Toronto *Globe,* March 15, 1910.
26. *Ibid.,* March 16; *The Washington Post,* March 16.
27. *Can. Tar. Negot.,* p. 12; Stratford *Herald,* February 21, 1911.
28. Washington *Herald,* March 16, 1910.
29. Telegram to Knox, March 17, 1910. *State Department Archives.*

day, were opened by a private talk between the principals, during
which Fielding stated why his government felt entitled to the American minimum without conceding the Canadian intermediate rates.
Pepper was then called in to review the State Department's view of
the American position. Taft reiterated his inability to give Canada
the minimum rates without return concessions. Each side having
clarified its position for the record, Taft asked point-blank whether
Canada could not grant a series of intermediate rates in return for
the American minimum. Fielding hinted that if the list "were not
too large something might be done." He and Pepper then conferred
and determined upon a tentative list, on the understanding that the
President would invite Fielding to Washington to conclude the negotiations. At some point in the conference the question of reciprocity
was definitely broached as a *quid pro quo* for Canadian complaisance
in the immediate circumstances. Fielding and Knox exchanged notes
on March 26 and in Fielding's is the statement that "it was represented to me that the settlement of our present tariff differences and
the opening of the way for negotiations having in view a broader
scheme of reciprocal trade would be facilitated by Canada making
some reductions in its present scale of duties as applied to products
of the United States."[30] The two undoubtedly left the conference
committed to the idea of future negotiations for reciprocity. Taft
asked the omnipresent Macdonald to

assure the people of Canada that it is my deliberate purpose to promote, in such ways as are open to me, better trade relations between the
United States and Canada than at present exist. I am profoundly convinced that these two countries, touching each other for more than
three thousand miles, have common interests in trade and require special arrangements in legislation and administration which are not involved in the relations of the United States with nations beyond the
seas. We may not always have recognized that in the past, but that
must be our viewpoint in the future. Say that for me to the people of
Canada, with all the earnestness and sincerity of my heart.[31]

The Ottawa correspondent of the Toronto *Globe* aptly said that this
message "was the most conciliatory and friendly official statement

30. *Can. Tar. Negot.*, p. 14; *Tar. Rel.*, pp. 7–8.
31. Toronto *Globe,* March 21, 1910.

from Washington in the matter of trade relations which has been received for many years, and practically marks a turning point in the relations which for years past have been decidedly strained."[32]

The final settlement involved granting the United States intermediate rates on a selected list of commodities which left Canadian industries unscathed, in return for which formal concession Taft proclaimed that since Canada was not exercising "undue discrimination" against the United States, American minimum rates would apply to imports from Canada.[33] More important to the present study was the exchange of March 26, wherein Knox expressed by Taft's direction "the desire . . . that your Government will find it convenient to take up with this Government, at such time and in such manner as may be mutually satisfactory, the consideration of a readjustment of our trade relations upon the broader and more liberal lines which should obtain between countries so closely related geographically and racially, as indicated by the President in his recent public utterances." To this Fielding replied that "the Canadian Government . . . will gladly avail themselves of the invitation of the President to take up with your Government, at such time and in such manner as may be mutually satisfactory, the consideration of a readjustment of these relations upon broad and liberal lines."[34]

Thus an immediate emergency had aided both parties to a mutually desired end. Reciprocity, brought forward by the United States at Ottawa, found ready Canadian acceptance in principle, but was nearly sidetracked by each nation's insistence upon its own position relative to the Canadian intermediate tariff. Taft, more anxious for tariff peace and reciprocity than his official standpat attitude indicated, stepped into the picture and through Macdonald arranged a meeting with Fielding at which he proposed the settlement whereby, in return for almost purely formal concessions, Canada received the United States minimum tariff and was invited to future negotiations looking to reciprocity. The Canadian part, while passive, was nonetheless important. By virtue of the facts in a favored position, the Laurier government was quickly receptive to

32. March 22, 1910.

33. *Can. Tar. Negot.*, pp. 15–19, contains the Knox-Fielding correspondence and an analysis of the specific rates involved.

34. *Tar. Rel.*, pp. 9–10.

American overtures and as soon as a workable scheme was presented fell in with the American idea of formal concessions. This at once allowed the President to maintain his dignity and get out of his dilemma, permitted the Dominion to insist upon all its important rights, and opened the way to what both chiefs of state desired—reciprocity negotiations.

CHAPTER V

RECIPROCITY MARKS TIME:
MARCH–DECEMBER, 1910

THE spring and summer months of 1910 witnessed renewed pressure on the administration by the publishers, who were not immediately aided by the March arrangements; an abortive presidential effort to realize on the March promises of broader parleys; and Pepper's tentative and unsuccessful feeler toward reciprocity with Newfoundland as a makeweight in the Canadian negotiations. In the autumn matters were opened in earnest in an attempt to achieve some concrete results in time to influence the Congressional election. This failing also, November and December were used in setting the stage for the final and successful January sessions in which reciprocity was embodied in a formal agreement.

Less than a fortnight of April had elapsed before Sir Lomer Gouin told the Quebec Parliament that provincial restrictions on the export of pulpwood cut from Crown lands would take effect May 1, 1910. Knox promptly instructed Foster to protest to the Dominion government in the hope of obviating this potential threat to future good feeling. Laurier, however, soon reported Gouin's refusal to modify provincial policy.[1] Late in the month the Publishers Association at its annual meeting authorized Ridder to try to stimulate the President to action. Urgency was added by a strike in the mills of the International Paper Company which resulted in considerable price advances and fear of greater exactions in future contracts. Quebec's action was a source of further danger and Ridder asserted that the "American supply of pulp wood is almost exhausted." The remedy which the publishers sought was immediate Congressional action on Representative Mann's bill allowing free entry of wood pulp and printing paper from Canada in return for removal of all Canadian restrictions on exports of pulpwood and wood pulp.[2] The pub-

1. Foster to Knox, April 14; Knox to Foster, same date; Foster to Knox, April 26, 1910. *Can. Tar. Negot.*, pp. 19–21.
2. Ridder to Taft, April 28, 1910. *Taft Papers*.

lishers evidently tried to use the provincial export restrictions as a bugbear to induce administration action. That this was a trumped-up danger is indicated in repeated official reports showing that only a small proportion of total pulpwood exports was cut from Crown lands and furthermore that the International had protected itself by felling quantities of timber in considerable excess of immediate needs, felled timber being exempt from the restrictions. So much timber had been cut that Pepper reported in May that "there is no danger of a shortage of raw material which need restrict the output of print paper during the next two years."[3] Norris, acting for the Publishers Association, arranged for an interview with Taft on May 6, against which Pepper prepared an analysis of the situation and a proposed line of action for the use of Knox and the President. In this he reported that the publishers' design had been, as indicated by Ridder, a trade with Canada whereby in return for free entry of print paper Canada would remove export restrictions on wood pulp and pulpwood. The object of this, he asserted, was to secure an unrestricted supply of ground wood pulp which would be converted into print paper in a mill in New York harbor. Between the meeting of the publishers and the formulation of the memorandum Pepper had evidently been informed that the former had undergone a change of heart. It was intimated privately that they might request negotiation of a special treaty limited to wood pulp and print paper, which it was hoped the Senate would pass before adjournment of Congress. This line was recommended as less apt to open up the whole tariff question than a legislative proposal, which would have to pass both Houses. Pepper opposed this scheme and suggested the inclusion of the paper and pulp question in a general trade treaty. He noted that during the recent conferences the Canadians had hesitated to take further action until Parliament had been prorogued. This had just occurred, and he proposed a plan which so closely forecasts later events as to be worthy of quotation at some length:

After a week or ten days if nothing is heard from Ottawa on the subject it might be desirable to ascertain by private inquiry whether the

3. Memorandum to Knox, May 5, 1910. *Taft Papers. Cf.* also Department of Commerce, *Daily Consular and Trade Reports,* Washington, 1910, August 8, and October 26.

Dominion is ready to enter upon negotiations, not with a view to concluding a treaty before the present session of Congress is ended, but with the purpose of securing deliberate and full examination of all the questions which would be involved in a trade agreement. If negotiations should be entered upon, although the details would necessarily be confidential, there would be no objection to giving publicity to the main fact and especially to the intention to include wood pulp and print paper. This would be treating the publishing interests on the same basis as the food consumers' interests which are chiefly concerned with reciprocity in agricultural food products. It would be fair to all interests and while the publishers in the present crisis might not at first be ready to accept it as a satisfactory solution of the situation, they would probably reconcile themselves to this line of action as the best that could be done.[4]

Accordingly on May 12 Knox launched inquiries designed to ascertain whether Canada was ready to talk reciprocity.[5] As before, the approach was made through Lord Bryce, who at once forwarded Knox's request for action to the British and Canadian authorities.[6] Five days later he retailed to Knox Earl Grey's statement that the Canadian officials believed that Taft had not wanted to open negotiations until later, "probably in the autumn," that Parliament had adjourned, the Ministers had scattered, Fielding had arranged to go to England, and the whole business would have to wait.[7] Fielding informed Knox, in a personal note on May 19, that delay was now unavoidable and laid the blame on the British Embassy which had some weeks before informed Canada that it would not be convenient for the United States to take up the matter until autumn. He intimated that newspaper pressure might account for American haste and warned Knox that "as matters stand now, we could not give you any relief on that score." He also remarked: "I anticipate

4. Memorandum to Knox, May 5. *Taft Papers.*
5. The official correspondence upon which the following account is mainly based is found in Part 2 of *Can. Tar. Negot.*, pp. 23–30.
6. Knox to Bryce, May 12; Bryce to Knox, May 13. *Can. Tar. Negot.* Bryce to Governor General Earl Grey, May 12; Bryce to Sir Edward Grey, British Foreign Secretary, May 13. *Reports from His Majesty's Ambassador at Washington respecting a Reciprocal Tariff Arrangement between Canada and the United States. Commercial Dispatch No. 1, 1911,* London, 1911, p. 1.
7. Bryce to Knox, May 17, 1910. *Can. Tar. Negot.*, p. 24.

difficulty in the handling of the subject on both sides of the boundary
line. . . . Powerful influences in Canada, including influential
boards of trade, are setting themselves against the whole movement."
However, he indicated, through Foster, his willingness to negotiate
and said he would, if the United States desired, make a declaration
to that effect.[8]

Fielding's intimation that the British Embassy had led his government to the belief that delay was in order elicited explanations from
Lord Bryce, who told Huntington Wilson, Assistant Secretary of
State, that his impression had been gained from a general conversation with the President. During the talk Taft indicated that the
busyness of Congress with many matters would make it unlikely that
the Canadian negotiations would be reached before fall.[9] This statement, relayed to Canada, helped to spoil the executive plan for early
parleys. If the facts are as reported they indicate that newspaper
pressure may have influenced the administration to seek an early
negotiation. Fielding's letter of May 19 to Knox, while giving no
dates, stated that his information had been received "several weeks
ago," which might well place it prior to the publishers' agitation of
late April, resulting in the Pepper memorandum of May 5 and
Knox's move of May 12 for immediate action. At any rate, Taft's
chance remark was of no help in reaching his goal.[10]

The late summer found the publishers viewing with alarm and the
State Department quietly gathering information on the pulp and
paper question. August 6 the A.N.P.A. warned its members that the
Quebec pulpwood supply might be further curtailed by provincial
prohibition of exports of wood cut on "location tickets." These were
permits for clearance of land by prospective settlers. The prohibition was based on the allegation that most of the locations were
bogus and were "made for the purpose of cutting the wood for sale
and not for settlement." It was asserted that this prohibition would

8. *Can. Tar. Negot.*, pp. 25–27.   9. *Ibid.*, p. 27.
10. It should be noted that Knox intimated to Fielding that the President
had at no time desired to postpone the whole subject, but was merely waiting for the adjournment of Parliament before bringing it up. He mentioned
the representations of the publishers and cautiously inferred that their influence was negligible. May 28, 1910. *Ibid.*, pp. 28–29.

deprive United States mills of upwards of 200,000 cords of pulp-wood.[11] This was soon called to presidential attention by Norris.[12]

As early as July 11 the idea of starting a backfire against the agitation of the A.N.P.A. came under consideration. In a memorandum of this date Pepper discounted the publishers' cries of calamity, but indicated the "urgent need of considering other sources of supply, such as Newfoundland and Mexico, with a view to the influence on Canada." He added that the present favorable conditions, making for reasonable contract figures, were not permanent, and urged the desirability of taking "some measures which will insure the United States larger supplies from other countries than Canada. Newfoundland is furnishing proof of its ability to meet this demand."[13] The way was opened for him to conduct negotiations with Sir Edward Morris, Premier of Newfoundland, and some time after mid-September a series of conferences occurred in which he tried vainly to procure the withdrawal of export restrictions similar to those of Quebec in return for free importation of fish into the United States.[14]

As part of his trip to Newfoundland, Pepper gathered information in the Maritimes on the state of public opinion toward reciprocity in general and on the wood and pulp situation in particular. His observation confirmed his opinion of the spring that the publishers exaggerated the emergency created by Provincial restrictions, and that the best plan was to let the newspapers take their chances of gaining their objectives in connection with a general reciprocity negotiation.[15] He suggested that the Dominion government be held to its promises of March and placed on the defensive if it had not in-

11. A.N.P.A. *Bulletin,* No. 2251, August 6, 1910, quoted in *Sen. Doc.* 56, 62d Cong., 1st Sess., p. 1230.

12. A letter of Pepper to Taft's secretary, August 15, indicates that Taft had been addressed by Norris sometime prior to August 7. *Taft Papers.*

13. *Newfoundland Tariff Negotiations,* p. 6. This pamphlet, marked EXCEPTIONALLY CONFIDENTIAL, and subject to release only upon the written order of the Secretary of State, is in the *Knox Papers.* It details the inception and progress of unsuccessful contacts between Pepper and the Newfoundland authorities looking to reciprocity.

14. *Ibid.,* pp. 8–25.

15. To Knox, from Halifax, N.S., September 7, 1910. *Can. Tar. Negot.,* pp. 37–38.

timated its willingness to go ahead by the first week in October.[16] By
the end of September the United States was ready to proceed, and
Pepper summarized the situation to date and proposed a plan of action in a memorandum of the twenty-ninth in which he indicated
that the United States was in a strong tactical position, with the
Dominion placed on the defensive and unable longer to point to
American rebuffs as an excuse for inaction. He noted Laurier's reception in the West as a further factor which must influence his government. Against these favorable influences were arrayed the Canadian Manufacturers' Association and a group which feared that
reciprocity might weaken ties with Britain. He outlined tentative
bases for the proposed agreement which, as in an earlier instance,
furnished so much of the actual program of the United States as to
merit more extended comment.[17]

His proposals included broad concessions on the natural products, considerable concessions on manufactured articles, and drastic
reductions on pulp and paper. He urged that "the United States
should not only be ready to concede free wheat, free cattle, and free
fish . . . but that the list of non-dutiable agricultural products
should be considerably enlarged, while radical reductions might be
made on products on which some duties are retained." This suggestion accorded with his observation of world conditions where he remarked that the tendency "to remove all artificial restrictions, such
as tariff duties, on food products is growing stronger every day. It is
now becoming world-wide and there is no prospect that it can be
checked. The wisest policy, therefore, would seem to be to give the
movement the fullest recognition in effecting a trade agreement with
Canada." He would also bow "to what seems to be the prevailing
sentiment in the United States for lower duties on manufactured articles which may result in congressional action." He reiterated his
opinion that the Provincial restrictions upon wood-pulp exports
would not affect the supply for an indefinite period, and proposed to
place information supporting this contention before the publishers
in private with a view to inducing them to merge their special interest in a larger negotiation. Specifically, he recommended abolition

16. To Knox, from St. John, N.B., September 12, 1910. *Ibid.,* p. 40.
17. *Ibid.,* pp. 42–45.

of the retaliatory and countervailing duties on ground pulp and print paper, amounting in one case to $1.67 and in the other to $2.00 per ton. This he justified on the ground that its object, to force Provincial concessions on exports, had not been realized. Finally, he would reduce the duty on print paper from $3.75 to $2.00 per ton. Thus matters stood when, on September 30, Fielding notified Knox that his government was ready to resume negotiations.[18]

The domestic situation caused Fielding to urge that the United States take the next step; he therefore suggested that Knox come to Ottawa to open the discussions, which might then be adjourned to Washington.[19] Pepper and Henry M. Hoyt, Counselor of the State Department, advised Knox that the Canadian proposal should be acceded to, but that for the present informal negotiations through subordinates might be preferable. The advice closed on an urgent note: "It is highly important that the opportunity of clinching this matter now should not be lost."[20] November was not far off. Knox presently announced to Fielding his willingness to proceed, but suggested the appointment of plenipotentiary commissioners.[21] Fielding's reply disclosed a note of hesitancy—he now preferred to conduct preliminary negotiations informally rather than through plenipotentiaries, evidently fearing the results if negotiations began on a plane of high formality and then came to nought.[22] Pepper interpreted this to mean that Fielding had reversed his attitude of September 30 looking to formal action, probably with a view to postponing action if possible until reciprocity might be made an issue in a Dominion election, due at the latest in 1912—certainly until after the November Congressional elections in the States. This, he said, should be checkmated, perhaps by framing an answer explaining that any visit of Knox to Ottawa must be made in the immediate future.[23] Knox urged that, the preliminaries being cleared away, the time had come to work through fully accredited plenipotentiaries. The United States, he said, was ready for such action and he hoped

18. *Ibid.,* p. 47. Part 4 of this pamphlet contains correspondence with Canada and departmental discussions pertaining to the resumption of negotiations, pp. 47–68.

19. *Ibid.,* pp. 47–48.

21. *Ibid.,* pp. 50–51. October 5, 1910.

23. *Ibid.,* pp. 54–55.

20. *Ibid.,* p. 49.

22. *Ibid.,* pp. 52–53.

that appointment of Canadian plenipotentiaries "would not involve much delay."[24]

This pressure induced a reply favorable in principle, but Fielding indicated that delay would still be necessary since the King would have to designate the Canadian delegates. He suggested that meantime the United States might be willing to come to Ottawa for informal discussions, in which case Canadians were ready to proceed.[25] Pepper advised accepting this proposal, which left the administration in the position of having put its best foot forward. Moreover, under the circumstances the United States could formulate its proposals for presentation to Congress and the country for effect on the domestic political situation should the negotiations fail to be carried through to final fruition. And finally: "Mr. Fielding's letter offers a means for the negotiations to be begun with the widest possible publicity before November 8. This is highly desirable. The general public will be interested in the resumption of the negotiations and will not be concerned as to the method of procedure."[26] Accordingly Knox indicated Taft's willingness to proceed temporarily through informal negotiations, and promised that agents with full authority to canvass the question would be ready to proceed to Ottawa so as to hold the initial conference not later than November 5.[27] Thus through a month of sparring both parties shifted ground somewhat, starting from the original proposal of each that the negotiations should open on a plane of high formality. To this the Canadians at first demurred but later acceded in principle, under some pressure from the United States. Practical difficulties intervening, the United States substantially agreed to the Canadian proposal of informal negotiations. There seems no doubt that political exigency governed in each case, with the emergency being somewhat greater in the United States, where the administration was anxious to have something in the record prior to the Congressional election and was therefore ready to fall in with the Canadian proposal for informal discussions as the best that could be had prior to November 8.

As a result of these preliminaries Pepper and Hoyt went to Ot-

24. *Ibid.,* pp. 57–58. October 20, 1910.
25. *Ibid.,* p. 65. October 24, 1910.
26. To Hoyt, October 27, 1910. *Ibid.,* p. 66.
27. *Ibid.,* p. 67. October 28, 1910.

tawa to act with Foster in conferences with Fielding and William Paterson, Minister of Customs. These negotiators in meetings on November 5, 7, 8, and 10 canvassed the situation thoroughly and prepared the way for formal action at Washington in January, 1911. Original statements of position indicated widely divergent viewpoints—so divergent, in fact, as to create grave doubts of continued successful action. The controversy turned on whether, and to what extent, the proposed arrangement should include manufactured articles. The resultant compromise, whereby the United States modified its demands and Canada broadened the field open to discussion, was an immediate concession to Canadian fears, made possible continued negotiation, and forecast with some accuracy the nature of the final arrangement.

Departmental instructions to Hoyt and Pepper were very broad in scope; they included (a) free interchange of a wide range of natural products such as wheat, cattle, foodstuffs, dairy products, eggs, fish, fruits and vegetables, and coal; (b) an effort to secure free interchange of certain manufactures, such as agricultural machinery and its parts and, where this was not feasible, an attempt to secure an approximation of the lowest rates on manufactures prevailing either in the United States minimum or the Canadian intermediate schedules; (c) a duty equivalent to $2.00 per ton on print paper and reductions on other types coming from Provinces not taxing or prohibiting exportation of pulpwood to the United States; and (d) free rough lumber.[28] At the initial session the presentation of American views was received cordially but with evident reservations. Hoyt's introductory remarks suggested the exchange of natural products either freely or at a low rate, and of manufactures "on a basis of equivalency approximating the lowest rate prevailing in either country in every case and allowing in both the natural and manufactured categories for such limited number of exceptions as various manifest exigencies would call for in reference to one country or the other." For the immediate future Canada could look forward to being the exclusive recipient of such favors, subject to simi-

28. *Ibid.*, pp. 69–71, 77. Part 5, pp. 69–89, contains the instructions as above, the story of the November negotiations told in a series of letters and telegrams from Ottawa to Washington while the meeting was in progress, and the minutes of the meetings themselves.

lar arrangements with other countries in this hemisphere and to the
ever-imminent proviso of a general Congressional tariff revision.

Pepper and Fielding next exchanged views. The breadth of the
proposal evidently surprised the Canadians, who avoided immediate
acceptance, alleging various factors which would render passage of
an agreement in Canada difficult. Among these were "the political
difficulties of the Canadian Government, the strength of the imperialist sentiment, the general growth of strength of protectionist views,
the strength and engrossing opposition of the manufacturing interests, the indifference even of the farming classes and the alleged but
largely illusory (as he claimed) support of reciprocity from the
Canadian northwest." Fielding was disposed to carry out the agreement by concurrent legislation rather than by the treaty which he
himself had favored in the spring. There was no further formal discussion at this meeting. The American delegates gained the impression that the Canadian position had shifted since March, probably
"under pressure by the British Government," and felt that the obstacles alleged, though real and growing, were otherwise insufficient
to account for the "apparent total unwillingness to make any concessions on manufactures." As matters were left for the day, Fielding intimated clearly that, while holding manufactures open for discussion, Canada could not go far in that direction, and the Americans
"made it clear . . . that we could not be satisfied with an agreement
as to natural products alone, and could not deal except on the basis
of a comprehensive inclusion of manufactured articles."[29]

Fielding opened the meeting of November 7 by stating that the
government "had reached a conclusion in regard to manufactures,
and would be unable to include them in any proposed arrangement."
Negotiations could be continued on natural products, and the desire
for concurrent legislation was reiterated. He supported his position
by asserting that the banks had joined the manufacturers' protest
against lower duties, and had expressed fear that a panic might result. The manufacturers, he claimed, could not hold their own against
the United States under equivalency of rates. This was answered by
Foster and Pepper, who reminded the Canadians of their own attitude of March, when Laurier had expressed his personal willingness

29. *Ibid.*, pp. 72–73, 80–81.

to go to Washington for what was understood to be a comprehensive agreement, and Fielding had suggested reciprocity in manufactures as well as natural products. During the subsequent discussions Fielding "modified the first declaration by an incidental suggestion as to the possibility of a few manufactured articles, but indicated that they would have to be of trifling importance." Hoyt proposed to start a general discussion, beginning with natural products, in the hope that by the time manufactures were reached a way might be opened. This was done without much success and the day's conference ended with Fielding's suggestion that each side frame a definite list of agricultural products for consideration on the morrow.[30]

Before the conference of the eighth Hoyt, who was ill and unable to attend, in a discouraged note to Fielding virtually threatened to abandon the negotiations.[31] Faced with this prospect, the Canadian attitude became somewhat more conciliatory and the conference developed into a contest of maneuver during which the United States representatives began to qualify their interpretation of the term "comprehensive," and the Canadians tried unsuccessfully to obtain an American list of manufactures on which reciprocity was desired. At the start Canada again insisted that only natural products could be considered. Presently Fielding was informed that "if he understood by 'comprehensive' that we meant it to relate to the number, his interpretation might not be justified, but as to the principle it

30. *Ibid.,* pp. 73–74, 82–83.

31. He wrote, apropos of Fielding's position of the seventh, "that, feeling deep regret and disappointment at the situation now reached, by which it appears clear that you can make no arrangement based on manufactures, while we regard some comprehensive arrangement on that subject as essential, we shall be greatly indebted to you if you will tell us to-day frankly whether, except for form or appearances which may suggest one or two more meetings, we have not reached a finality so that our departure from Ottawa would be in order." *Ibid.,* pp. 74–75. A similar note of discouragement was struck in a note to Knox, written before the conference, in which he reiterated his opinion that Imperial reasons were behind the Canadian shift, and added that "it seems likely that the present government is tottering to its fall, and they evidently have no confidence that they could carry a reciprocity agreement through Parliament; and they tell us that they would have no opportunity to go to the country under these circumstances if they were defeated, but would merely go out of office and give way to the opposition, which plainly they do not want to do." *Ibid.,* pp. 75–76.

would have to stand. We further explained that we made this statement in order that natural products should not be considered and
then a few unimportant manufactured articles be taken up as a
proper basis for continuing the negotiations." After some discussion
the Americans were asked to submit a list of manufactures on which
reciprocity was desired. This was refused on the ground that the
United States desired to establish the principle of equivalency of
rates rather than any special list, and a counterrequest was made for
a list which Canada could grant with the least inconvenience. This in
turn was refused and again Canada asked for a list. Pepper then
reminded Fielding that at the spring negotiations such a list had
been submitted by the United States and disregarded—an experience which it was not desired to repeat. After this coy exchange
agricultural implements were discussed as one manufactured item
which might be included, along with some others. The meeting closed
with Fielding again asking for a list and, more particularly, for an
intervening day before the next conference in order to sound out his
colleagues.[32]

On the morning of the ninth the American delegates still further
qualified their interpretation of "comprehensive" in an informal note
to Fielding and Paterson. They explained that they had not meant
"that every paragraph or number in both tariffs should be included"
and, while still reluctant to submit a specific list of manufactures,

it may well be that if we can present lists mutually of agricultural and
other natural products, and discuss them, with the idea that when we
come to the categories of manufactures we shall not find the problem to
be absolutely insoluble, a comparatively limited list selected from the
two tariffs might present the comprehensive scheme which we have in
mind. . . . If you will be prepared tomorrow to exchange tentative lists
on the question of agricultural products and other natural products,
and of manufactures from the point of view now indicated, we will be
similarly prepared.[33]

This suggestion that a more limited list might be deemed "comprehensive" elicited from Fielding a note later in the day assuring the
Americans that "my colleague and myself do not at all regard the

32. *Ibid.*, pp. 76–77, 83–84.
33. *Ibid.*, p. 78.

problem as insoluble. On the contrary, we continue to be hopeful that in the end we should find a ground of common action."[34]

The final conference, something of a love feast, was marked by relief on both sides and renewed hope for the future. Fielding opened by stating that there would probably be no great difficulty on natural products. As to manufactures, the Canadians were cognizant of the "substantial and liberal offer" made by the United States, and "they were ready to say that they would now take the matter up from their hearts." They found it necessary, however, to ask for a postponement, because of the ill-health of Fielding and the need of time to "educate members of the Government and influential people among the opposition" to the notion of reciprocity in manufactures. He suggested that the next conference be held at Washington and that the agreement be couched in legislative rather than treaty form. In reply Hoyt indicated that the Americans had not attached a "numerical significance" to the word comprehensive, nor had they intended by it "that a large list of the Canadian tariff numbers on manufactures should necessarily be included." He then "expressed the very great appreciation and warm and responsive feeling with which he and his colleagues had heard Mr. Fielding's words, and said they were sure, with the spirit animating both sides, that a satisfactory result was now most hopeful." To pave the way to that happy consummation he suggested,

as a point meriting consideration, in reference to the objection of Mr. Fielding and Mr. Paterson, that the real thing which the Canadian industries feared was the capitalization and scientific organization of American industries; that in taking up the manufacturing schedules in detail the effort on our part would be as much as possible to differentiate and segregate those articles affecting the smaller industries on both sides of the water [sic], so that they might compete on equal terms and leave the rates on the industries of the great combinations unchanged where they involved Canadian objection.[35]

There followed a tentative discussion of what manufactures might be included in a further negotiation. It was agreed that some reduction on agricultural implements would be necessary. Substantial

34. *Ibid.*
35. *Ibid.*, p. 86.

agreement was reached on a $2.00 rate for print paper and the Canadians intimated that they would raise no objection to the later consideration of the pulpwood question. Other manufactures and natural products were discussed verbally and the Canadians were shortly in virtual possession of the American lists of both kinds of goods on which concessions would be expected. This device was used in order to avoid an exchange of lists which might be embarrassing in case of legislative requests for documents on either side of the border. It was suggested that both parties should deposit formal lists with Foster, who could show them confidentially to each principal. The conference then adjourned.[36]

Thus compromise had turned a threatened stalemate into a hope of substantial agreement. The discussion opened with a statement of diametrically opposed views on manufactures. Eventually Canadian reluctance had whittled down American insistence on a "comprehensive" list to a point where it was understood that a "principle" could be maintained with a shortened list of goods planned to avoid antagonizing the great manufacturing interests which might make trouble for the Canadian government. On the other hand, the thinly veiled threat to abandon the negotiations entirely had indicated to the Canadians that their long desire for concessions on natural products would be balked unless they broadened the base of the discussion to include some manufactures. The very real danger to the scheme through opposition of powerful Canadian interests had been made apparent. For the moment both sides had gained by making concessions.

36. *Ibid.*, pp. 79, 85–89.

CHAPTER VI

AGREEMENT REACHED: JANUARY, 1911

THE memory of reciprocity was kept green on both sides of the border during November and December. The Dominion Parliament convened in mid-November and while the debate on the Speech from the Throne mainly centered around Opposition efforts to make capital of the Drummond-Arthabaska election and the Government's naval policy, reciprocity received some attention. In an exchange between Mr. Robert L. Borden, Opposition Leader, and Laurier, the former cautiously opposed reciprocity, and was answered stoutly by the Premier to the effect that while an effort would be made to draw closer to the United States commercially, Canada's interests would be protected.[1] Taft's message of December 6 summarized developments and concluded that previous accomplishments justified "further efforts for the readjustment of the commercial relations of the two countries so that their commerce may follow the channels natural to contiguous countries and be commensurate with the steady expansion of trade and industry on both sides of the boundary line."[2]

Preparations were accordingly made to resume discussions at Washington early in January. Here again, as well as can be educed from the scanty records available, American insistence overcame Canadian reluctance but did not achieve all the ends desired.[3] For the United States the principal figures were Knox, Pepper, and Chandler Anderson, who had replaced the deceased Hoyt as Counselor of the Department. Fielding and Paterson again represented the Dominion, assisted by several tariff experts. Preparatory to dis-

1. Toronto *Globe,* November 22, 1910; *Official Report of the Debates of the House of Commons of the Dominion of Canada,* 3d Sess., 11th Parl., Ottawa, 1910–11, I, 22–34, 46–54 (cited subsequently as *Hansard*).

2. *Record,* 61st Cong., 3d Sess., p. 19.

3. The material preserved in the *Knox Papers* and in the State Department is much less satisfactory for this culminating episode than for the preliminaries. The careful record of events through the November negotiations, found in *Canadian Tariff Negotiations,* was either not continued or not deposited in the Library of Congress with the Knox documents. Fragmentary data have been utilized in the following unsatisfactory account.

cussion the Bureau of Trade Relations drafted a memorandum indicating what the United States had in mind to give and ask. The offer comprised first a list of Canadian goods which would be allowed free entry, including substantially food products in the natural state and a few other articles: wheat, cattle, sheep, swine, fresh fish, fresh fruits, dairy products, eggs and poultry, rough lumber, coal, farm machinery, and vehicles. A second list, mainly of secondary or partly manufactured food products, would be admitted at reduced rates: potatoes and other vegetables, barley, hay, oats, rye, bacon, ham, lard, canned meats, canned vegetables, and flour. "Various manufactured commodities," not listed, were also to be admitted at lowered rates intended to approximate the lower Canadian levies. Newsprint was to come in at $2.00, instead of the existing rate of $3.75, with the removal of countervailing and retaliatory duties.

In return for these concessions the United States would ask for:

(a) Reciprocal free rates on all articles we make free, and possibly on cotton seed oil.

(b) Canadian French treaty intermediate rates on articles not included in the agreement of last March, with some exceptions due to unreadiness of the Dominion to antagonize certain industries.

(c) Intermediate or special rates for some additional articles such as paints and varnishes, roofing slate, paving stones, etc.

With the realization that this proposal might not be accepted in full, it was further noted that compromise rates on coal and on farm machinery would be accepted, and that the print-paper proposal might be modified "if in view of the unwillingness of the Canadian Provinces to remove their pulp-wood restrictions except in return for outright free paper the President thinks the American publishers are entitled to this concession."[4]

The conferences opened on Saturday, January 7, and continued through Saturday, the twenty-first, when agreement was announced. Strict secrecy was maintained and the newspapers could only report successive meetings and speculate vainly as to what was going on. Behind the scenes the discussions opened with a preliminary statement of position. Knox announced his understanding that the pre-

4. Memorandum of January 5, 1911, in *Knox Papers*.

vious exchanges indicated the probability of an agreement including natural products, with some inclusion of manufactured articles. Fielding's first remarks were directed to further insistence on legislative rather than treaty action, a procedure to which Knox assented. When the actual discussion of rates opened Fielding reiterated much of what he had said at the Ottawa meetings and indicated that he was "earnestly desirous" of meeting the American wish for an agreement on a basis broader than merely natural products, "if it could be done." Next arose the question of using such items of the French treaty rates as had not been granted to the United States in March as the basis for discussing manufactured articles. It had been the understanding at Ottawa in November that this would be done. Fielding hoped that the United States could see its way clear to leaving some of these items as they were without reduction by Canada, in view of the superior organization of the American firms producing them. Pepper countered by asserting his opinion that Canada could grant practically all the French treaty rates without serious danger to her industries. The Canadians insisted that the Dominion could not grant free agricultural implements, but was prepared to consider a rate lower than the existing one. Knox reiterated the American position that "something substantial" must be done in the field of manufactures. Adjournment was then taken after each side had promised to submit formal lists at the next meeting.[5]

The formal Canadian list of January 9 can be compared only with the preliminary American memorandum of the fifth, as the American list of the ninth has not come to light. Its shortcomings from the American standpoint may be analyzed by indicating comments of M. H. Davis, of the United States delegation.[6] It was evidently a minimum list, far short of the preliminary understanding, and designed for bargaining purposes. The free list included live cattle, horses, and sheep, but excluded swine, poultry, and other food animals. A limited list of fresh fruits was included, whereas the United States desired wide reciprocity in this item. Dairy products proposed to be reciprocally free included butter and cream but not fresh milk

5. Typed memorandum, undated: "Rough Draft of MINUTES OF CONFERENCES AT WASHINGTON." This memorandum, covering only the initial meeting, is in the *Knox Papers*.

6. Both the Canadian list and the Davis comments are in the *Knox Papers*.

or cheese. Barley was the only grain listed, whereas the United States wished wheat, oats, and rye as well, Davis asserting that the "opportunity for the transportation, handling and manufacture of wheat and oats into food products should be one of the prime incentives to the United States for a reciprocity agreement." Of farm and garden products the Canadians listed only potatoes, whereas Davis now urged "all other vegetables in their natural state . . . beans and pease, as dried and prepared for market; and would include hay and straw, and all fodder foods for animals. The minor food products of agriculture, such as eggs, honey, horticultural stock, dried fruits, etc., should also be included; as well as all fresh meats, beef, veal, mutton, lamb, pork, etc., whether fresh or refrigerated." It was suggested that all kinds of ore should be free in the unworked state. The Canadians proposed free rough lumber, as well as lath and shingles, but exception was taken to the last two. The Canadian proposal for free "fish of all kinds, salted or preserved in any form" was considered too broad, as allowing all kinds of canned fish. In addition to the Canadian proposals Davis suggested numerous items for the free list, including agricultural machinery and parts, fertilizers, paving brick and stone, and print paper, "providing restrictions and prohibitions are removed."

Naturally the Canadian dutiable list included numerous items on which the American commentator desired reciprocity, such as meats, bacon, hams, eggs, cheese, oats, pease, beans, wheat, bran, and others. Davis proposed a long list on which the United States should be placed on a par with France and granted the Canadian intermediate schedule. The proposals above, Davis indicated, were not an irreducible minimum or ultimatum, but marked a general standard from which departure in either direction would involve dangers. Politically it might be wise, he admitted, to cut the American demands somewhat in order to avoid jeopardizing ultimate agreement. Commercially, however, "very little could be gained by extending the above lists, and much would be lost by both countries if any decided reduction is made in the articles above enumerated."

From this point, until agreement was reached on the sixteenth, the information at hand is fragmentary. Taft's letter of the tenth to Theodore Roosevelt indicated the "probability . . . that we shall reach an agreement with our Canadian friends by which all natural products—cereals, lumber, dairy products, fruits, meats and cattle —shall enter both countries free, and that we shall get a revision (not as heavy a one as I would like, but a substantial one, and equivalent certainly to the French reciprocity treaty, and probably more) on manufactures."[7] Things came to a head on the fourteenth, for on this date Knox asked Taft for his final instructions, in view of the possibility of substantially closing the negotiations that evening.[8]

Agreement was reached on the sixteenth. It included:

First. An identical free list, embracing practically all the natural products, especially agricultural products, which have been under discussion.

Second. A list of articles, both natural products and manufactured commodities, on which identical rates will be levied by both countries. This includes secondary food products, the majority of the items in the French Treaty (textiles being excepted) of preponderant value, and additional articles submitted by both countries. All these rates are considerably lower than the present ones.

Third. A small list of articles on which the United States is not able to come to the Canadian rate, but concedes a lower rate than the existing one.

Fourth. A small list on which Canada is not able to come to the United States rate, but concedes a lower rate than the existing one.

Fifth. We do not accept the suggestion of a reduced duty on print paper unconditionally. We stand on free print paper, on condition of the removal of restrictions on the exportation of pulp wood by the Canadian provinces. The Canadian negotiators assent to our putting this condition precedent in our legislation, while at the same time not including it in the proposition which they will lay before Parliament. . . .

Seventh. The method of procedure will be an exchange of notes between the Canadian Minister of Finance and the Secretary of State, in which the agreement reached will be described, and the details as to rates, etc., set forth. The Dominion Government will present a bill to Parliament, and the President will send a message to Congress giving

7. *Taft Papers.* The same letter contained the prophetic statement: "I think it may break the Republican party for a while." Roosevelt replied two days later that the Canadian scheme seemed to him "admirable from every standpoint," and agreed that the party might suffer "damage" for a time, but would benefit in the long run.

8. Knox to Taft, January 14, 1911. *Ibid.*

the details as set forth in the agreement, and will have a bill introduced to carry them into effect.[9]

On the twenty-first a joint public statement announced agreement and provided for simultaneous announcement of specific terms on the twenty-sixth. On the same date official letters were exchanged between Fielding and Knox indicating the details of schedules, the text of which follows:

I. THE CANADIAN LETTER

The negotiations initiated by the President several months ago through your communications to his Excellency, the British Ambassador, respecting a reciprocal tariff arrangement between the United States and Canada and since carried on directly between representatives of the Governments of the two countries have now, we are happy to say, reached a stage which gives reasonable assurance of a conclusion satisfactory to both countries. We desire to set forth what we understand to be the contemplated arrangement and to ask you to confirm it.

It is agreed that the desired tariff changes shall not take the formal shape of a treaty but that the Governments of the two countries will use their utmost efforts to bring about such changes by concurrent legislation at Washington and Ottawa. The Governments of the two countries having made this Agreement from the conviction that, if confirmed by the necessary legislative authorities, it will benefit the people on both sides of the border-line, we may reasonably hope and expect that the arrangement, if so confirmed, will remain in operation for a considerable period. Only this expectation on the part of both Governments would justify the time and labour that have been employed in the maturing of the proposed measure. Nevertheless, it is distinctly understood that we do not attempt to bind for the future the action of the United States Congress or the Parliament of Canada, but that each of these authorities shall be absolutely free to make any change of tariff policy or of any other matter covered by the present arrangement that may be deemed expedient. We look for the continuance of the arrangement not because either party is bound to it, but because of our conviction that the more liberal trade policy thus to be established will be viewed by the people of the United States and Canada as one which will strengthen the friendly relations now happily prevailing and promote the commercial interests of both countries.

9. From a "Summary" memorandum in the *Knox Papers*.

With respect to the discussions that have taken place concerning the duties upon the several grades of pulp, printing-paper, etc.—mechanically ground wood-pulp, chemical wood-pulp, bleached and unbleached, news-printing paper and other printing paper and board made from wood-pulp of the value not exceeding four cents per pound at the place of shipment—we note that you desire to provide that such articles from Canada shall be made free of duty in the United States only upon certain conditions respecting the shipment of pulp-wood from Canada. It is necessary that we should point out that this is a matter in which we are not in a position to make any agreement. The restrictions at present existing in Canada are of a Provincial character. They have been adopted by several of the Provinces with regard to what are believed to be Provincial interests. We have neither the right nor the desire to interfere with the Provincial authorities in the free exercise of their constitutional powers in the administration of their public lands. The provisions you are proposing to make respecting the conditions upon which these classes of pulp and paper may be imported into the United States free of duty must necessarily be for the present inoperative. Whether the Provincial Governments will desire to in any way modify their regulations with a view of securing the free admissions of pulp and paper from their Provinces into the markets of the United States must be a question for the Provincial authorities to decide. In the meantime the present duties on pulp and paper imported from the United States into Canada will remain. Whenever pulp and paper of the classes already mentioned are admitted into the United States free of duty from all parts of Canada, then similar articles, when imported from the United States, shall be admitted into Canada free of duty.

II. THE UNITED STATES LETTER

I have the honour to acknowledge the receipt of your communication of this date in relation to the negotiations initiated by the President several months ago for a reciprocal trade arrangement between the United States and Canada, in which you set forth and ask me to confirm your understanding of the results of our recent conferences in continuation of those negotiations. I take great pleasure in replying that your statement of the proposed arrangement is entirely in accord with my understanding of it. It is a matter of some regret on our part that we have been unable to adjust our differences on the subject of wood-pulp, pulp-wood and print-paper. We recognize the difficulties to which you refer growing out of the nature of the relations between the

Dominion and Provincial Governments and for the present we must be content with the conditional arrangement which has been proposed in Schedule "A" attached to your letter.

I fully appreciate the importance, to which you call attention, of not permitting a too rigid Customs administration to interfere with the successful operation of our Agreement, if it is approved by the Congress of the United States and the Parliament of Canada, and I desire to confirm your statement of our understanding on this point. I am satisfied that the spirit evinced on both sides gives assurance that every effort will be made to secure the full measure of benefit which is contemplated in entering into this arrangement. The assurance that you give that the Dominion Government proposes to require only a nominal fee from the fishing vessels of the United States for the privilege in Canadian waters for which heretofore a charge of $1.50 per ton for each vessel has been required is most gratifying. I heartily concur in your statement of the purposes inspiring the negotiations and in the views expressed by you as to the mutual benefits to be derived by both countries in the event our work is confirmed, and I take this opportunity to assure you, on behalf of the President, of his appreciation of the cordial spirit in which you have met us in these negotiations.[10]

The foregoing will indicate that the settlement foreshadowed at Ottawa in November had been partly fulfilled, but that in some respects Canadian qualms had prevented realization of American hopes. The free list included substantially all the important natural products, a much more inclusive list than that proposed by Canada in her list of January 9, and in line with the desires of the United States. American wishes concerning manufactures had been catered to in principle but not in practice. An imposing list of articles was placed upon an identical basis, but the American desire for freer exchange had fallen before Canadian fears of domestic hostility. The lowered rates satisfied no one entirely; they gained the American manufacturer little in the Canadian market; the reductions on agricultural machinery were insufficient to suit the Canadian prairie farmer; and the reductions, harmless as they were, presented to the Canadian industrialists the "thin edge of the wedge" which would some day be driven home to destroy the protection as dear to them as to their prototypes south of the border. On the one side Mr. Taft had tried,

10. *Can. Ann. Rev.,* 1911, pp. 26–30.

not entirely successfully, to open Canada to American manufactures; he had given Canadian natural products almost free access to the American market. He had opened the question of trade relations, had taken a positive step, and had secured an agreement which he hoped would be of political avail in the coming months. On the other hand Mr. Fielding had opened the huge American markets to Canadian natural products; he had delivered the Canadian manufacturer from danger but not from fear; and he had placed Laurier's feet in a position which the rumblings of Canadian sentiment even now indicated was likely to be a stormy one.

It remains only to describe such newsprint phases of the negotiations as are apparent from the record. The publishers' prediction that "the commercial representative of the State Department is tenaciously clinging to a duty of $2.00 per ton on print paper" was borne out by the American proposal of January 5, as was also the prediction that "the Canadians will refuse anything less than free print paper in exchange for free pulp wood."[11] Norris and a delegation from the Publishers Association saw Knox during the negotiations and urged "the importance of an insistence upon free pulp wood from Canada in exchange for free print paper and wood pulp"[12] into the United States. Two days before the details of the agreement were made public Ridder was able to communicate its pulp and paper provisions to his Association, a fact which irked the papermakers not a little.[13] And in commenting on the agreement the Association's *Bulletin* remarked contentedly: "This draft is entirely satisfactory to publishers."[14] As may be noted in the exchange of official letters, above, the pulp and paper matter occupied more space than was given to any other single commodity. The agreement as finally worked out represented at once an effort to avoid disturbing Canadian Provincial autonomy and to please the American publishers by securing free raw materials. As such it was a triumph of negotiation and an earnest of powerful support for the agreement in the States.

11. A.N.P.A. *Bulletin*, No. 2338, December 24, 1910, p. 1105.

12. Norris to Knox, January 16, 1911. *Knox Papers*.

13. His circular letter of January 24 is quoted in *Sen. Doc.* 56, 62d Cong., 1st Sess., p. 1008.

14. No. 2361, January 28, 1911, p. 81.

At the outset of the discussions the American object was to secure "an agreement under which the United States would get pulp wood from Canada free from Canadian restrictions . . . and give therefor free admission for Canadian paper and pulp wood." This the Canadians refused to promise, since the export restrictions were Provincial levies with which the Dominion officers did not wish to interfere. In deference to American importunity a provisional section was inserted in Schedule "A" (the free list), designed to induce removal of these restrictions. Under it, once the general agreement had been ratified by the United States, whenever the Provinces lifted their restrictions on exports of pulpwood, such pulpwood, and Canadian newsprint, would be placed on the United States free list. Until such action by the Provinces, the duties levied by the Payne-Aldrich Act would continue to apply. Thus the club which that act had brandished at the Canadian Provinces was still held aloft to induce concessions. Implicit in the arrangement, however, was a solution of the difficulty which the publishers were not slow to recognize. It permitted Congress, while retaining the tariff wall against products of the Crown lands, *to allow free importation of similar products of private lands.* Thus the publishers would secure their cheap raw materials and the pressure upon the Provinces to relax export restrictions would be continued by holders of Crown-land timber rights. Attention was called to this possibility in a letter written by Knox to Chairman Payne of the Ways and Means Committee on February 4, and even earlier the A.N.P.A. *Bulletin* had jubilated that the agreement "will provide for the immediate entry of print paper and wood pulp from Canada. The snarl with the provinces of Canada has been completely avoided by an entirely new turn to the stipulations, which now follow the wood—not the province. If wood is free from restriction, such as wood from private lands the products of that wood will come into the United States free of duty."[15] Thus had Taft strengthened his right arm to fight for reciprocity.

15. A.N.P.A. *Bulletin,* No. 2361, January 28, 1911, p. 81. Knox sent Senator Boies Penrose, June 5, a copy of his letter of February 4 to Payne, in which the following carefully couched language tells the story: "Inasmuch as this proposed conditional arrangement has not been accepted by Canada as a part of the agreement, except in the sense that, when, and if, it is made operative by American legislation to secure free admission of these articles

into the United States from all parts of Canada, Congress may, without impairing the agreement arrived at by the negotiators, work out this result in its own way. As, for instance, by maintaining the present status until the Provincial restrictions are removed, *or, by presently admitting free paper and pulp manufactured in Canada unaffected by the restrictions, should Congress believe this latter method of dealing with the subject would expedite the removal of the restrictions." Knox Papers.* Author's italics.

CHAPTER VII

OPINION DEVELOPS:
MARCH, 1910—FEBRUARY, 1911

IT must not be thought that the negotiations just described occurred in a vacuum. Indeed, the atmosphere of public opinion took on added density following the March meeting until by January Canada, at least, had been made thoroughly aware of the issues involved. In the States, reciprocity aroused little public attention and not until the finished agreement was published did other than metropolitan journals give much space to the matter. This disproportion of interest between the two countries continued roughly throughout the controversy and was doubtless inevitable considering the facts of the situation: to Canada reciprocity was of vital economic and political import, touching closely the deepest springs of Imperial connection and of national partisanship and prosperity; to the United States, though of considerable moment to particular interests and of some importance in national economic and political affairs, it was of less transcendent significance. The present account, therefore, will concern itself first with developing Canadian opposition to reciprocity, then with the reactions of each country to the January discussions and to the finished agreement.

The Canadian interest most likely to be adversely affected was of course the manufacturer. The report of its Tariff Committee to the Canadian Manufacturers' Association indicated fear that the ministers might, in such negotiations as those of March, injure the manufacturers without consulting them, and that during the March meetings the manufacturers felt "very nervous."[1] In the Commons on May 3 Mr. Borden, harassed leader of a disunited Conservative Opposition,[2] cautiously indicated a somewhat hesitant antagonism to the March settlement.[3] A few days later the Montreal Board of Trade passed resolutions directed to the attention of the government

1. *Industrial Canada,* 11:286 (October, 1910).
2. For a consideration of the factors leading to this lack of party unity in 1910, see *Can. Ann. Rev.,* 1910, pp. 287 ff.
3. *Ibid.,* 1910, p. 623.

in which they expressed fears lest reciprocity should mean a weakening of the Imperial tie and a needless concession since the United States was likely to reduce tariffs in the near future.[4] In June Mr. Borden could be somewhat more specifically skeptical of closer trade relations. At Finch, Ontario, on the twenty-fifth, he raised the question of Canada's ability to play her part in a needed scheme of Imperial trade coöperation if she fettered her fiscal freedom "by embarrassing commercial treaties and understandings" with foreign countries.[5] The summer numbers of *Industrial Canada,* organ of the Canadian Manufacturers' Association, carried an increasing volume of comment and criticism. By September and October the newspaper clans were gathering for the fray, giving principal consideration for the moment to the larger question of protection.[6]

In September the Manufacturers' Association carried the war into Africa. On the way to the annual convention at Vancouver (held September 20–22) stout efforts were made to convince the Prairies, where insistent farmers had so recently embarrassed Laurier, of the virtues of moderate protection. At Winnipeg, at Portage la Prairie and Brandon, Manitoba, at Moose Jaw, Saskatchewan, and at Calgary, Alberta, the advantages of protection and the needs of manufacturers were stressed.[7] At the Vancouver meeting President John Hendry's address, to the accompaniment of the wail of infant industries, asserted that Canada did not need reciprocity and could afford it only on a limited number of natural products. A nation-wide propaganda campaign was proposed to enlighten the people on the benefits of protection. Objections were made from the floor, however, and it was suggested that the Association had better not raise the issue but rather should wait until it came up and then try to secure its ends by working on the government at the proper moment. Policy was finally left to the Tariff Committee with power.[8]

4. *Sixty-Eighth Annual Report of the Council of the Montreal Board of Trade: Being for the Year 1910* (pamphlet), Montreal, 1911, pp. 54–55.

5. Toronto *News,* June 25, 1910.

6. The files of the Toronto *News, The Toronto World,* and *The Gazette* (Montreal) for these months furnish evidence of the Conservative-protectionist point of view, while the Toronto *Globe* may be cited on the other side.

7. Toronto *Globe,* September 14, 15, 17, 1910.

8. *Indust. Can.,* 11:251–333. A general campaign was evidently later determined upon. *The Daily Telegraph and the Sun* (St. John, N.B.), Febru-

Late in September Senator Sir George W. Ross, formerly Liberal Premier of Ontario, in two important communications to the Toronto *Globe,* questioned the value and the wisdom of reciprocity. These views were reiterated before the Toronto Board of Trade, November 3, and, reprinted in pamphlet form, became one of the principal opposition documents.[9] This precocious statement set forth most of the telling arguments used later when reciprocity became the subject of formal consideration. Asserting that the proposal stemmed from domestic political exigencies rather than real desire for improved commercial relations, he alleged that an earlier American desire for annexation of Canada had not died out. Canadian conservationists were urged to remember that the larger market for their lumber would also deplete their forests. Canadian transportation interests would be endangered. Existing commercial prosperity would be placed at the mercy of a binding treaty. An entanglement with the United States would imperil the Imperial connection and the British market. Finally, why not let well enough alone? In the December number of the *University Magazine* George E. Foster went over the ground of opposition, furnishing further ammunition for the battle of 1911.[10] On December 29 T. A. Russell, chairman of the Tariff Committee of the Manufacturers' Association, addressing the Toronto Canadian Club in what the *Grain Growers' Guide* denominated the official reply of that organization to the farmers' delegation to Ottawa, canvassed the opposition yet again. He too would let well enough alone in view of inevitable tariff reductions in the

ary 3, 1911 (cited subsequently as St. John *Telegraph-Sun*), reprinted a letter allegedly sent by the Association to all its members urging that "in view of the strong and persistent agitation for tariff reduction now being carried on by the Grain Growers, it is urgently necessary for every manufacturer to give the widest circulation to the arguments advanced by the manufacturers for the maintenance of the tariff as it now stands. A carefully prepared statement of the manufacturers' case was presented to the government a few days ago. This will be printed and sent to you in any number you wish, free of charge, for general distribution. It is especially desirable that this should be sent to your western agents and customers. An antidote for the present free trade propaganda is very necessary in Western Canada."

9. Toronto *Globe,* September 27, 30, 1910; Ross, Sir George W., *Reciprocity* (pamphlet), n.p., n.d.

10. "Reciprocity with the United States," *University Magazine,* 9:550–562 (December, 1910).

States. He viewed political union as the only way in which reciprocity could benefit Canada, and objected to any time arrangements likely to be made as endangering the stability of markets.[11] Thus before Laurier and Fielding had their agreement formulated their enemies were preparing for the inevitable clash and many of the most potent arguments had already been brought forward.

Public opinion as reflected in the newspapers was not particularly excited about the January negotiations. The most numerous expressions of opinion were from Ontario and Quebec, by opponents of reciprocity. This dearth of comment was largely due to the close censorship placed by the negotiators upon news. It may have been, as suggested in some quarters, because there was little feeling that anything important would come from the parleys.[12] Where opinion found expression it formulated arguments which were to be of considerable moment in the following months. A treaty, it was urged, would endanger Canada's fiscal freedom.[13] The United States could best initiate proceedings by reducing rates to the Canadian level.[14] The Imperial tie would be weakened or endangered by assuming obligations outside the British commonwealth.[15] Furthermore, Canadian national development would be made subservient to "the com-

11. *Grain Growers' Guide,* January 11, 1911. January 13 a small "but exceedingly representative" delegation handed Laurier the Association's plea for continued protection. An accompanying argument by Russell reminded the farmers that the home market was best. Laurier replied that the Government would do nothing to disturb the national prosperity. Toronto *News,* January 13, 1911.

12. In estimating the growth of public opinion as registered in the press an effort has been made in this as in subsequent chapters to cover a leading journal of each party in each Province, in the belief that such a procedure gives a reasonable cross section of opinion. Frequently more papers have been read; occasionally the collections of the Dominion Archives and the Parliamentary Library, where the Canadian research was primarily done, were so limited as to make necessary dependence upon fewer than the intended minimum.

13. Toronto *News,* January 6, 1911. It was generally assumed that any agreement would take the form of a treaty; in fact long after the proposal was published it was thus referred to.

14. Toronto *News,* January 6; *Halifax Herald,* January 24; *The Ottawa Evening Citizen,* January 7, 1911.

15. *The Sentinel* (Toronto), January 19; *The Montreal Daily Star,* January 13, 1911.

mercial exigencies of the United States."[16] Finally, why not let well enough alone? As the Montreal *Gazette* put the matter: "Never, therefore, has there been less justification for advocating a radical change in the principle on which the tariff is based, substituting uncertainty for certainty, checking the growth of industrial enterprise and imperilling the success of that which is now helping to build up the country's wealth."[17] *The Montreal Daily Star* at this stage bore the brunt of the attack. In the Maritimes, on the Prairies, and in the Far West little editorial comment appeared prior to the announcement of January 26.

This mild Canadian interest in what was doing at Washington was more than matched below the border. Outside the metropolitan dailies, which carried moderate news coverage with slight editorial comment, the negotiations went almost unnoticed. Examination of the news and editorial columns of twelve papers, representing a like number of northern border States where interest would if anywhere be expressed, discloses that only four commented editorially and but two carried any significant news items. Thus neither public was adequately prepared for the bombshell which the announcement precipitated into both legislatures. In Canada, however, the case had been argued in various quarters and opposition cohorts had been marshaled for the fray.

When, as prearranged, Fielding took the floor in the House of Commons to render an account of his mission, his remarks were received with unmixed surprise that Washington had conceded so much. Beyond this point analysis is difficult. The Conservatives were undoubtedly taken aback, particularly those from the West who saw in reciprocity a start toward what the Prairies had been so loudly demanding.[18] Fielding's stout apology emphasized the large concessions made by the United States and the opportunity offered the Canadian farmer to enter the American market and to obtain agricultural implements on more favorable terms. To forestall expected criticism he insisted that Canada's fiscal independence was unimpaired and that Dominion concessions ought not to injure Canadian

16. Montreal *Star*, January 12.

17. January 14; *cf.* also Toronto *News*, January 9; Montreal *Star*, January 6, 7, 1911.

18. *Reciprocity: A Retrospect* (pamphlet), Ottawa, 1915, p. 5.

manufacturers.[19] Borden replied for the Opposition. His remarks, compounded of desire to place the Government in the wrong without committing the Opposition to too much, repeated several stock arguments and concluded on the note which, in the week of stocktaking that followed, was to be sounded most loudly in the Conservative press.

While not able to apprehend the full meaning and scope of these proposals or the exact results which will ensue from this tariff policy now proposed, I believe it is open to severe and grave criticism by reason . . . of the fact that it does not sufficiently regard the position of this country as an integral and important nation of the British Empire and does not sufficiently regard the purpose, the object and the scope of the policy to which Liberals and Conservatives alike, as I understand the records of the past have been committed with respect to the development of Canada and its status as a nation of the British Empire.[20]

There followed a period during which the Conservatives waited to hear from home, meantime saying for the most part as little as possible. A week end intervened shortly after the announcement, which afforded many, particularly the Ontario members, a chance to go home and talk with their people, and others for whom this was impossible an opportunity to receive letters or telegrams. The Ontario members returned from their week end at home with their attitude noticeably strengthened by contact with their constituents.[21] By the midweek following the announcement the party had begun a series of caucuses which, opening with sentiment still divided and somewhat uncertain, resulted in the eventual decision to make opposition a party matter.[22]

19. *Hansard,* II, 2440–2478; Toronto *Globe,* January 27, 1911.

20. *Hansard,* II, 2497–2502.

21. Borden, Henry (ed.), *Robert Laird Borden: His Memoirs,* 2 vols., New York, 1938, I, 303–304. The late Sir Robert Borden kindly permitted the writer to read this work in manuscript, without privilege of quotation. The present volume had been completed when the *Memoirs* appeared, but there is nothing in Sir Robert's account which essentially alters the narrative or interpretation herein presented.

22. Montreal *Star,* February 1, 2, 3, 1911. The present discussion of the development of Canadian sentiment has been arbitrarily broken off at the end of the first week after the announcement. The story will be resumed at a later point. *Cf.* below, Chap. X.

Meantime various influential interests had been less hesitant in opposition. These open expressions, coupled with the private pressure which was undoubtedly being exerted upon party and leaders, were important in aiding the group to reach a decision, and as such merit sampling. Transportation men generally feared a loss of the long haul from the Prairies, part of which would be diverted to the seaboard through the United States. Sir William Mackenzie of the Canadian Northern was reported from London as opposed. Sir William Whyte of the Canadian Pacific, while fearing the effect on Montreal shipping interests, indicated that his road would suffer less than others, and concluded: "On the whole I do not think that the proposed tariff is a bad thing for the country." Sir Thomas Shaughnessy, president of this road, was at first careful of his opinion, venturing only that it was likely to endanger particular interests. He did not wish to talk about its effect on transportation interests without further study. Only one railroad executive came out flat-footedly in favor of the agreement. E. J. Chamberlin, general manager of the Grand Trunk Pacific, asserted that his road saw "nothing to be alarmed about in the new tariff, either for the company or the country."[23] The spokesman for the Massey-Harris Company, leading Dominion manufacturers of agricultural implements, naturally viewed with alarm and was quoted as considering the agreement "a very serious matter" for his interest, which had "been made the scapegoat as usual."[24] *The Canadian Journal of Commerce* asked pertinently, "who pays the piper?"[25] At St. Catharines, Ontario, the City Council convened to hear a delegation of Niagara Peninsula fruitgrowers assert that the earlier season in the States would ruin their business.[26] The Montreal Board of Trade, after the bitterest discussion on record, adopted resolutions asking that the matter be submitted to the people. The vote, however, was sixty to forty-four, indicating that opinion was by no means unanimous at this stage.[27] In Toronto Mr. (later Sir Joseph) Flavelle,

23. *Edmonton* (Alta.) *Daily Bulletin,* January 28, 1911; *Grain Growers' Guide,* February 8, 1911.
24. Edmonton *Bulletin,* January 30, 1911.
25. February 3, 1911.
26. Toronto *Globe,* January 31, 1911.
27. Montreal *Star,* February 1, 1911. Meeting of January 31.

then the representative of a large meat-packing establishment, and soon one of the agreement's leading opponents, listed several cogent reasons why it should not pass.[28] And in the Commons A. C. Boyce launched a bitter attack on Fielding in connection with the testimonial purse of the preceding spring. The Finance Minister replied, precipitating a discussion in which considerable soiled linen was aired and not a little potential campaign thunder placed in the record.[29] Thus a week of discussion and expression demonstrated to the still hesitant Parliamentary Opposition that a body of sentiment was developing to support legislative obstruction. This becomes still more evident upon surveying the development of public opinion as registered in the press.

Extensive examination of newspaper files indicates a general cleavage along party lines, with an occasional Conservative journal supporting the agreement in the early stages only to swing back into the party line later.[30] Following the example of the party in Parliament, some Conservative sheets hesitated to make definite commitments at first.[31] Geographically, the Ontario, Quebec, and British Columbia papers were predominantly hostile, both in volume and tenor of opinion expressed. In the Maritimes and the Prairie Provinces the burden of opinion was favorable, with a touch of regret in the latter area at the slight reduction on agricultural implements. As is inevitable in any tariff discussion, the herrings of local interest obscured the trails of both sides.

Conservative arguments were widely varied and combined an economic approach with a more concentrated attack on the agreement's dangers to national and Imperial welfare which was the chief characteristic of Conservative opinion at this early stage. Foreshadowed, too, were certain lines of attack which later flowered into venomous appeals to party and to racial prejudice. From the economic stand-

28. *The Toronto Daily Star*, January 27, 1911.

29. *Hansard*, II, 2748–2827, January 31.

30. The following discussion is based upon editorial opinion gathered from twenty-eight papers, divided geographically as follows: Ontario, 10; Quebec, 5; the Maritimes, 6; the Prairie Provinces, 6; British Columbia, 1. The two Conservative papers which reversed themselves were the *Edmonton* (Alta.) *Journal* and *The Evening Journal* (Ottawa).

31. Montreal *Star*, January 28; Montreal *Gazette*, January 27, 1911.

point it was urged that the many concessions to the United States would be disastrous to Canadian producers.[32] The Toronto *News* argued that the higher American market would determine agricultural commodity prices, resulting in increased living costs to Canadian industrial and salaried classes.[33] The future security of Canadian railroads, constructed at huge governmental expense from east to west through long stretches of unproductive territory between Ontario and the Prairies, would face the competition of American roads which would divert much traffic to north-and-south channels.[34] Relaxation of border restrictions would cause the closing of American branch factories, recently become a source of revenue and a labor outlet.[35] Conservation of Canadian forests was incompatible with the operation of the agreement.[36]

More numerous and more heavily emphasized than these economic pleas were others directed to the possible loss of national integrity and Imperial solidarity. Attention was early and often called to the threat to national independence which might follow on the heels of such close economic relations with so powerful a neighbor.[37] The argument most frequently and cogently used was the threat of reciprocity to Canada's place in and relations with the Empire. This at once appealed to patriotism and purported to elevate the matter above mere partisan bickering. The Conservative journals rang the changes on this theme with vigor and enthusiasm, urging particularly that the Imperial preference was in jeopardy, with consequent fears for the integrity of the Imperial connection. The Toronto *News* remarked early in the discussion that "if . . . this agreement goes into effect it seems impossible that we can hope for a preference in British markets. . . . We take this step just when 48 per cent. of the British people have declared for tariff reform, and thus Canada

32. *The Mail and Empire* (Toronto), quoted in Toronto *News,* January 27, 1911.

33. January 27, 30, 1911. Echoed by Halifax *Herald,* February 1, 1911.

34. Toronto *News,* January 30; Montreal *Star,* February 1, 1911.

35. Toronto *News,* January 30, 1911.

36. Montreal *Star,* January 28, 1911.

37. Toronto *World,* January 27 (quoted in Ottawa *Citizen,* January 28); Toronto *News,* January 28; Toronto *Sentinel,* February 2, 1911. The *News* remarked that "the ultimate political results may be disintegrating to a serious degree."

probably will wreck the whole movement for interimperial preferences." The Toronto *Sentinel* saw ultimate free trade, absorption,
and loss of the British connection in the offing, and the Montreal
Star, somewhat less pessimistic, still felt that "free trade in food
stuffs between Canada and the United States spells death to a preferential arrangement between Canada and the United Kingdom."
In the Maritimes the Halifax *Herald* feared for the future of Imperial relationships, and *The Standard* (St. John, N.B.) saw in the
agreement "a deliberate effort on the part of the Laurier government to take Canada out of the Empire."[38]

Even thus early two factors appeared which became more prominent in the later and more vindictive stages of the debate—appeals
to race feeling and slurs on the Government's administrative record.
The Montreal *Star,* after commenting on the likelihood that reciprocity would weaken the Imperial tie, inquired how this would affect the French-Canadian elements of Quebec's population. "Can
they afford to see the British flag run down and the American flag
run up? With the British flag will go all the guarantees to the
French language and the Roman Catholic religion which were
granted by the conquerors to the conquered on the Plains of Abra-
ham and which have been included in every national constitution
from that day down to the British North America Act." With all
these privileges now in possession, it was asked, "Would they enjoy
this protection if the Provinces should become part of the American
Union?" A reply was suggested by inquiring as to the position of
the French language in Louisiana. This was a definite plea addressed
to a racial and religious element whose allegiance to the party in
power had already been sorely tried by the Laurier navy.[39] And the
Halifax *Herald* attacked Fielding for alleged inefficiency in connection with the Farmers' Bank episode, to be noted more fully subsequently, and for accepting the testimonial without insisting upon
full publicity concerning the contributors.[40]

On the other hand, the protagonists of the agreement had to
shoulder a double task, which throughout the discussion was to di-

---

38. Toronto *News,* January 27; Toronto *Sentinel,* February 2; Montreal
Star, January 30; *The Standard* (St. John, N.B.) (quoted in St. John *Telegraph-Sun,* January 31, 1911).

39. January 31, 1911.   40. January 30, February 1, 1911.

vide their energies. In the first place the bargain must be proven a bargain to Canada—converts must be won by positive arguments. In the second place opposition arguments must be refuted and overborne. From the start this duality confused and weakened the Liberal press, and the first week's discussion was directed almost as much to saying "No" to Conservative charges as to introducing reciprocity's positive advantages. As to positive arguments, the most obvious and important point to be made was the advantage gained by giving Canadian natural products access to the "larger market" to the south. This applied alike to Maritime fish, potatoes, and fruits, to Saskatchewan cattle, and to Manitoba wheat, and was everywhere acclaimed by the Liberals as an outstanding triumph.[41] Aside from this, principal attention was devoted to warding off opposition shafts. The Liberals vigorously scouted the fear of annexation which had been sounded by the Conservatives during the negotiations and which was implied in their fears for national integrity after the agreement was announced. The Toronto *Globe* scathingly inquired in reply to such insinuations: "What sort of base-born, nation-bartering men do these faint hearts think Canadians are?"[42] Thus the ghost was raised which would not down, and which during the campaign assumed all the proportions of a very flesh-and-blood bogey. Again it was asserted that the deflection of trade from established east-west channels, abnormal as these were geographically, would either not occur or would be of slight consequence.[43] As might be expected, the loudest counterblast was directed against the important opposition argument anent Canada and the Empire, and it was stoutly averred that both the preference and the Imperial tie would remain unimpaired under reciprocity.[44]

Ottawa and Washington alike registered surprise at the scope of the agreement. Taft's message announcing it to Congress received

41. *The Island Patriot* (Charlottetown, P.E.I.), January 27; St. John *Telegraph-Sun*, January 27; Ottawa *Citizen*, February 1; Toronto *News*, January 27; *Grain Growers' Guide*, February 1; *The Morning Leader* (Regina, Sask.), January 27; *The Winnipeg* (Man.) *Evening Tribune*, January 27; Winnipeg *Free Press*, January 28, 1911.

42. January 30; *cf.* also *Daily Witness* (Montreal), January 27, 1911.

43. Montreal *Witness*, January 31, 1911.

44. Toronto *Globe*, January 27; St. John *Telegraph-Sun*, January 27; Halifax *Chronicle*, January 31, 1911.

in the House the greatest ovation accorded any of his communications. There was less enthusiasm in the Senate, where only thirty members were present to hear the message read.[45] Political implications quickly appeared. Taft's stroke in advancing a program which would appeal to large groups regardless of party lines evidently strengthened his proposals.[46] On the other hand, the existence of disgruntled local interests and dissatisfied elements of his own party boded ill for his measure. To the important and already none-too-loyal Insurgent group reciprocity offered at once a challenge and an embarrassment. Coming largely from the agrarian Northwest, they saw in reciprocity's mutual lowering of barriers on farm products, particularly wheat, a blow at their sectional interests—a blow so severe as to demand their uncompromising opposition. In the record, however, were long speeches out of their own mouths demanding tariff reform. Here was that reform in an unwelcome and unexpected guise. The problem of reconciling local interest with previous protestations was easily solved, but in the solving the Insurgents left themselves out on a limb and exposed alike to the jeers of pro-Taft Republicans and of Democrats—jeers of Democrats, because it was early hinted that the President would find support in opposition ranks, support which time was to show would be necessary to the success of his agreement.[47] It soon became apparent that the President had raised an issue likely to be of national importance, that he had appealed widely to the consuming public, and at the same time had sowed some dragon's teeth which were likely to sprout into partisan conflicts.

Out of doors, affected interests were not far behind their Canadian compeers in making their ideas heard. Most vociferous were farmers, speaking through the Grange and a majority of the farm journals. The Executive Committee of the National Grange promptly adopted hostile resolutions and issued a statement to be circularized

45. New York *Tribune,* January 27; *The American Banker,* 76:247–248 (January 28, 1911). The present account confines itself to the reception of the agreement and to early statements by affected interests and in the press. The legislative story will be told below.

46. *Harper's Weekly,* 55:4 (February 11, 1911).

47. *The Independent,* 70:219, 265–266 (February 2, 1911); Washington *Herald,* January 28; New York *Tribune,* January 27, 1911.

to its 7,500 locals. These resolutions took the position that tariff reduction was being undertaken at the expense of the farmer, whose products received less protection than manufactures, and who would by reciprocity be forced to compete with Canada's exports of food-stuffs without adequate compensatory reduction of the burden on manufactures. This opened a strong campaign in which, as will appear later, the Grange was used as the willing tool of other interests, with more cash but a smaller clientele, to influence the farmer against trade concessions to Canada. Several State Granges soon followed the national body into opposition.[48] Early issues of the farm journals were sometimes temporizing in their remarks but more often they were openly opposed; in very few instances was comment favorable.[49] The lumber interests, also subjected to reduced protection, were largely opposed in early statements.[50] Several financial sheets, on the other hand, recorded themselves as favorable to the deal.[51]

Newspaper publishers were naturally well pleased with their prospective gains. Ridder promptly wrote the members of the Association:

Users of print paper have a direct and immediate interest in securing this relief from combinations of papermakers which have been taxing

48. New York *Tribune*, February 5, 9, 1911.

49. Opposed were such papers as *The American Cultivator* (Boston), February 4, 1911, p. 8; *Michigan Farmer and Live Stock Journal* (Detroit), 136:118 (February 4, 1911); *The New-England Homestead* (Boston), 62:180 (February 4, 1911); *The Journal of Agriculture* (St. Louis), February 9, 1911, p. 8. *The American Agriculturist* (Springfield, Mass., etc.), 87:176 (February 4, 1911), urged delay until the fall to give time for development of informed opinion. *The Progressive Farmer and Southern Farm Gazette* (Raleigh, N.C.), 26:19 (February 4, 1911), was mildly favorable.

50. See for example *American Lumberman* (Chicago), February 4, 1911, pp. 30, 35; *The Mississippi Valley Lumberman* (Minneapolis), February 3, 1911, p. 31; *The Southern Lumberman* (Nashville and Memphis), February 4, 1911, pp. 15–16. The editor of *Hardwood Record* (Chicago), however, was of opinion that "it will not make a Continental cent's difference to the industry whether lumber is on the free list or not." February 10, 1911, p. 30.

51. *The Commercial & Financial Chronicle* (New York), 92:216–217, 289–290 (January 28, February 4, 1911); *The Financial World* (New York and Chicago), 16:12 (February 4, 1911); *Commercial West* (Minneapolis), February 4, 1911, p. 7.

publishers to the extent of $5,000,000 per annum. Free print paper
from Canada should reduce print paper prices promptly and materially.
The reciprocity arrangement is urged also on the broad lines of conserving our forests and of removing a tax upon knowledge.

Will you not promptly communicate with your Senators and Representatives in Congress and urge favorable action?[52]

Manufacturers were correspondingly downcast and their organ asserted that free imports of wood pulp and print paper meant "virtually assigning the business to Canadian interests. . . . The paper
manufacturers justly regard themselves as having been unduly discriminated against."[53] The American Paper and Pulp Association,
lobby organization of the manufacturers, circularized its membership, dolefully asking, "Do you know what reciprocity means to
you, as a paper manufacturer or as a jobber?—free paper from
Canada . . . the disorganization of the paper business."[54] Thus in
the States as in Canada interested groups contended for their own
ends. American opposition, however, had not had the training in self-
expression which more widespread Canadian attention had developed,
and was to wait longer to reach its full volume.

The press also took a remarkably unanimous stand, regardless of
political or sectional allegiances. The tendency of early discussion
was to commend the agreement on the basis of its advantage to local
interests or to preserve a rather noncommittal attitude—again doubtless because of local interests. On the whole the atmosphere was one
of benevolent approval. Where possible, local interests became the
basis of favorable arguments, as in the case of Maine potatoes and
fish.[55] Elsewhere general arguments, such as cutting the high cost of

52. January 27. Quoted in *American Economist*, 47:81 (February 10,
1911).

53. *Paper, Inc.* (New York), 2:14 (February 1, 1911).

54. Quoted in *The Paper Mill and Wood Pulp News* (New York), February 4, 1911, p. 1 (cited subsequently as *Paper Mill*).

55. *Lewiston* (Me.) *Evening Journal*, January 27, 1911. The conclusions
presented herewith are based upon information gathered from twenty-seven
papers grouped geographically as follows: New England, 5; New York and
Pennsylvania, 3; Middle West, 4; Far West, 3; South, 2. The papers were
examined for the two weeks following the announcement of the agreement,
and not for a single week as in the case of Canada, in order to secure a better
picture of the more slowly developing newspaper sentiment in the States. It

living, acquisition of new markets, mutual advantage, etc., were ad-
duced.[56] Occasionally the agreement was supported without giving
any adequate reasons for such action. Several Midwestern editors
delighted to hold up to public view the Insurgents, squirming on the
griddle of their own heating.[57] One element of later press propaganda
was conspicuously absent—the drive to convince the farmer that
reciprocity was for his good. The argument that reciprocity would
reduce the cost of living received more attention now than it did
later on, since it was easy for opponents to ask how this could be
true unless the farmer had to take less for his produce—a question
which the friends of the agreement found it difficult to answer to the
satisfaction of the other side.[58] And finally, the dominant newspaper
motive in supporting reciprocity—private advantage through free
newsprint—was now as later seldom mentioned.[59]

Thus by early February both countries had been given the issue.
Canada had canvassed it the more thoroughly, as behooved the smaller
party to a big contract. United States opinion had begun to survey
the economic aspects. On each side considerable underbrush had been
cleared away by those who wished to clarify the issue; those who
wished to obscure it to their own ends were preparing the planting
of other and thicker underbrush behind which they might attack or
support it. To the south reciprocity quickly became the center of a
legislative fight in which Taft was to match first wits and then power
with the members of his own party to secure passage of his agree-

should be noted, too, that sixteen papers, in addition to the ones covered in
the following analysis, carried no editorial comment.

56. *Idaho Statesman* (Boise), February 5; *Philadelphia Press* (quoted in
New York *Tribune*, January 31); *Salt Lake* (Utah) *Tribune*, January 28,
1911.

57. *The Milwaukee* (Wis.) *Sentinel*, January 29; *Sioux Falls* (S.D.)
Argus-Leader, February 1; *Sioux City* (Ia.) *Journal*, January 28, 1911.

58. *Morning Oregonian* (Portland), January 31; *The Manchester* (N.H.)
Union, February 1, 1911. The Sioux City *Journal*, May 2, 1911, called attention to this dilemma, as did other papers.

59. A few journals proved exceptions to this generalization. *Cf. Concord*
(N.H.) *Evening Monitor*, January 27; Salt Lake *Tribune*, January 28; *New
York American*, January 27, 1911. However, practically every paper examined printed the pulp and paper schedule *in toto* in its first announcement
of the agreement.

ment; wits failing in the first round, power was to win the second—power compounded of loyal Republican and opportunist Democratic support of a Republican President who wished to be reëlected. To this battle we now turn.

CHAPTER VIII

CONGRESS FAILS TO ACT

THE presidential message of January 26 stoutly defended reciprocity in principle, and as proposed in practice. A bill, drafted in the State Department, followed shortly and was referred in a routine manner to the Committee on Ways and Means, setting in motion a remarkable train of events.[1] To carry his scheme, born in fear of the future of his party and the success of his own administration, Taft was to be forced to use executive pressure unprecedented during his incumbency; he was to find himself allied with the Democrats against a large portion of his own party to pass a measure which many Republicans opposed as a repudiation of sound doctrine; he was to find the alliance, gleefully accepted by the Democrats, made an entering wedge to pry open the whole tariff question, which neither he nor his party wanted attacked in that manner; he was to alienate even more thoroughly the Insurgents, already at the point of dissolving party allegiance; and he was, despite his immediate victory, to drive several large-sized nails in the coffin which was to house Republican hopes in November, 1912. Of all this he could, however, have had small inkling as he wrote Senator Aldrich of his hope to save the protective principle as applied to industry by establishing reciprocity in natural products.[2] Suiting action to words, he went promptly to work, and by all the devices of publicity, cajolery, and propaganda

1. For the message and text of the agreement, *cf. Record,* 61st Cong., 3d Sess., pp. 1515–1519. The bill (H.R. 32216) was introduced January 28. *Ibid.,* p. 1618.

2. January 29. *Taft Papers.* He wrote: "Many say that if this bill passes, it is the beginning of the destruction of the system of protection. I can not see this result. . . . The movement against high prices now can only be properly moderated so as to prevent its giving us free trade by withholding high tariff rates where they are not needed. . . . If I could secure the passage of the present bill, I could put myself in a strong attitude to resist any excessive reduction of the duties on manufactures which would destroy them. . . . If this agreement is adopted we shall have largely satisfied the demand for the removal of obstruction to lower prices in the necessities of life, and with the report of the tariff commission to set the proper limit to any reduction, I can save our policy of protection. If not, I feel sure we are going to

at his command sought action despite the conviction that success might be disastrous to him personally.[3] Before the fight was well under way Archie Butt, his military aide, could write his opinion that the President was "putting on his fighting clothes" and quote Taft as saying: "I think I have got far enough now in my administration to let some of the timber I don't like drop overboard, and I propose to begin from now on to show my teeth."[4] During the committee hearings of early February the executive branch prepared a series of attacks on the enemies of reciprocity which, delivered during the short session, form a background of legislation altogether new in the Taft administration—so new as to deserve first chronicling in this story of legislative action under executive spur. Since time was short (the session expired by limitation on March 4), prompt action was necessary. It included suggestions to commercial organizations, prepared statements from the State Department for use of interested parties, a presidential barnstorming tour, speeches at strategic points by Cabinet officers, and the exertion of individual pressure upon doubtful Senators in the debate's late stages—all coupled with increasing general pressure upon Congress and a threatened special session in default of action.[5]

Four days after the announcement of the agreement the New York *Tribune* referred to the President as believing that the time had come for consumers to express their views to their representatives as

be beaten in the next presidential election and then the Democracy without restraint will play havoc with our industries and create chaos in business from which we shall be a long time recovering." He insisted that all this could be done without harm to the farmers, who were disturbed at the prospect of reciprocity.

3. January 30 he wrote to O. T. Bannard: "My judgment, before I sent in the message . . . was that this will blow me up politically." *Taft Papers.*

4. January 28. These statements were made apropos of the Lorimer case, then pending before the Senate, but are indicative of a changing presidential attitude. Butt, Archie, *Taft and Roosevelt: The Intimate Letters of Archie Butt, Military Aide,* 2 vols., Garden City, N.Y., 1930, II, 584–585.

5. The hostile *American Review of Reviews* remarked in July, when the fight bade fair to succeed, that "Mr. Taft's fight to carry a reciprocity measure, that no party or faction in Congress believed in or desired upon its intrinsic merits, must rank with the most extraordinary political feats in the history of any American administration." 44:5 (July, 1911). *Cf.* also *Paper,* 4:14 (July 19, 1911).

an offset to the paid lobbies of the protected interests.[6] To a New York correspondent he expressed his thanks that the matter was to be put before the Chamber of Commerce and similar organizations, "because it is by arousing public opinion that we can hope to enact the agreement into law."[7] Pepper suggested to the President's secretary the advisability of making contact with the Chicago Association of Commerce, since if that organization "could be waked up and would take some action, good results will follow."[8] The Bureau of Trade Relations of the Department of State prepared a series of articles outlining the advantages of the agreement to particular localities. These showed how both farmer and manufacturer would benefit from the mutual exchanges facilitated by reciprocity.[9]

Sensing a hard fight, the President went directly to the people over the heads of Congress and in a series of speeches fought hard for his agreement. Speaking before a farm audience at the National Corn Exposition at Columbus, Ohio, February 10, he addressed himself to the general merits of reciprocity, stressing particularly its value to the Northwest and the fact that the farmer need not fear its effects.[10] To the Illinois State Legislature the following day he repeated the argument of his Aldrich letter to the effect that a judicious abandonment of unnecessary protection was essential to maintenance of the protective system against unreasoning attacks.[11] Back in Washington, before the Pan-American Commercial Conference he advocated reciprocity not only with Canada but with all of North and South America. That this was regarded as something of a tacti-

6. January 31, 1911.

7. To Eugene H. Outerbridge, January 31. *Taft Papers*.

8. January 31, 1911. *Ibid.*

9. Sample statements, applying to North Carolina and Illinois, respectively, may be found in *Record*, 61st Cong., 3d Sess., p. 2448, and *The Chicago Daily Tribune*, February 17, 1911. Norris, calling on Pepper "in a very good humor," promised to begin distribution at once. Pepper to Knox, February 7, 1911. *Knox Papers*.

10. His speeches at Columbus and at Springfield are printed in *Reciprocity with Canada: Papers in the Consideration of Bill (H.R. 32216) Relating to Reciprocity with Canada*, Sen. Doc. 862, 61st Cong., 3d Sess., Washington, 1911, pp. 31–41 (cited subsequently as *Sen. Doc. 862*). *Cf.* also New York *Tribune*, February 11, 1911.

11. New York *Tribune*, February 12, 1911.

cal blunder is evidenced by his hasty insistence that he spoke in the abstract and contemplated no other immediate action, though willing to approve any such agreement under favorable conditions.[12] During his remarks he announced that he had already forgathered with Champ Clark, slated as Speaker of the next House, who was present at the meeting. Later the two retired to a private room and made plans for the forthcoming fight, which Clark warned Taft would be a bitter one. That the scrambling of party lines had begun was indicated by Archie Butt's rather plaintive note to "Dear Clara": "It does seem strange, seeing the President and the leader of the Minority hatching plots to defeat the plans of the Republican party in the House and Senate. But such is the case. The President declared himself and Champ to be partners in this business."[13] The last public presidential pronouncement was a letter to Nahum J. Bachelder, president of the National Grange and archenemy of the agreement, after it was evident that a special session would be necessary. This letter put into the record for the continued fight Taft's opinion that the agreement would not injure the farmer.[14] Several of these statements reflect, as well as the President's determination, the main line of opposition—a line to become even more evident as the story unfolds. The farmer had been pushed out on the stage as the main target of propaganda and his welfare was already being made the bone of contention between enemies and friends of reciprocity—a sudden solicitude for the tiller of the soil which was to issue strangely from the lips of his new-found advocates.

The President's voice was not the only one to be raised in praise of the agreement. Cabinet members and interested friends were drafted to spread the gospel. Secretary of State Knox, in speeches at Chicago (before the local Association of Commerce, February 15) and Pittsburgh (February 19), dwelt on the historical aspects of the problem and deprecated the abandonment of reciprocity in the

12. February 13. New York *Tribune,* February 14, 15, 1911. *The Indianapolis Star,* February 15, 1911.

13. Butt, *Taft and Roosevelt,* II, 594. This prospective alliance with the Democrats is further foreshadowed by Taft's letter of February 6 to Frank A. Day, Chairman of the Democratic State Central Committee of Minnesota, in which he stated that he hoped "ultimately, with the aid of my co-workers and your co-workers in politics, to get it through." *Taft Papers.*

14. New York *Tribune,* March 4, 1911.

nineteenth century. He also devoted considerable time to laying the bogey of annexation which the Congressional debates had raised.[15] At Chicago he was aided by James J. Hill. Secretary of Agriculture James Wilson entered the lists on February 9 with a long letter to the Legislative Committee of the National Grange answering its telegram of the fourth. Later in the month he spoke at Buffalo. He then shared the platform with Hugh Guthrie, M.P., in an official defense of the agreement.[16] Both his defense and its method were something of a liability. It was gleefully pointed out that he had been dragooned into supporting the President after many years of advocacy of protection for the farmer.[17] One of his arguments which called forth mild amusement in the farm journals was that the agreement would be a boon to the farmer because it allowed free importation of barbed wire from Canada; this because it was soon discovered that no barbed wire was being imported.[18]

Finally, through personal conference, telegraphic communication, and friendly intermediaries the President endeavored to turn the tide. After the Western trip he put considerable pressure upon House leaders, who were hesitant to push the matter to his liking. Particularly recalcitrant were Speaker Cannon and John Dalzell of Pennsylvania, an influential member of the House.[19] When need arose he did not hesitate to speak sharply to those whom he considered doubtful. In point is his letter of February 27 to Republican Senator William O. Bradley of Kentucky: "I regard this as the most important measure of my administration. . . . I can say to you that I shall be very bitterly disappointed if I can't count on your support when I need it. . . . I must say that you are the last man in the Senate that I thought would hesitate to support me in a matter in which I have given all my heart and strength."[20] Bradley and his Democratic colleague, Thomas H. Paynter, were subjected to con-

15. New York *Tribune*, February 16, 20, 1911.

16. *Buffalo Evening News,* February 23. His letter is printed in the New York *Tribune,* February 10, 1911, and in *Sen. Doc.* 862, 61st Cong., 3d Sess., pp. 42–46.

17. Portland *Oregonian*, February 11, 1911; *Record*, 61st Cong., 3d Sess., *Appendix*, p. 106.

18. *The Prairie Farmer*, April 15, 1911, p. 20.

19. Butt, *Taft and Roosevelt*, II, 595–597.

20. *Taft Papers.*

siderable executive pressure through friends in Louisville and Chicago, through Kentucky commercial associations, and through individual communications engineered by the President's newspaper connections.[21] Thus presidential initiative combated the inertia of a divided and uncertain Congress—an inertia which was to show itself temporarily the stronger and to compel the President to call a special session wherein his insistence tilted against the balanced forces on either side of his proposal.

The first rebuff was not long delayed. Despite his urgent personal request Sereno E. Payne of the Committee on Ways and Means refused to sponsor the bill enacting the agreement, and it was necessary to call upon Samuel W. McCall of Massachusetts to do the honors.[22] After McCall had obliged, Taft urged Payne to expedite the hearings, indicating that, if a favorable recommendation should result, he would then ask the Rules Committee to "give us the benefit of a rule for the immediate consideration of the bill without amendment."[23] Committee hearings opened on February 2 and continued with some interruptions through the ninth. They were devoted almost entirely to opponents, including the fishing interest, manufacturers of paper and lumber, and producers of dairy products and of barley malt. Few favorable witnesses appeared; some evidence was introduced indicating that not all interests connected with the fish business were hostile, and John Norris and Don C. Seitz assured the committee of the publishers' satisfaction.[24] The committee reported

21. Numerous letters and telegrams in the *Taft Papers* outline this campaign, especially J. G. Schaffer to Taft, February 6, March 2; Schaffer to Charles D. Norton (Taft's secretary), February 28; George Du Relle to Taft, March 1; Taft to Du Relle, March 3, 1911.

22. The request was made in a letter of January 26 in which Taft wrote: "As this is an administration measure, I should very much like the Chairman of the Ways and Means Committee to act as the representative of the Administration in this movement, the importance of which I do not think can be exaggerated. . . . I should feel disappointed if the measure here in the American Congress did not have the prestige of your introduction and support." *Taft Papers.*

23. January 30, 1911. *Ibid.*

24. New York *Tribune*, February 3–10, 1911. *Reciprocity with Canada: Hearings before the Committee on Ways and Means of the House of Representatives 61st Congress 3d Session on H.R. 32216*, Washington, 1911. These hearings were not given a number in the regular document series. Since

the bill favorably by a vote of twelve to seven on February 11, after a sharp split which found half of the twelve Republican members joining one Democrat to oppose a majority divided equally between Republicans and Democrats.[25]

McCall's majority report set forth the mutual benefits of reciprocity: to Canada it would mean that the slow growth enforced upon the Dominion by artificially nurtured east-west communication between widely separated productive areas would be exchanged for natural north-south commerce and rapid growth in national stature; the United States by removing the tariff barrier to the north would stimulate her trade by the equivalent of "another Louisiana Purchase." Answering the objections already raised he argued that the farmers, particularly the wheatgrowers, would not be injured, since the tariff had never influenced the domestic price of wheat, which had always been fixed in the Liverpool market. Furthermore, the time was not far distant when the United States would cease to export wheat, in which case access to the Canadian market, sans tariff, would be a blessing. The agreement was immediately beneficial, even with both countries exporting wheat, since large amounts needed by the Minneapolis milling interests could come in from Manitoba, freeing like amounts for export purposes, with consequent profits to the United States in handling and processing. Similar arguments were advanced to show that producers of barley and corn would gain. In summary, prospective advantages of the proposed schedules were asserted to be: "First, that they will act as regulators of the prices of very many necessary articles generally consumed by our people, and in times of scarcity in particular articles will tend to keep prices down; and, second, by augmenting the prosperity of the country, which, according to her population is by far the best foreign customer we have, they will increase her purchasing power, and thus increase our own trade."

a more complete account of hearings will be given at a later point, comment on the early hearings will be limited.

25. New York *Tribune,* February 12, 1911; *Record,* 61st Cong., 3d Sess., p. 2375; *Reciprocity with Canada, House Report 2150,* 61st Cong., 3d Sess. Consists of a report by McCall for the majority and one signed by six Republicans, headed by Dalzell, for the minority. R. F. Broussard, a Louisiana Democrat, reported in the press as opposed to the agreement in committee, did not sign the minority report.

The minority report objected in principle and detail. The bill, hastily presented without consulting members of Congress, involved tariff revision and had received insufficient consideration. Specifically, it revived the type of agreement in vogue from 1854 to 1866, which proved "disastrous" to the United States; it was un-Republican, calling for reciprocity in competing products, contrary to the accepted principle; finally, it was "class legislation of the most obnoxious character. It singles out from all the beneficiaries of tariff legislation the farmer. Everything he produces is put upon the free list—everything he buys is a protected article." Thus the agreement's opponents sought to show that the farmer was the scapegoat for the administration's sins of commission.

The House debate opened with reciprocity facing rather heavy odds—odds created on the one hand by other issues competing for attention before Congress and the country, and on the other by indifference and hostility within the President's own party which were to be offset only by the adherence of numerous Democrats to his standard. Congress faced several problems, each of some intrinsic importance and all, with their demands on the short time left, dangerous rivals of the administration's pet measure. Secretary Ballinger was under fire in the House, as was a move by Robert E. Peary's friends to secure promotion for the polar explorer. Also to the fore was the discussion of a bill creating a new Tariff Commission—perennial refuge of antireform Republicans. Senatorial oratory, not so easily curbed in response to executive behest, heatedly discussed related problems in the effort to expel William Lorimer, accused of having secured his Illinois seat by improper means, and the proposal to amend the Constitution to provide direct election of Senators. Congress and country alike were concerned over the formation of the National Progressive Republican League (January 21) to focus the dissatisfactions which had been gathering for years; nine Senators and thirteen Representatives had been on its original roster, all Republicans and each a potential factor in the reciprocity decision. Nor were Insurgents alone a danger to the measure—party wheel horses evinced open opposition or lukewarm support.

The same papers which reported the President's speech at Springfield, the very day the bill was introduced, carried the text of a letter written by Speaker Cannon to State Senator Martin B. Bailey of

Illinois opposing the plan.[26] And two days later the Chief Executive was to write in vain to Dalzell, Chairman of the Committee on Rules and a signer of the minority report against reciprocity, to ask him to call a meeting of his committee to report a special rule to expedite the bill's passage.[27] No rule was forthcoming, and the bill had to take its parliamentary chances. To offset this obvious hostility and less obvious indifference in his own party, the President gained aid from the other side, for the Democrats had caucused on the sixth and voted, ninety to twenty-two, to support reciprocity.[28] Thus the President went into his biggest fight minus the help of party leaders in each House (for Senator Aldrich had been absent most of the winter nursing his health) and dependent upon a substitute captain leading an army largely composed of Democrats to win the battle.

The result was a two-day fight as bitter as the House had witnessed in years, with arguments running the gamut of opposition and defense, with most of the time occupied by the bill's opponents, with troubled Insurgents generally in opposition, and with delighted Democrats taunting their Republican opponents and finally making possible the passage of the bill.[29] During the debate Champ Clark, Democratic Speaker-designate, made unfortunate remarks on annexation which furnished Canadian opponents of the pact with some of their most explosive ammunition. Possibly stimulated by the frequent laughter and applause which punctuated the earlier part of his address, he may have been led into unwitting exaggeration when he took up the annexation matter. Whatever his thought, his words were dangerous, as he said: "I am for it, because I hope to see the day when the American flag will float over every square foot of the British-North American possessions clear to the North Pole." These sentiments, promptly repudiated by Taft in a letter to McCall, by Knox in his Chicago speech, and by the daily and periodical press, called forth a question in the British House of Commons, angered Canadians, and furnished ideal propaganda material for those in Canada who claimed to see danger for the future of the British connection.[30]

26. New York *Tribune,* February 12, 1911.
27. February 13. *Taft Papers.*
28. Indianapolis *Star,* February 7, 1911.
29. New York *Tribune,* February 14, 15, 1911.
30. *Record,* 61st Cong., 3d Sess., p. 2520; Taft to McCall, February 15,

As has been noted earlier (in the survey of developing opinion, Chapter VII), the farmer became a major object of solicitude. This great producing class would be injured; this great producing class would *not* be injured. The farmer's situation constituted the most frequent if not the most important argument advanced on either side. Tactically the advantage lay with reciprocity's opponents, who could force its friends into the negative position of insisting that the common object of their devotion would *not* be hurt—thus leaving room for a lurking doubt. The obvious reason why he would be hurt, iterated and reiterated, was that he alone was deprived of protection and offered as a sacrifice on the altar of free trade. This, it was alleged, was discrimination and class legislation of the worst sort.[31] For good measure and for home consumption, arguments including the fishing and lumber interests among the endangered producers were added.[32] The agreement's proponents, if on the defensive, argued the farmer's case more adroitly. Several Democrats happily informed that worthy that so-called protection of his products was ineffectual anyway, though long used as a Republican vote-catcher.[33] Several pointed to the larger and expanding market which would lead to increased exports, especially of products which, because of seasonal or climatic factors, could be shipped advantageously to Canada.[34] Furthermore, he need not fear the small volume of Canadian products likely to come in; McCall, for example, noted the fact that the United States

1911. *Taft Papers; Nation,* 92:181 (February 23, 1911); New York *Tribune,* February 16, 1911; *Commercial & Financial Chronicle,* February 25, 1911. It is difficult to determine his real feeling from the context. The press, at first silent, and then anxious to play down the significance of the remarks by intimating that Clark was joking, is an unsafe guide.

31. *Cf.* the language of the minority report, quoted above and repeated by Dalzell in the debate, *Record,* 61st Cong., 3d Sess., p. 2513. Other speeches ringing the changes on this theme will be found in *ibid.,* pp. 2440, 2458, 2516–2517, 2533–2536, 2538, 2539, 2540, 2546, 2548, 2550, 2558; *ibid., Appendix,* pp. 90–91, 101, 106–107, 113, 114, 127, 131, 139, 143, 148, 163, 167 ff., 182.

32. *Record,* 61st Cong., 3d Sess., pp. 2517, 2527, 2534, 2548, 2558. The Congressional debate on the agreement is covered in Swartz, W. G., "The Proposed Canadian-American Reciprocity Agreement of 1911," *Journal of Economic and Business History,* 3:118–148 (November, 1930).

33. *Record,* 61st Cong., 3d Sess., pp. 2446–2447, 2451, 2509, 2546.

34. *Ibid.,* pp. 2436, 2446, 2452, 2520.

exported to Canada over the tariff wall more than twice as much butter and fifteen times as many eggs as came south.[35] Some attention was called to a matter more prominent in the second debate— the position of the Northwestern wheatgrower. McCall tried to show that this interest need fear nothing from the influx of Manitoba wheat, since so long as both countries produced a surplus the price was fixed in a world market.[36]

Having paid their respects to agriculture, both sides advanced other arguments which will be presented, as far as possible, as antitheses, giving the defenders of reciprocity the first word. Urban representatives saw the high cost of living cut, to the profit of the consumer; this, indeed, without the farmer losing his profits. Here was a seeming contradiction which the other side wanted explained.[37] Opponents explained the high cost of living as due to middleman monopolies and high freight rates, which reciprocity would not help. Therefore, even though the price of farm products might be depressed the reductions would be absorbed on the way to the ultimate consumer.[38] One timid Republican insisted (under leave to print) that reciprocity did not violate the protective principle, only to be drowned out by a chorus of contrary assertions.[39] To offset the statement that the agreement was one means to keep the manufacture of paper south of the border it was charged that it would drive the mills to Canada.[40] When friends attempted to minimize dangers on the ground that the agreement was based on legislation and so amendable or terminable unilaterally, only once was the contrary danger (to be emphasized later) of lack of permanence brought forward.[41]

This balancing of arguments left the opposition with several more shafts to loose—shafts which were not parried, perhaps because of the short two days allotted to debate. Several Northwestern members alleged that the agreement aided the trusts, which would obtain free

35. *Ibid.*, pp. 2434, 2551; *ibid.*, *Appendix*, p. 104.

36. *Record*, 61st Cong., 3d Sess., p. 2551.

37. *Ibid.*, pp. 2451–2452, 2454, 2514, 2524, 2536, 2543.

38. *Ibid.*, pp. 2457, 2524, 2556; *ibid.*, *Appendix*, pp. 117, 168.

39. *Record*, 61st Cong., 3d Sess., pp 2510–2512, 2548; *ibid.*, *Appendix*, pp. 104–105, 135, 143.

40. *Record*, 61st Cong., 3d Sess., pp. 2517, 2532.

41. *Ibid.*, pp. 2451, 2549, 2551.

raw materials while retaining protection on finished products. The oppressed farmer was therefore urged to note that under reciprocity he would sell his wheat and live cattle in a free-trade market and buy his flour and dressed meat under protection.[42] Others called attention to the secrecy of negotiation and the hasty action in the Committee on Ways and Means, with the State Department refusing requested information.[43] This raised a delicate constitutional question which was suggested by several, involving the originating of revenue legislation in the executive department. The raising of this question was allegedly aimed both at the separation of powers and at the peculiar province of the House to initiate money bills.[44] One other point appeared which was to be urged more loudly later—that Canada must, under the European interpretation of the most-favored-nation clause, "give to every other nation with which she has a treaty containing the most-favored-nation clause the same preference that she gives to the United States under the proposed agreement and without any equivalent in exchange therefor."[45]

The debate closed at the end of two days under operation of a rule bringing the matter to a vote. Discussion had brought out most of the stock arguments which were to adorn the later controversy in Congress and country, though stressing but lightly many which were later prominent. The farmer had been pushed upstage as the hero (or villain) of the piece, at whose feet the wreaths of oratory pro and con were to be cast. The offerings to date indicated that the opponents had more numerous and perhaps more positive arguments to offer; friendly speakers were already somewhat on the defensive. On the whole, an effort had been made to clarify the issue and the arguments for the most part were intended to be to the point; the day of pettifogging and windjamming was yet to come.

The House passed the McCall bill by 321 to 92 in a vote remarkable in many ways. It was cast under the chairmanship of Ollie James of Kentucky, called to preside by Cannon—the first time, according to the press, that a Democrat had been so honored since the Republicans took over the House. It was made possible by a special rule discharging the Committee of the Whole from consideration of the

42. *Ibid.,* pp. 2539, 2556; *ibid., Appendix,* pp. 113, 114.
43. *Record,* 61st Cong., 3d Sess., pp. 2439, 2456, 2509–2510, 2633.
44. *Ibid.,* pp. 2527, 2533, 2544.   45. *Ibid.,* p. 2556.

bill—a gag rule such as the Democrats had long deprecated and to curb which they had recently shorn the Speaker of his power, but which they now supported enthusiastically. It was the first bill to pass the House under the new rules despite the open and expressed opposition of the Speaker. Its passage was made possible by the Democrats, who supported it 143 to 5, and against the wishes of a majority of the President's own party, which divided 78 ayes to 87 nays. Perhaps the most peculiarly situated were the 20 Insurgents, whose chief stock in trade had been tariff reduction, but who, coming mainly from the farm States, were placed in a dilemma. Few expressed themselves in words, but 13 voted aye, 6 nay, with one absent. With this send-off the measure passed to the tender mercies of the Senate Finance Committee and the upper house.[46]

Here it faced a perilous journey, what with the opposition of Senator Eugene Hale of Maine, a lame duck and acting Chairman in the absence of Aldrich, the press of other important legislation, and the brief time remaining before expiration of the session, to say nothing of Insurgent hostility and standpat qualms. The final outcome was forecast when the President called in Senators Murray Crane and Thomas H. Carter and threatened them with a special session unless reciprocity and the Tariff Commission bill were passed. It became more apparent when the Committee spent precious time hearing the agreement's enemies. It became a certainty when senatorial oratory swelled to such a volume that March 4 arrived ahead of a vote. Thus the President was forced to a special session, to dependence upon Democratic allies to pass his measure, and to the risk (or better, the inevitability) of general tariff discussions. The situation was not a pleasant one for Mr. Taft or his party.[47]

46. *Ibid.*, pp. 2552–2564; New York *Tribune,* February 15, 16, 1911; Toronto *Star,* February 15; *The Outlook,* 97:372 (February 25, 1911). No amendments were permitted save one sponsored by the committee clarifying the pulpwood and print-paper section by "providing for free print paper when made from free wood." *Sen. Doc.* 56, 62d Cong., 1st Sess., p. 1224.

47. New York *Tribune,* February 8, 19, 1911. On February 18 there remained for action ten general appropriation bills, the Tariff Commission bill, the Lorimer case, the direct-election-of-Senators amendment and proposals to fortify the Panama Canal, to pass old-age pensions and Congressional reapportionment.

Three days of hearings opened February 20 to the echoes of Taft's announcement through McCall that he would summon a special session in default of a vote.[48] Whether deliberately or not, this maneuver laid on hostile Republicans the responsibility of an extra session, with the prospective reopening of the tariff question nine months earlier than necessary, if they refused to allow reciprocity to come to a vote. Likelihood of success was momentarily increased by the reported promise that no Democratic Senator would filibuster, thus laying the blame for delay squarely on Republican doorsteps.[49] The hearings themselves were devoted mainly to allowing agricultural, paper, lumber, and fishing interests to howl calamity, under the expert tutelage of Senators Hale and P. J. McCumber of North Dakota. Norris' was the sole proreciprocity testimony. Most formidable of opponents were the Grangers, represented by eleven Masters of State bodies and shepherded by Aaron Jones of Indiana, for eight years Master of the national organization. These marshaled evidence of the disaster in store for the farmer under reciprocity and furnished the Congressional and farm-journal opposition with much thunder.

Three arguments were stressed principally. First, American lands were wearing out and under increasing production costs could not compete with the newer Canadian fields. This situation had been repeated on each new American frontier and would recur if the tariff barrier against Canada were destroyed.[50] Again, frequent mention was made of the lower standard of living prevailing in Canadian areas adjacent to New England, with the inference that reciprocity would drag the American farmer down to the lower level.[51] The equality-of-protection idea appeared in the argument that "so long

48. *Ibid.,* February 20, 1911. His correspondence indicates that his mind was made up as early as the sixteenth. To Horace, to S. J. Roberts, February 16; to John V. Farwell, February 18. *Taft Papers.*

49. New York *Tribune,* February 21, 1911.

50. *Reciprocity with Canada: Hearings before the Committee on Finance of the United States Senate on H.R. 32216 An Act to Promote Reciprocal Trade Relations with the Dominion of Canada and for Other Purposes,* Sen. Doc. 834, 61st Cong., 3d Sess., Washington, 1911, pp. 53, 88, 138, 142, 144, 257–258 (cited subsequently as *Sen. Doc.* 834).

51. *Ibid.,* pp. 45–48, 142, 143, 150.

as protection was to be the national policy, the farmers must receive the same degree of protection on their products as was given on manufactured articles."[52]

The papermakers argued that domestic spruce would supply the demand indefinitely, and that American paper ought to be made from American wood, free from the competition of cheaper Canadian raw materials and labor. C. W. Lyman, of the International Paper Company, denied the charges brought by the publishers that his concern was monopolistic and excessive in its charges, saying little on the merits of reciprocity as such.[53] The lumber manufacturers claimed that they stood to lose by free trade on rough lumber, lath, and palings and reduced duties on various grades of manufactured lumber. Therefore, speaking through Edward Hines of Chicago, president of the National Lumber Manufacturers Association, they charged that the agreement, by letting Canadian lumber in more freely, would take the bread out of the mouths of American workers in the mills of 48,000 lumber manufacturers. This disaster would be brought about by opening to Canada large Northern markets which Southern lumbermen would no longer be able to supply because of the existence of a transportation differential of from six to eight dollars per thousand feet in favor of the Canadian mills.[54] Finally, the plaint of the Gloucester fishermen was heard.[55] Norris' testimony in favor of the paper provisions of the bill was concerned mainly with an attack upon the monopolistic tendencies of the International Paper Company and with the need of his own interest for cheaper supplies.[56]

The McCall bill was reported to the Senate February 24 with the damning "without recommendation" attached.[57] Senator Hale informed his colleagues that "a large majority [of the Committee] was opposed to the reciprocity agreement and to reporting it favor-

52. *Ibid.*, pp. 37, 87, 147. It should be noted that none of these advocates of the farmer came from west of the Mississippi.

53. *Ibid.*, pp. 3–13, 272–274, 298–300.

54. *Ibid.*, pp. 16–29. Similar arguments were made by representatives of the lumber interest of the South and the Pacific Northwest. *Ibid.*, pp. 31–35, 119–124.

55. *Ibid.*, pp. 65–75.

56. *Ibid.*, pp. 217–229.

57. *Record*, 61st Cong., 3d Sess., p. 3309.

ably."[58] Debate was largely confined to three days, February 25, 27, and 28, and was of minor importance in reciprocity's progress. Northwestern Senators bore the brunt of the attack and practically no favorable comment was made. The only argument to receive extended airing was the danger to the farmer, and nothing was added to the House statements.[59] Other scattered arguments generally repeated those advanced in the lower chamber.

The net result of a complicated parliamentary and factional situation was failure to secure a vote and the issuance of a proclamation calling the Sixty-second Congress in special session April 4. Detailed explanation of this failure is not easy to formulate. Contemporary opinion and evidence generally point to lack of real sympathy with the plan and absence of Republican leadership.[60] Granted leadership, it seems likely that reciprocity could have been forced to a vote by tying it to one of the other issues upon which much time was spent. This seems particularly true of the vote seating Senator Lorimer, whose supporters could win a test in the old Senate, but could not hope to do so in the new.[61] As things came out, much of the final time was spent in filibustering and when William J. Stone of Missouri, self-appointed friend of the agreement, proposed during the closing hours to try to force a vote he was dissuaded by Taft, who feared that a motion to take up the bill might be tabled, with a bad effect in Canada.[62] The President's first chance was gone, and with it his only chance to keep reciprocity an end in itself, unencumbered by general tariff complications.

58. *Ibid.*, p. 3310.

59. *Ibid.*, pp. 3309, 3389 ff., 3395, 3578, 3659, 3664–3665.

60. New York *Tribune*, March 5, 1911; Chicago *Tribune*, March 3; *Nation*, 92:234 (March 9, 1911). The Chicago correspondent wrote: "It never has had and does not today have in the Senate one enthusiastic friend who is capable of leadership." And the *Nation* remarked truly that "lukewarmness and secret malevolence are sometimes worse than open antagonism."

61. *Cf.* the comment in the New York *Tribune*, March 1, 1911: "It is the conviction of many Senators that had a vote on the Canadian reciprocity agreement been made a condition of a vote on the Lorimer case at this session it could have been obtained and the necessity of a special session of Congress avoided, but the reciprocity agreement had no friends who were ready to make an earnest fight in its behalf when the crucial moment arrived."

62. New York *Tribune*, March 4, 1911.

Meantime the clans of propaganda manufacturers had been gathering and by the end of the session several lines of attack had been blocked out. (It will be remembered that the expression of opinion was traced through the two weeks following the announcement. This section carries the story through the adjournment of Congress.) The farmer spoke or was spoken for through the Grange and the farm press and, as became a rather inarticulate hero of the drama, found other and less fraternal champions anxious to speak for him. Indeed, one of the most significant features of early public discussion was the emergence of the farmer as the stalking-horse of widely varied interests manifesting a sudden concern for his welfare. The Grange through its Executive Committee, composed of Bachelder, T. C. Atkeson of West Virginia, and Jones, launched a spirited attack. By the time Taft spoke at Columbus, Grange machinery had begun to function and the local chapters were receiving prepared material picking flaws in reciprocity—material prepared, as the subsequent story will show, by expert hands whose interests were far from agricultural. On the thirteenth Bachelder's letter replying to Secretary Wilson's broadside deaconed off the tune for the farmers' chorus: "The sole question before the American people is whether we shall have free trade in all farm products and high protection for manufactured articles." After some further remarks Bachelder asserted: "We can only conclude that you have been deceived by the special interests, which have cunningly plotted to allay the country-wide clamor for an honest revision of the tariff, by making the farmer the scapegoat for the sins of the high protectionist."[63] The following day the Legislative Committee (Bachelder, Jones, and Atkeson) distributed the first medium for exerting pressure, a letter commenting on the bill, stating the Grange position "that the farmer should receive exactly the same measure of protection as the manufacturers," and enclosing forms of protest to be forwarded to Congressmen.[64] The reply to Wilson was widely quoted and, together with other Grange announcements, put the Grange in the limelight.

63. *Documents Relating to Reciprocity with Canada, Letter of N. J. Bachelder Relating to Reciprocity with Canada, Sen. Doc. 828, 61st Cong., 3d Sess.*, Washington, 1911, pp. 1–2.

64. *Sen. Doc. 56, 62d Cong., 1st Sess.*, p. 65.

In some quarters there was disposition to question Bachelder's authority to speak for his organization, or for his organization to speak for the farmer.[65] Strong hints, correct in principle but mistaken in detail, appeared to the effect that the Grange campaign was being financed by outside interests desiring retention of protection.[66]

The campaign to save the farmer was furthered by the farm press. The arguments advanced at this stage were not dissimilar to those of the Grange. Essentially, they asserted that the farmer was being discriminated against. After years of hearing that protection was a benefit, he was now asked to forgo that benefit just when it was about to become a reality.[67] Again, he was asked to bear the burden in the shape of Canadian competition with his products, while urban and industrial classes continued to reap the benefits of protection and whatever gain might come from Canadian natural products.[68] It was occasionally noted that the agreement was a political deal in which the administration sacrificed the farmer for partisan advantage.[69] One sheet suggested that reciprocity would force large emigrations of American capital and population.[70] One correspondent shrewdly pointed out that though the agreement was bad, the farmer ought to support it as an entering wedge toward tariff revision.[71] *The Farmers' Review* (Chicago) harped repeatedly on the discrimination against the farm interest, concluding: "The principle of true reciprocity is not on trial. It is the question of tariff discrimination against agriculture. Equity to agriculture is the one paramount issue—whether or not free trade shall be forced

65. Manchester *Union,* February 15; *The Anaconda* (Mont.) *Standard,* February 16, 1911.

66. Boston *Daily Advertiser,* February 14, April 8; Lewiston *Evening Journal,* February 10, 14, 20, 1911. It was asserted that Edward Hines, representing the lumber interests and a chief backer of Senator Lorimer, was financing the Grange in order to preserve protection and strike a blow at Taft, who wished Lorimer removed.

67. *Michigan Farmer,* 136:182 (February 18, 1911).

68. *Farm, Stock and Home* (Minneapolis), 27:202 (March 1, 1911); *The Farmer* (St. Paul), 29:244 (February 18, 1911).

69. *Farm, Stock and Home,* 27:202 (March 1, 1911); *The Country Gentleman* (Albany), 76:132 (February 9, 1911).

70. *American Cultivator,* February 18, 1911, p. 8.

71. *Farm and Fireside* (Springfield, O.), 34:23 (February 25, 1911).

upon the producer while the manufacturer is still treated to protection."[72]

The farmer's self-appointed friends were stirring. The Executive Committee of the National Association of Wool Manufacturers righteously declared that its members were "not among those men of business who would sacrifice the farmers' interests for their own supposed advantage."[73] The American Protective Tariff League's Circular No. 271, after indicating that the agreement involved abandonment of the protective policy for labor and industry, lamented that it "contemplates the withdrawal of Protection from American farmers, fishermen, miners, lumbermen and manufacturers of paper, while retaining full Protection for the general body of Manufacturers."[74] *The Bulletin of the American Iron and Steel Association* shed a tear because the farmer, just convinced that protection was good for him and beginning to realize that good, was now to be "stricken down."[75] Verily, the farmer was not to fight his fight unaided.

The passage of time showed division in the ranks of lumber interests, as compared with earlier opposition. It became evident that the agreement was objectionable to some, of indifferent importance to others, and actually advantageous to still others, with the result that the industry as a whole was badly split. West Coast interests feared inability to compete successfully with British Columbia lumber in the California market, chiefly due to a favorable differential in transportation costs owing to more stringent American shipping regulations.[76] Vermont dealers claimed that New England would not be much affected by the lowered duty on rough lumber.[77] Many Southern hardwood manufacturers would profit by the provisions allowing agricultural implements easier access to Canada, since their product entered extensively into the making of such tools.[78] The

72. 43:155, 215, 423 (February 18, March 4, April 29, 1911).

73. *Bulletin of the National Association of Wool Manufacturers* (pamphlet), Boston, 1911, p. 146.

74. Quoted in *American Economist*, 47:93 (February 17, 1911).

75. Quoted in *ibid.*, 47:113 (March 3, 1911).

76. *The Seattle* (Wash.) *Post-Intelligencer*, February 12; Portland *Oregonian*, February 14, 1911.

77. *Burlington* (Vt.) *Daily Free Press*, February 15, 1911.

78. *Southern Lumberman*, February 11, 1911, p. 23. On the other hand,

official attitude of the National Lumber Manufacturers Association remained hostile.[79]

Milling sentiment was likewise divided on the free wheat and lowered duty on flour (reduced from 25 per cent ad valorem to 50 cents per barrel) carried in the agreement. Except in one quarter little opinion was expressed at this stage of the discussion.[80] *The Northwestern Miller* (Minneapolis) urged support, even though free wheat might eventually result in free flour, on the ground that access to Canadian raw materials would enable the American miller to compete in British and continental markets and thus regain the export trade which had been hurt by the high cost of living.[81] The real argument on the wheat question was yet to be developed.

Papermakers rose in arms at the threat to their industry in the pulp and paper sections, laying the blame upon the publishers' selfish desire for free newsprint. The net result would be, it was asserted, the ruin of the industry. An effort was made to enlist the American Protective Tariff League in blocking the legislation.[82] The publishers soon opened an earnest propaganda campaign. On February 9 Norris dispatched a circular calling general attention of publishers to the advantages of the bill through "providing for free print paper when made from free wood." He enclosed material furnished by the State Department detailing special advantages to particular localities. It was also suggested that the publishers induce State legislatures and local commercial and industrial organizations to pass resolutions addressed to the President and both Houses of Congress. On February 17 Ridder sent out a communication which was to cause the publishers some embarrassment later: "By request, private

the Hardwood Manufacturers Association passed a resolution condemning the agreement, but the vote was not unanimous and it was asserted that the majority of the membership had left the hall when the vote was taken. *The Nebraska State Journal* (Lincoln), February 17, 1911.

79. *Southern Lumberman*, March 4, 1911, p. 24.

80. *Modern Miller* (St. Louis) opposed the agreement and asserted that the majority sentiment was in this direction. February 4, p. 12; February 18, 1911, p. 11.

81. 84:643 (December 14, 1910); 85:267, 327; 86:339 (February 1, 8; May 10, 1911).

82. *Paper Mill*, February 11, p. 1; March 4, 1911, p. 1; *American Economist*, 47:81 (February 10, 1911).

to editors. It is of vital importance to the newspapers that their Washington correspondents be instructed to treat favorably the Canadian reciprocity agreement, because print paper and wood pulp are made free of duty."[83]

The press campaign assumed clearer outline late in the short session.[84] The argument *ad agricolam* emerged as the favorite weapon, appearing most frequently of all the proreciprocity points. The few papers whose agricultural constituency constrained them to oppose the agreement despite their interest in free newsprint almost unanimously insisted that the farmer would be hurt by it.[85] The proreciprocity sheets faced a double task: they must persuade the farmer, bombarded by the farm journals with antireciprocity arguments, that reciprocity would not hurt his interest, and then go on to show its positive benefits. That most attention was devoted to the former indicates that the press was somewhat on the defensive. In discussing the first phase the tendency was to rely upon simple assertion that the farmer would not be hurt.[86] On the positive side it was argued that reciprocity would open a larger market to the farmer, thus extending the scope of business transactions.[87] There was some tendency to admit that the immediate results would be bad in lowering

83. Reprinted in *Sen. Doc.* 834, 61st Cong., 3d Sess., pp. 212–213; *Sen. Doc.* 56, 62d Cong., 1st Sess., p. 1224. Included in the February 9 circular were the advantages of reciprocity to the following areas: Florida, Georgia, Maryland, Illinois, Ohio, North Carolina, Michigan, Minnesota, Nebraska, and Wisconsin.

84. It will be remembered that the preceding chapter surveyed the attitude of the press during the first two weeks after the agreement was announced. The following discussion is based upon examination of forty-four daily papers for the period covered, February 9–March 4, 1911.

85. Two of three antireciprocity papers, all in the Dakotas, used one or another form of this argument. *The Fargo* (N.D.) *Forum,* February 28; *The Evening Times* (Grand Forks, N.D.), February 13, 16, 1911.

86. *Cf.,* as samples of numerous statements on this point: *The Cincinnati* (Ohio) *Enquirer,* February 14: the farmers are "needlessly alarmed"; Burlington *Free Press,* February 10: "We are waiting patiently to discover a specific case in which New England farmers will be injured"; Chicago *Tribune,* February 15; *The Register and Leader* (Des Moines, Ia.), February 24, 1911.

87. Des Moines *Register and Leader,* February 11; Burlington *Free Press,* February 18, 1911.

the price of his commodities, but this was to be offset by long-time good to the country at large and by more immediate gains to the farmer himself on other commodities such as lumber and fish.[88] The consumer, who was to be helped by reciprocity, came in for some attention.[89] Several papers called attention, with approval, to the fact that reciprocity began a breach in the protective tariff.[90] As earlier, few papers avowed their interest in free newsprint.[91]

Numerous other arguments were advanced, some of which were to be of importance later, but only one deserves present comment. Second in number to arguments directed to the farmer were those called forth by Champ Clark's annexation speech. A few bolder sheets feared or expected that annexation might result.[92] After Clark's remarks a veritable barrage of editorials was launched to counteract its effect. Canada was assured over and over again that nothing was farther from American thoughts; the assurances, however, were to receive far less notice in Canada than the remarks.[93]

Two figures emerged from the smoke of battle beclouding the short session: William H. Taft and the American farmer. The President had at long last assumed the habiliments of command, only to find that he must lead a motley army through second lieutenants. His own party, weakened by Insurgent defections, broke beneath him and forced the enlistment of Democratic volunteers who joined the fray as mercenaries rather than as patriots, seeking by reciproc-

88. The *Nebraska State Journal* hammered home this idea through a long series of editorials beginning early in the discussion and continuing through several issues. *Cf.*, for example, January 30, February 7. *Cf.* also *The Omaha* (Neb.) *Daily Bee*, February 16, 1911.

89. Cincinnati *Enquirer*, February 14; *The Houston* (Texas) *Post*, February 15, 1911.

90. Indianapolis *Star*, February 16; *The Atlanta* (Georgia) *Constitution*, February 15; *The Atlanta Journal*, February 15, 1911.

91. Sample exceptions are: Milwaukee *Sentinel*, February 19; Sioux Falls *Argus-Leader*, March 1; Portland *Oregonian*, February 17, 1911.

92. Fargo *Forum*, February 17; Grand Forks *Evening Times*, February 20, 1911.

93. Samples will be found in *The News and Courier* (Charleston, S. C.), February 20; *The Minneapolis Morning Tribune*, February 21; New York *American*, February 16, 22, 1911. It should be noted that this bellwether of the Hearst flock gave considerable space to the campaign, as became the largest consumer of newsprint in the country.

ity to attack protection. Winning the first round with his makeshift forces, he was defeated in the Senate by secret hostility, bankruptcy of leadership, and press of other matters, and was forced to continue the fight under circumstances in which his Democratic reciprocity friends were to become his tariff enemies. Thus he lost twice: once by failing to put his scheme into law and again by continuing the battle on enemy territory. He had, however, gone so far that he had to continue the fight; only by going on and winning could he redeem the mortgage he had laid upon his reputation when he raised the issue and assumed leadership in the reciprocity struggle. The American farmer took on new stature. Asked to bear the immediate burden of the agreement in reduced protection of his products, he was courted assiduously, one group of suitors insisting that he was being made the goat and the other shouting that he was the gainer. On both sides there was room for doubt as to whether the son of the soil was being loved for himself alone. The succeeding story will make it increasingly clear that he was not. But at any rate, he was loved, and courted.

CHAPTER IX

THE PRESIDENT SUCCEEDS

WHILE a pleasant Washington spring melted into a hot Washington summer reciprocity's fate became increasingly enmeshed in intra-Republican quarrels, Democratic tariff revision, and the background of a presidential election. Under the spur of its alliance with the President, the obliging Democratic House passed the agreement fairly promptly in order to get to its real business, a piecemeal attack upon the tariff as a promise for 1912. The Senate, where stand-patters, Insurgents, and Democrats were hopelessly scrambled, insisted upon holding long hearings and making long speeches. It early became evident that here there was no disposition to pass reciprocity and go on to other things; the agreement's enemies would attach tariff revision, which they wanted, to reciprocity which they did not, in order to kill the latter. In the resultant tangle tempers rose with the thermometer, but Insurgent tactics eventually failed and the bill passed as ordered by the President. His victory was a Pyrrhic one, however, won at the expense of the last vestige of party harmony and followed by the threatened Democratic assaults on the citadel of protection in a series of popgun bills whose explosions, however petty they might seem, did much to undermine the foundations of Republican control.

As before, executive pressure was stoutly exerted, particularly during the crucial month while the bill was being bombarded in the Senate Finance Committee hearings. As before, the State Department furnished informational propaganda. Again the President was compelled to go over the heads of Congress and appeal to the people personally. The alliance with the Democrats was cemented shortly after the regular session when a White House conference offered the services of the Tariff Board to Oscar Underwood, Chairman of the Ways and Means Committee.[1] Aldrich was early urged to use his influence with Senator Boies Penrose to keep the new Finance Committee from being so organized as to give control to the Insurgents and the Democratic opponent of reciprocity, Joseph W. Bailey of Texas.

1. Norton to Knox, March 8, 1911. *Knox Papers.*

This because, as Taft wrote to Knox, "we are greatly at a disadvantage because we haven't anybody who has the courage and real sympathy with us in this fight."[2]

The State Department prepared and circulated considerable material directed mainly toward turning the agricultural interest to reciprocity. No Republican had been "able or willing," according to Pepper, to make a speech during the short session which could be used as a document. However, thanks to Senator Carter, most of the material prepared by the Department had found its way into print in *Senate Document* 862, 61st Congress, 3d Session.[3] Pepper took responsibility for having 100,000 copies of this prepared for franking in the farm areas, and urged distribution of a million copies to combat the Grange propaganda, "which it is generally supposed is being financed by the lumber trust." Friendly newspapermen received propaganda as rapidly as it could be absorbed, and the Carter compilation was distributed to lists furnished by John Norris and others.[4] The Tariff Board prepared informational propaganda for use by the newspapers.[5] The Department of State drafted detailed replies to be sent to honestly inquiring farmers, designed of course to make clear the advantages of reciprocity to their particular interest.[6] Pepper tried to rebut the antireciprocity arguments before the Senate Finance Committee by suggesting that the President ask James J. Hill to send from the Northwest "two or three intelligent farmers or a college professor."[7]

2. Taft to Aldrich, March 11, 1911; to Knox, same date. *Taft Papers*.

3. Included was a general analysis of the bill from which many of the defense arguments were to be taken, the text of the agreement, the President's speeches at Columbus and Springfield, and other material.

4. Pepper to Norton, March 17; to C. D. Hilles, who succeeded Norton as Taft's secretary, April 11, 1911. *Taft Papers*. Coöperation between Norris and the administration was evidently close. *Cf*. Hilles to Norris, April 6, 1911. *Ibid*.

5. *Cf*., for example, a State Department release of late March, based upon a Tariff Board Report and directed to proving the substantial equality of land values and farm wages north and south of the boundary. *The Detroit News*, March 29, 1911. This was one of the articles furnished by Pepper to Norris and circulated by the A.N.P.A. *Cf. Sen. Doc*. 56, 62d Cong., 1st Sess., pp. 1239–1240.

6. A sample was enclosed in Pepper to Hilles, May 10, 1911. *Taft Papers*.

7. Pepper to Hilles, May 1, 1911, enclosing draft letter to Hill. *Ibid*.

Twice during the thick of the hearings official reports were issued designed to influence opinion. On May 16 Knox submitted through Chairman Penrose an opinion scotching rumors that other nations could capitalize upon American concessions to Canada through the most-favored-nation clause.[8] The next day the Tariff Board published a long-awaited report on newsprint indicating that costs of both labor and raw materials in the United States exceeded those in Canada, resulting in a more costly finished product which reciprocity might make less expensive.[9] Thus the President's hands were diligently and variously upheld by the State Department.

Shortly after the bill passed the House, Taft, sensing that the real battle was ahead, turned on the pressure in an address before the joint banquet of the Associated Press and the American Newspaper Publishers Association in New York on April 27—as excellent a sounding board for executive opinion as could be desired. A fatally effective sounding board, in fact, for from it the Canadian press quoted statements which helped measurably in building up the hostile opinion so inimical to reciprocity north of the border. In this "now or never" speech he set forth the critical juncture which reciprocity created in Canadian-American and Anglo-Canadian relations.

I have said that this was a critical time in the solution of the question of reciprocity. It is critical because, unless it is now decided favorably to reciprocity, it is exceedingly probable that no such opportunity will ever again come to the United States. The forces which are at work in England and in Canada to separate her by a Chinese wall from the United States and to make her part of an imperial commercial band reaching from England around the world to England again by a system of preferential tariffs, will derive an impetus from the rejection of this treaty, and if we would have reciprocity with all the advantages that I have described and that I earnestly and sincerely believe will follow its adoption, we must take it now or give it up forever.

Again, speaking of the condition of affairs in Canada, he said:

The government is one controlled entirely by the people, and *the bond uniting the dominion with the mother country is light and almost im-*

8. New York *Tribune*, May 17, 1911; *Record*, 62d Cong., 1st Sess., p. 1223.
9. New York *Tribune*, May 18, 1911; *Pulp and News-Print Industry: Report by the Tariff Board Relative to Pulp and News-Print Industry*, Sen. Doc. 31, 62d Cong., 1st Sess., Washington, 1911, p. 134.

perceptible. There are no restrictions upon the trade or economic development of Canada which will interfere in the slightest with her carving out her independent future. The attitude of the people is that of affection toward the mother country and of a sentimental loyalty toward her royal head. But for practical purposes the control exercised from England by executive or Parliament is imponderable.

These statements, together with one of January 26 in the message transmitting the agreement to Congress, form a dangerous trilogy. In the message he said, referring to the Dominion, that "it has an active, aggressive, and intelligent people. *They are coming to the parting of the ways.* They must soon decide whether they are to regard themselves as isolated permanently from our markets by a perpetual wall or whether we are to be commercial friends." These pronouncements, obviously from their context referring to trade matters, were distorted in the heat of the election campaign in Canada into a threat to Imperial political solidarity, and rank with Champ Clark's ill-omened annexation remarks in raising the temperature of Canadian loyalty to the Empire to a high pitch in August and September.[10]

Later in his remarks Taft pooh-poohed the annexation threat. And again he directed his main batteries against agrarian hostility to prove that the farmer would not suffer under reciprocity. To offset prospective opposition strategy he insisted that his plan ought not to be tied in with any efforts at tariff revision—it ought to stand or fall alone, irrespective of other considerations. And to silence critics concerned because the arrangement was not broad enough, he announced that it was not his fault, but Canada's, for, said he, "We tendered the Canadian commissioners absolute free trade in all products of either country, manufactured or natural, but the Canadian commissioners did not feel justified in going so far."

The same day the press announced that long Finance Committee

10. The italicized sentences were widely stressed in Canadian reprints. The New York *Tribune* of April 28, 1911, prints the address. The message of January 26 is found in *Record*, 61st Cong., 3d Sess., pp. 1468–1470. The Montreal *Star* began reprinting parts of the three statements quoted above as early as August 25, displayed in a prominent box, and repeated them at frequent intervals until the date of the election. Other papers followed the *Star's* example. *Cf.* Montreal *Star*, September 1, 2, 5, 9, 11, 13, 19, 20.

hearings would kill time while the House passed the popgun tariff bills held in abeyance during reciprocity's passage. These hearings, opened early in May, prolonged themselves into June. They evidenced so much hostility and danger of death-dealing amendment that the President felt constrained to make a second direct appeal to public opinion. At Chicago, June 3, he addressed the Western Economic Society, a largely academic organization. He struck from the shoulder, explaining why he had journeyed so far from the Senate to try to push a measure through that body: "It is because this bill will pass, if it passes at all, because of the force of public opinion in its favor." Thus, having unlimbered the big stick, he proceeded to wave it vigorously under the noses of special interests which he asserted were bunkoing the farmer into opposition; he named the lumber trust and the manufacturers of print paper, charging these with creating a fictitious impression of hostility belying the facts. Furthermore, those who purported to speak for the farmer, in cahoots with the special interests, were deceiving those whom they claimed to represent. Point was given to his remarks by the Senate hearings, which a few days earlier had disclosed the activities of a firm of New York lobbyists, paid to concoct antireciprocity propaganda for use by the Grange. (See below, page 121, for the story in full.) It was, as *The Nation* remarked, a weighty speech, and one which created a deep impression.[11]

Five days later he spoke before the dinner of the Interstate Cotton Crushers Association. After paying his respects to the industry in a few graceful sentences, he again lashed out at his enemies, trying to prevent what then seemed likely, the attachment to the reciprocity bill of the so-called "farmers' free list." He pointedly suggested pressure upon Southern senators to prevent this. In his insistence upon keeping the two subjects separate he asserted that "the situation in the Senate is one that can be described as calling for the bill, the whole bill, and nothing but the bill." He repeated his earlier insistence that reciprocity would not injure the farmer.[12] By July 4 when

11. Reprinted as a pamphlet: *Reciprocity with Canada: Address of President Taft before the Western Economic Society at Orchestra Hall, Chicago, June 3, 1911*, Washington, 1911; Chicago *Tribune*, June 4; New York *Tribune*, June 4; *Nation*, 92:567 (June 8, 1911).

12. New York *Tribune*, June 9, 1911.

he delivered his final address at Indianapolis the defeat of one of the most dangerous amendments had eased the situation somewhat and he could afford to be less belligerent. He therefore addressed himself mainly to the agricultural aspects of the agreement.[13]

Thus on four major occasions the President had read into the record vigorous attacks upon his opponents. From four platforms, only one of which any stretch of the imagination could connect with farming, he had wooed the farmer as assiduously as had ever the "interests" against whose blandishments he was so loudly trying to warn the object of their mutual affections. The farmer, if he read the papers, must have begun to swell with importance that such great and mighty folk were his suitors.

The special session had opened April 4 with the Democrats in control of the House, with reciprocity to the fore, and with general tariff revision a thinly veiled threat. As the legislative campaign opened the President considered it one of his main tasks to prevent attachment to reciprocity of a rider revising one of the regular schedules. Could he stave off this unholy alliance and get reciprocity through, he felt confident of preventing a general revision.[14] This contingency was averted in the House by the development of Democratic strategy calling for the passage of the "farmers' free list" bill, which removed duties from a number of articles useful to farmers and acted as an offset to the alleged losses to this interest through reciprocity. It was a shrewd move to make party capital in the rural districts, particularly in the South, and to cut the ground from under the Senate Insurgents, who had planned to amend the reciprocity bill in the direction of the farmers' free list.[15] To a point this strategy suited the President, for it would help reciprocity through the House; beyond this point, however, it would not avail, because the free list itself was general tariff revision which he sought to avoid, as well as a virtual amendment of reciprocity.

A party caucus voted on April 11 to put reciprocity ahead of tariff reform, defeating a move to attach the free list. Chairman Underwood of the Ways and Means Committee introduced both bills the following day. The reciprocity measure was identical with the

13. Indianapolis *Star,* June 30, July 5, 8, 1911.
14. To Aldrich, March 30; to Underwood, April 10, 1911. *Taft Papers.*
15. *The Literary Digest* (New York), 42:765–766 (April 22, 1911).

McCall bill except for a request to the President to treat with Canada for further concessions.[16] While the committee considered the bill the House passed to other legislative measures. Debate opened April 15 and continued through the twenty-first. The free-list bill was reported on the nineteenth. The majority of the committee rendered a routine report favoring the bill and John Dalzell and J. W. Fordney spoke for the minority.[17] Their constitutional attack alleged that Taft's action was "an invasion of the constitutional prerogative of the House of Representatives to originate revenue legislation." Specifically, it charged that the proposal was un-Republican in proposing reciprocity in competing products, was class legislation detrimental to the farmer, and was an abandonment of the protective principle.

Underwood preferring to close for his side, Representative Claude Kitchin of North Carolina opened debate for the Democrats. His three-hour campaign speech twitted Republicans and Insurgents both before exposing the sham of protection for farm products and asserting that the real opposition came not from the farmer but from monopolistic interests which stood to gain by protection. Names were now beginning to appear in the discussion, and Kitchin referred specifically to the International Paper Company and the lumber trust.[18] Several days following were devoted mainly to opposition arguments, Underwood evidently being content to let the opposition talk and his side vote. Discussion rang the changes on the farmer's fate under reciprocity. Arguments were refined and pointed up somewhat but the refrain was the same. Consumers were again advised of the alleged dangers in reciprocity, and the trust argument was somewhat more prominent than before.

Analysis of the agricultural aspects of the argument yields the following pros and cons. The points most generally discussed were two: the effect of removing the tariff barrier upon wheat prices and the influence of newer and cheaper Canadian lands competing with those of the United States. The wheat argument was essentially that

16. New York *Tribune*, April 12, 13, 1911; *Record*, 62d Cong., 1st Sess., p. 183.

17. *Reciprocity with Canada, House Report 3*, 62d Cong., 1st Sess., Washington, 1911.

18. *Record*, 62d Cong., 1st Sess., pp. 273–287.

the prices of No. 1 Northern and No. 1 hard spring wheat, blended with softer grades by the flouring industry, were fixed by demand at Minneapolis and Duluth and had been kept considerably above the Winnipeg level by the protective tariff. Figures demonstrated this price discrepancy in detail, and also showed that the Winnipeg price rose and stayed up, while that of Minneapolis dropped and dropped again after January 26.[19] Defenders of reciprocity urged as before that the "man in North Dakota does not compete with the man across the line in Manitoba directly, but he competes with him 4,000 miles away in the Liverpool market. We have an exportable surplus of something like 100,000,000 bushels a year, and Canada has an exportable surplus of, perhaps, half that amount, and those surpluses are both taken by the Liverpool market." The differing price levels above and below the border were laid to local conditions.[20]

It was argued again that the farmers east of the Mississippi had long been put to it to compete with the cheaper and more productive lands to the west. Only recently, due to readjustment of production to local needs and to the growing scarcity of Western lands, had older lands and their products begun to appreciate to the point where, aided by the protective tariff, these farmers could view the future with other than gloomy alarm. Now reciprocity threatened reinauguration of decades of depression and poverty through an influx of Canadian foodstuffs.[21] Reply was made that the post-Civil War movement across the Mississippi, which caused the disturbed equilibrium, was due to overbuilt railroads, overstimulated immigration, and the Panic of 1873, resulting in overproduction of farm products. There was no accurate parallel, it was urged, between this situation and that involving the Canadian West.[22]

The only other prominent opposition argument was directed to the consumer interest, where it was urged that the agreement would not cut the cost of living, would not aid the consumer, but would aid the trusts and monopolies. The dilemma of the former session reap-

19. This point, of course, was vastly important to the members from the Prairie States. The argument of C. R. Davis of Minnesota may be noted as a sample. *Ibid.*, pp. 488–489. Other examples: *ibid.*, pp. 466, 491, 498, 507.
20. *Ibid.*, p. 527; for other arguments, *ibid.*, pp. 347–350, 417, 535–536.
21. *Ibid.*, pp. 288–295, 375–382, 396–400, 425–426.
22. *Ibid.*, p. 526.

peared and reciprocity's friends were asked to explain how consumer prices could be lowered without hurting the farmer. Again it was argued that even injurious reductions in farm prices would never bring down retail consumer prices; any savings would be dissipated into the pockets of the middleman.[23] Rather ineffective efforts were made to answer these arguments, mainly by mere assertion that living costs *would* be cut.[24]

Other arguments, pro and con, were scattered. Lumber received some attention, with assertions that free rough lumber would aid the farmer and strike a blow at the lumber trust as well.[25] Reply was made that the provision was inadequate, since little lumber reached the ultimate consumer in the rough state. The result would be that the American mills would receive the benefit of free rough lumber, which they would then machine and sell to the consumer at a price based upon the protection accorded the Canadian finished product.[26] Little attention was paid to newsprint, though some were bold enough to charge that the publishers were trading off the farmer's welfare for their own selfish interest.[27] Several argued that both the farmer and the manufacturer would benefit.[28] Annexation, so prominent during the first debate, was barely mentioned.

The bill passed April 21, two days after the free-list bill was introduced. McCall concluded the debate for the proreciprocity Republicans, Dalzell for Republican opponents, and Underwood for the Democrats. McCall deftly exposed the saviors of the farmer by paraphrasing their gloomy picture of their hero: "According to his eulogists here, the American farmer is a very serious-minded individual, with his wife and numerous progeny gathered about him . . . desperately and with great solemnity endeavoring to cling to a precarious existence. These orators lament over his rugged qualities, they almost brood over his virtues." The farmer he himself had known was "not the sad-eyed monstrosity, always staring destiny in the face, that we have had painted here." McCall even permitted

23. *Ibid.*, pp. 427, 466. Also pp. 346, 421, 423, 462, 463, 471, 479, 490, 491, 495, 504, 515.

24. *Ibid.*, pp. 338–340, 358–363, 373–374, 517.

25. *Ibid.*, pp. 334, 370, 417, 534.   26. *Ibid.*, pp. 468, 489.

27. *Ibid.*, pp. 330, 404–405.

28. *Ibid.*, pp. 457, 505, 533–534; *ibid., Appendix,* p. 8.

himself to wonder whether the farmer had ever been as agitated over reciprocity as his new friends would have the world believe.[29]

After over thirty destructive amendments had been defeated, the vote stood 268 to 89. In the negative were ten bolting Democrats, one Independent, and seventy-eight Republicans, as against sixty-seven Republican ayes. The President had failed to carry his party, though he had carried his bill with Democratic assistance.[30] The emphasis in debate remained as before, primarily directed toward the farmer. The arguments were largely repetitious. Within the larger frame of agrarian appeals emerged two points not much noticed in the first debate: namely, the position of the wheat producer and the feared competition of new and fertile land with older areas. The agreement's alleged failure to benefit the consumer received considerably more attention. The House debate wrote the opening bars of the Hallelujah Chorus to be rendered in the Senate.

As if realizing the impending crisis, opponents marshaled in stout array for the hearings before the Senate Committee on Finance. Few new interests appeared, but old ones were out in greater force. The sessions served various purposes: they registered enemy arguments; they took time, which irked the President and allowed the lower house to discuss tariff revision measures; they showed a sharp division within the committee, frequently manifested by heckling of witnesses, particularly favorable ones; and they showed again what Taft had known long since, that outspoken friends of reciprocity were hard to find. Again the farmer interest was to the fore, with lumber, paper, and the A.N.P.A. as companions.[31] Furthermore, the few favorable interests appearing seemed either less adept at self-expression than their adversaries or more susceptible to the tactics of antireciprocity committee members.[32]

Nearly sixty spokesmen took the floor for the farmer, of whom twenty-four represented the Grange or other farm organizations. Their reiterated arguments added only weight of numbers.[33] Per-

29. *Record,* 62d Cong., 1st Sess., pp. 525–536, 559–560.

30. New York *Tribune's* analysis of vote, April 22, 1911.

31. *Cleveland Plain Dealer,* May 15; Chicago *Tribune,* May 18, 22, June 15, 22; Boston *Daily Advertiser,* May 19, 1911.

32. For example, the representatives of commercial associations. *Sen. Doc.* 56, 62d Cong., 1st Sess., pp. 551–610.

33. *Ibid.,* pp. 16–531.

haps more significant of tendencies were two episodes demonstrating at once the attitude of the administration toward the Grange opposition and the somewhat synthetic character of that opposition. On May 8, shortly after the hearings opened and the day the free-list bill passed the House, a delegation of twenty-five protesting Grangers was shepherded to the White House by N. P. Hull, Master of the Michigan State Grange. Ushered into the presidential presence, Hull read a prepared address not notable for its tactful handling of a delicate relationship. He practically read Taft a lesson on policy, asserting that reciprocity would force the farmer to take lower prices for his wheat and produce, and intimated that continuance of the present course would endanger the loyalty of the border States, backbone of the party. As the reading progressed, the President visibly lost his temper, and at its conclusion replied hotly that the farmer was not in the least likely to lose by breaking down the Canadian tariff wall. He explained later to Archie Butt that he thought someone had put Hull up to the whole performance, and was inclined to give Hines, of the lumber trust, the credit. Later, when his feelings had cooled somewhat, he prepared to tone down his remarks for release to the press, but was persuaded by Butt to let them stand as spoken.[34]

It had often been intimated that the farmer opposition derived counsel and financial support from other than dirt farmers. Point was given to these suspicions by revelations during the hearings that the Grange propaganda had been largely prepared by a New York firm, Allen and Graham. Though this was neither new nor necessarily underhanded, it permitted the administration and the newspaper press to assert that the farmers were not their own men, particularly when it became clear that Allen and Graham had expected, if not solicited, contributions from the protected interests for their services to the farmers. The matter was emphasized sufficiently through the hearings and publicized sufficiently through the press to minimize considerably the effect of the farm delegations before the

34. New York *Tribune,* May 9, 1911; Butt, *Taft and Roosevelt,* II, 643–644. The President was correct in his inference that Hull was primed for his address, but was mistaken as to the instigator. The whole meeting was prepared by Allen and Graham, whose activities are to be detailed forthwith, and Hull's speech was written by the latter. Interview with Whidden Graham.

committee, to the advantage of the administration. The story opens on May 10 when Pepper wrote to C. D. Hilles, Taft's secretary: "I have given the New York Herald the name of the firm of lawyers who are engineering the 'spontaneous' movement of the grangers, for consideration, and the Herald may find something of interest in that connection before long."[35] The following day *The New York Herald* broke the story in an article which was widely quoted, indicating that Grange propaganda had been supplied largely by the firm, for which one member, Whidden Graham, did the writing, and the other, Joseph H. Allen, maintained the necessary contacts.

The article purported to be a first-person direct quotation from an interview with Allen and Graham by an unnamed individual representing firms which had been approached for a subscription. This anonymous informer was quoted as saying that "the National Grange also wants it to go on record that if the Canadian agreement is passed through the failure of the manufacturers to give proper financial support, they declare they will do all they can to defeat the Republican party for the next twenty years." Allen was reported to have solicited some of the manufacturers personally. On May 12 Senator Stone requested the presence of Allen and Graham, with copies of all antireciprocity literature for which they had been responsible.[36] Nothing having come of his request, he engaged on May 25 in a heated discussion with Senator Jacob H. Gallinger, during which he moved for the issue of subpoenas. Gallinger hinted pointedly that Allen and Graham's activities had been discovered to the pro-reciprocity Stone by the A.N.P.A. Finally it was agreed to invite them to appear, without issuance of the subpoenas.[37]

Their examination, May 31, with information furnished by Bachelder, clarified the situation considerably. Bachelder testified

35. *Taft Papers.* The following account is based, in addition to references given in the notes, upon an interview with Whidden Graham in the summer of 1936, and upon correspondence with him covering the episode. Though he was seventy-three years old at the time of the interview, his story checks sufficiently with that told by the documents to warrant including in the narrative details not covered by the printed evidence available.

36. *Sen. Doc.* 56, 62d Cong., 1st Sess., p. 292.

37. *Ibid.,* pp. 459–461; New York *Tribune,* May 25, 1911. Graham's explanation is that their activities were exposed to the newspapermen by a disgruntled former employee.

that Allen and Graham had been employed by the Grange since 1905 in preparing "petitions, arguments, and so forth" relative to proposals in which the Grange was interested, including the denatured-alcohol bill, good-roads legislation, and parcel post. Since announcement of reciprocity the firm had worked with Grange executives in preparing various documents which were circularized to the Granges and other farmer organizations. Stone endeavored to trap Bachelder into admitting that Allen and Graham were employed by the Grange but paid by other interests—for example that the automobile people paid for good-roads propaganda furnished by Allen and Graham and put out by the Grange. The object, of course, was to find out who was paying for the Grange propaganda. It appears that the actual technique of coöperation was that Allen and Graham prepared material and sent it to Bachelder, who accepted it for use, sometimes after consultation with other Grange leaders. Allen and Graham had it printed and shipped to Concord, New Hampshire, whence it was distributed through the local post office under Grange auspices.[38]

Allen, in his examination, could not remember approaching any manufacturers, but admitted that some had come to see him. He admitted further that he had suggested to such that they should contribute. However, he asserted that to date but one contribution had been received, through the Grange, from a manufacturer who was connected with neither the paper nor the lumber business. Further, all the arguments which his firm had furnished had been directed to the injuries the farmer would suffer through reciprocity. He had had, so he said, conferences with C. W. Lyman of the International Paper Company, and with Arthur Hastings of the American Paper and Pulp Association, though neither of these had so far contributed. It was his understanding that any money coming from the paper interest would be from the American Paper and Pulp Association. He side-stepped Stone's question as to whether his firm was "not now collaborating with the lumber interests and the paper

38. *Sen. Doc. 56,* 62d Cong., 1st Sess., pp. 52–87. Included, pp. 60–82, are the documents circulated by the Grange, including communications between Grange officials and various members of the government, and a series of articles prepared to show the advantages of reciprocity to the Canadian farmer and its harmful effects south of the line.

manufacturing interests" by asserting that "the work that I am now doing is wholly with the National Grange and wholly with reference to agriculture."[39]

Graham, on examination, was somewhat more explicit as to the firm's relations with manufacturers and the Grange. He admitted quite frankly that their earlier work for the Grange had been paid for by other interests—by a committee of manufacturers using alcohol on the denatured-alcohol bill, by the automobile manufacturers on the good-roads bill. He insisted that the whole business was "a mare's nest instigated by the New York Herald, and we are brought down here to furnish some news items on which garbled reports are sent out to the papers, misrepresenting the position of the grange." He insisted further that neither his firm nor the Grange had had anything to do with Hines of the lumber trust, whose name had been linked with the matter because he had been placed before the public in connection with the Lorimer case in an unfavorable light. Asked point-blank by Stone whether his firm was being paid by outside interests, he declined to answer, as, not being on oath, he could do.[40] Thus, though the inquisitors were unable to secure direct admission that outside interests had paid for the Grange propaganda, sufficient information had been put into the record to enable the newspapers to discount thenceforward the farm furor over reciprocity. A reasonable supposition had been created—a supposition tardily confirmed by Graham's admission to the writer that the International Paper Company later paid his firm at the rate of one thousand dollars per month and expenses for a six-months campaign for the Grange.

The lumber manufacturers were represented by several individuals from the sections most likely to suffer from the agreement—the South and the Pacific Northwest—and by Leonard Bronson, chief lobbyist of the National Lumber Manufacturers Association. The rising price of lumber and the concentration of standing timber in a few hands had created a public opinion unfavorable to the lumber interest, particularly in New England and the North Central and Prairie States. Free rough lumber was doubtless included in the agreement partly to offset the probable hostility of the latter

39. *Ibid.*, pp. 4–14.   40. *Ibid.*, pp. 242–257.

area on the free-wheat issue.[41] The principal difficulty advanced by the West Coast lumbermen was that free rough lumber would enable the British Columbia producers to drive out American competition in the prairie and California markets; in the latter case because Canada's lax shipping laws made possible cheaper transportation. This factor, it was alleged, would ultimately give Canada the Eastern United States market after the opening of the Panama Canal. The principal Southern argument was that favorable production and transportation costs would give Canada the advantage in the East.

The inevitable clash between the makers and users of paper marked the hearings, with the former being the more numerously represented.[42] The burden of their plea was again that reciprocity, by removing the duty on low-cost paper, would drive the business to seek cheaper Canadian labor and materials. Arthur Hastings, president of the American Paper and Pulp Association, which performed for the papermakers propaganda functions similar to those of the A.N.P.A. for the publishers, entered a denial that his organization fixed prices. He did admit, however, that he sometimes suggested curtailing production, not with the idea of raising prices, but in order to "keep a more uniform price." Norris, heckled by Senators Weldon B. Heyburn and Reed Smoot and supported by Stone, rehearsed the now familiar story of Provincial efforts to force the paper industry to Canada by export restrictions. He explained the compromise which had been worked out in the Payne bill and defeated in the Senate "at the instigation of Senator Hale and of the extreme standpatters among the paper makers [who] upset that arrangement and undertook to bulldoze the Canadian Provinces by the imposition of retaliatory duties to let the pulp wood come into the United States without restriction." This, he asserted, provoked such complications that the paper clause of the agreement

41. *Documents . . . .: Papers Relating to Reciprocity with Canada, Sen. Doc.* 862, 61st Cong., 3d Sess., Washington, 1911, pp. 13–14; U.S. Tar. Comm., *Rec. with Can.,* pp. 68–69. The Senate hearings, principal points of which are herewith summarized, are found in *Sen. Doc.* 56, 62d Cong., 1st Sess., pp. 711–859.

42. *Sen. Doc.* 56, 62d Cong., 1st Sess., pp. 961–1163, gives the text of the hearings on the paper matter.

offered "the only immediate and promising solution" by exerting counterpressure upon the Provinces to relax their export restrictions to permit free entry to the United States of paper made from free wood—i.e., wood not subject to export restrictions. Under questioning he admitted sponsoring the preparation of articles pointing out the advantages of reciprocity to the farmer, but asserted that the fact that none of these mentioned free newsprint was "purely an oversight" to which his attention had but recently been called.[43]

Perhaps the most significant development of the hearings relative to the paper interest was Senator Elihu Root's introduction of an amendment designed to prevent free entry of paper and pulp until all the Canadian Provinces had repealed their export restrictions. It was probably forced upon the proreciprocity Root by his Northern New York papermaker constituents. Taft admitted that it was in accord with the agreement, but felt that it was bad tactics as it would endanger the bill in the Senate and might involve a dispute, since the House had sought a different path to the same goal.[44]

The hearings occupied a month, largely devoted to threshing old straw exceeding fine. They added little to the arguments already presented and demonstrated beyond peradventure that the farmer, whatever his real attitude, was the target of press and Grange arguments on the one hand disingenuous and on the other prefabricated. This, to say nothing of the President's pleas to the farm interest. The hearings brought out a further important issue in the Root amendment. And they formed a background against which legislative pressure for tariff revision through the farmers' free list had vied for public attention with executive pressure for singlehanded action on reciprocity. This rivalry furnishes the key to much that happened in the final debate. Could the President hold his leaderless and none too enthusiastic Senate in line and prevent the saddling of tariff revision upon reciprocity? To this story, with its accompaniment of Insurgent frustration, we now turn.[45]

43. *Ibid.*, pp. 1023–1028, 1137–1163.

44. *Ibid.*, pp. 1321–1325, gives Root's appearance before the committee in support of his amendment. Taft's letters to his brother Horace (May 25) and to St. Clair McKelway (June 13, 1911) give his point of view. *Taft Papers. Cf.* also Indianapolis *Star*, May 19; New York *American*, June 15, 1911.

45. He expressed his hopes and fears in a letter to Horace, May 25, 1911:

The Senate housed various interests: standpat Republicans backed the President for party reasons; stalwart Democrats backed him on reciprocity but fought him on the tariff; Insurgents fought to discredit him; and a few mavericks fitted into none of these categories. The resultant of these complex forces was a long discussion, forced by Insurgent efforts to defeat the President's version of the tariff reduction they had so ardently espoused in 1909, and watched by Democrats who were only waiting to revise the tariff themselves. Insurgents and Democrats in coalition finally accomplished tariff revision after Senate and country alike wearied of reciprocity talk. In the shuffle the President's bill passed, unamended as he had wished. "1912" was writ large upon the record, as all sought to make capital for the coming fight. Under these circumstances the legislative history of reciprocity must be considered as part and parcel of the party melee; arguments on the merits had long since been thoroughly rehearsed and, but for slight changes in emphasis, need little comment. As in the House debate, the tendency was to let the opponents do most of the talking; reciprocity's friends were content to await the victorious vote which from the first seemed a foregone conclusion.[46]

Penrose reported the bill in the Senate on June 13, without recommendation and accompanied by the Root amendment. Three minority reports were appended; R. M. LaFollette and P. J. McCumber each handed in unfavorable recommendations, and John Sharp Williams, John W. Kern, and Stone, favoring reciprocity in principle, attacked the Root amendment in a report prepared by Williams.[47] There was some surprise at LaFollette's action though in Insurgent conferences he had "frankly asserted that the reciprocity agreement

"I am still very hopeful in thinking I can get it through. But of course, I labor under very serious disadvantage in not having any very earnest supporter to take the lead. Some of my supporters disgust me more than I can say. . . . However, we can count the votes, and if I can keep the Democrats from attempting to put in the so-called 'farmers' free-list' I can get the bill through." *Taft Papers.*

46. A poll of May 2 in the *Knox Papers* showed 55 definitely favorable, 31 definitely opposed, and 6 doubtful; a line-up surprisingly close to the 53–27 vote by which the bill finally passed.

47. *To Promote Reciprocal Relations with Canada, Sen. Rep. 3, 62d Cong., 1st Sess., Washington, 1911.*

must not be approved, because it would reflect credit on the Taft administration."[48] McCumber opened the formal debate on the fourteenth. He admitted from the first that opposition would be unavailing, as the bill would pass by two to one. This admitted, he and other Insurgents, aided by a few Republicans and stray Democrats, proceeded to the fray. Again the farm interest was stressed, with the wheat situation to the fore. Again the bogey of Canadian hard wheat as a price depressant in the Northwest was flaunted in the record. Many followed McCumber's opening admission, that Liverpool generally fixed the world price, and copied him in spending hours refuting the general by citing the particular, their point being that Northwestern farmers needed protection from Canadian hard wheat, free importation of which would create unfavorable conditions for the American product by lowering prices in the Minneapolis flouring market.[49] The bill's leading supporters rallied to counter this interpretation, reiterating that Liverpool fixed the price or insisting that if there was any leveling the Canadian price would rise more than the American price would drop.[50]

The very length of the discussion helped increase the number and variety of arguments, but old stand-bys continued to receive considerable attention. Again it was asserted that the cost of living would not be cut.[51] The principle of protection was still endangered.[52] Again accusations of executive usurpation of functions of both Senate and House raised a constitutional question, and in reply it was asserted that Taft was within his rights.[53] Once more the trusts were brought forward as beneficiaries and once more the argument was refuted.[54] Among the few who came up to defend the President might be noted Senators Stone of Missouri, Theodore E. Burton of Ohio, Norris Brown of Nebraska, and Wesley L. Jones of

48. New York *Tribune,* June 9, 1911.

49. *Record,* 62d Cong., 1st Sess., pp. 2006 ff. *Cf.* also remarks of Knute Nelson, *ibid.,* pp. 2071 ff.; R. J. Gamble, pp. 2610–2611; A. J. Gronna, pp. 2681–2686, as samples and variants of this argument.

50. T. E. Burton, *ibid.,* p. 2630; Stone, p. 3065; Norris Brown, one of Taft's few Insurgent supporters, p. 3039.

51. *Ibid.,* pp. 2704, 2711, 2773–2774.

52. *Ibid.,* pp. 2503, 2577–2578, 2609.

53. *Ibid.,* pp. 2071, 2371, 2572, 2573, 2677, 2769, 3035, 3036, 3094.

54. *Ibid.,* pp. 2575–2576, 2753, 2906, 3099, 3145 ff.

Washington, the last two Insurgents. The debate contributed little save variety and verbosity, and was mainly a sounding board for more important events now to be described.

The discussion had opened with opponents admitting likelihood of defeat, with friends by and large willing to listen and vote, and with public counting of noses of those who were likely to support the measure.[55] The first important issue was the Root amendment, which was considered on June 19, 21, and 22, and defeated without a record vote. Root himself was convinced that it could not pass and said that he was satisfied to have brought the matter to public attention.[56] Routine consideration of reciprocity was shortly upset by a tariff bombshell. On June 20 the House passed a bill revising the wool schedule and the following day a combination of Democrats and Insurgent opponents of reciprocity voted to throw the tariff into the Senate arena. This was done by passing the Gore resolution directing the Finance Committee to report the wool bill not later than July 10. On June 22 the committee passed the buck to the Senate by reporting both the wool and free-list bills adversely. This put both reciprocity and tariff revision on the floor, assured each of open discussion and, as the gleeful Insurgents asserted, marked the beginning of the end of reciprocity, which would be smothered by tariff talk.[57] At any rate, early adoption could not be hoped for, and its death through tariff-revision amendments was to be feared. In fact, Borah and Albert B. Cummins, leading Insurgents, openly threatened to propose many such amendments before letting reciprocity pass.[58] It was frequently asserted that the alliance had been entered by the Insurgents in order to defeat reciprocity and thereby injure the President's prestige and his chances in 1912.[59]

This was a blow to Taft's program, a threat to his highest hopes, and a danger to his newly found leadership. He announced bravely, however, that he was not worried by developments, and it soon be-

55. New York *Tribune*, June 16, 17, 1911; *Independent*, 70:1289 (June 15, 1911).

56. *Record*, 62d Cong., 1st Sess., pp. 2279–2288, 2376, 2454–2527.

57. *Ibid.*, pp. 2381–2403; New York *Tribune*, June 21, 22, 23; *Literary Digest*, 42:4–5 (July 1, 1911).

58. New York *Tribune*, June 22, 1911.

59. Boston *Daily Advertiser*, Sioux City *Journal*, New York *Tribune*, June 23, 1911.

came evident that his equanimity was justified, at least as far as the
Democrats were concerned, for Senator Thomas P. Gore asserted
that his party would not hinder reciprocity; many Democrats evidently preferred reciprocity first and tariff revision second.[60] The
first-fruits of this decision was the defeat of the Root amendment
already noted. Thereafter the Insurgents loosed their batteries and
in the face of increasingly hot weather Borah, Benjamin L. Bristow,
A. J. Gronna, and Cummins addressed themselves to a series of
amendments proposed by Cummins—and to empty benches.[61] As the
debate dragged its weary length it became increasingly apparent
that the amendments were the basis of a filibuster, that they were
doomed to defeat, and that the President was finally receiving some
expert assistance from Penrose and Burton who became the parliamentary and the forensic champions of the agreement. One by one
the Cummins amendments were rejected.

Presently a much-remarked alliance between LaFollette and
Bailey appeared as the principal obstacle to an early vote. Bailey
secured control of the floor on July 11 and held it, avowedly because
he had promised LaFollette, who was not yet ready to speak, to prevent a vote on a pending resolution.[62] LaFollette finally took the
floor for a speech marking his final departure from Republican
ranks—one which proved to be a bitter attack upon the President,
and his own bid for consideration as Taft's successor. It also closed
the door on any possible hope of holding standpatters and Insurgents together. His attack on reciprocity, bitter though it was,
merely served as the vehicle of his larger purposes.[63] Tempers were
by this time becoming frayed and the matter of a quorum developed
into a serious problem. On July 14, under the impetus of Penrose's
driving, dates were set for voting on several measures, including
reciprocity, the wool bill, and the free-list bill, with reciprocity head-

60. New York *Tribune,* June 23, 24, 1911.

61. The debates, covering June 28 through July 7, will be found in *Record,* 62d Cong., 1st Sess., under these dates. The setting of heat and empti-
ness is described in the New York *Tribune,* June 29–July 8, 1911. Cummins held control of the floor during most of the period.

62. *Record,* 62d Cong., 1st Sess., p. 2818; New York *Tribune,* July 12,
1911.

63. *Record,* 62d Cong., 1st Sess., pp. 2899–2906; New York *Tribune,*
Boston *Daily Advertiser,* July 14; *Literary Digest,* 43:161 (July 29, 1911).

ing the list.[64] The filibusterers against a foregone conclusion had encountered an increasing desire for a vote and an end of talk. After more maneuvering and the defeat of more amendments the bill passed the Senate July 22, by fifty-three to twenty-seven.[65] Taft had won his fight. So, too, had the A.N.P.A., since Section 2 was so drawn as to be effective as soon as the President signed the act. The vote presented a curious line-up indicative of the unstable equilibrium to which reciprocity had so largely contributed. The Republicans were split, the Democrats were split, and even the Insurgents were divided. The fifty-three affirmative votes included thirty-two Democrats and twenty-one Republicans, of whom three were Insurgents. The negative counted three Democrats (generally referred to as servants of corporate interests) and twenty-four Republicans of whom ten were Insurgents holding out to the bitter end. Verily, the political eggs were badly scrambled.

In its larger aspects the story just presented has had much to do with the making of a presidential reputation and the unmaking of a President. Taft's tardy assertion of leadership had driven through a program which many of his own henchmen viewed with indifference if not with alarm. The road to this end, however, was marked by much maneuver and the appearance of factors ominous for the future. To gain his ends the President had been forced to ally with the Democrats and had made the Insurgents look ridiculous. The Democrats accepted the alliance only as a means to their larger end of tariff revision, to which they proceeded apace, with Insurgent assistance. Thus the Insurgents, who had shouted for tariff reform since 1909, opposed it in the form of reciprocity but supported the Democratic wool and free-list bills. This inconsistency showed quite clearly that hostility to the President was to them at least on a par with tariff reform, and demonstrated, if proof were needed, the sharp split in Republican ranks. The President was momentarily triumphant and could go on to veto the popgun bills; the Insurgents were in disgrace for their factious opposition. But in the long run the important thing was that the Republican party was divided—a division to which the discussion of reciprocity contributed in no small measure.

64. *Record,* 62d Cong., 1st Sess., pp. 2923–2931.
65. *Ibid.,* pp. 3167–3175.

Turning from Congress to country, the farmer and the farmer's friends continued their hostile campaign, albeit somewhat less vigorously after the Allen and Graham revelations and after it became evident that the Senate would pass the bill. Bachelder protested to Senator Gallinger at Senator Stone's revelation of the Allen and Graham matter in a telegram which the author has not found printed in any of the Eastern papers examined. In it he charged that the whole thing was hatched up by the A.N.P.A., and insisted that if his own activities were scrutinized the relations of the publishers to the reciprocity movement ought to be investigated also.[66] He asserted in a letter to a complaining Pennsylvanian that reciprocity was Taft's bribe to the publishers.[67] The scanty evidence available indicates that Grange influence was decreasingly important after June 1 and was directed finally to killing the bill by amendments rendering it unacceptable to Canada.[68] It is the author's opinion, after study of the Grange activity, that the organization created a stir out of proportion to its clientele (Bachelder placed its proven membership at 425,033 as of June 30, 1910), and covering a much wider area than would have been possible except for the hearing provided for its propaganda by the International Paper Company's subsidy.[69]

As before, the farm press stressed numerous variants of the idea that the farmer was being made to bear reciprocity's burdens for the benefit of the city dweller, the manufacturer, and the middleman.[70] The selfish attitude of the publishers was emphasized frequently.[71] Again it was asserted that reciprocity would not lay the specter of

66. Salt Lake *Tribune,* May 15, 1911.

67. To A. B. Farquhar, May 17, 1911, sent by the latter to Taft and found in the *Taft Papers.*

68. *American Cultivator,* June 10, 1911, p. 8.

69. *Cf.* Lewiston *Evening Journal,* May 29, 1911.

70. The following references voice this geographically: *Farm, Stock and Home,* 27:258 (March 15, 1911); *Farmer,* 29:448 (March 25, 1911); *Farm Life* (Chicago), April, 1911, p. 1; *The National Stock Grower and Farmer* (St. Louis), April, 1911, p. 8; *The Ohio Farmer* (Cleveland), 127:434 (April 1, 1911); *American Agriculturist,* 87:574 (April 8, 1911).

71. *The Northwestern Agriculturist* (Minneapolis), 26:532 (April 29, 1911); *Ohio Farmer,* 127:434 (April 1, 1911); *Michigan Farmer,* 136:636 (June 17, 1911); *Farmers' Review,* 43:595 (July 8, 1911).

high living costs.[72] The argument of falling values in face of new and fertile Canadian lands was occasionally presented, perhaps a reflection of this oft-repeated Congressional argument.[73] An occasional journal looked forward to annexation with some favor on the ground that if Canada were to share American markets a sharing of political responsibilities was no more than fair.[74] Some fear was expressed lest reciprocity depress the price of wheat.[75] Toward the end of the discussion the farm press clung to the principal anti-reciprocity argument used from the beginning; there is some evidence, however, of greater variety of argument, largely copied from other fountains of opinion. Some journals, too, slackened their efforts, evidently sensing that the fight was lost. And a very considerable proportion of the papers on which the foregoing discussion is based paid little or no attention to the matter.[76]

As always, the farmer had friends to advise and help him for his —or *their*—own good. The Allen and Graham revelations somewhat weakened the Grange influence, but the American Protective Tariff League ably filled the void. Its organ, *The American Economist*, showed vividly how badly the farmer would fare under the agreement; its columns carried long quotations from antireciprocity organs; it even occasionally indicated its real fear, that reciprocity would breach the tariff wall. It solicited editorials from the farm papers, an earnest of coöperation which was accepted in some quarters and rejected in others. It quoted in its own columns one such rejection, *The Michigan Dairy Farmer*, March 18, commenting editorially that it did not "care to exchange editorial courtesies with a

72. *The Rural New Yorker* (New York), 70:324 (March 11, 1911); *Ohio Farmer,* 127:288, 434 (March 4, April 1, 1911); *Prairie Farmer,* June 15, 1911, p. 12.

73. *American Agriculturist,* 87:708 (May 13, 1911); *Ohio Farmer,* 127:434 (April 1, 1911); *Rural New Yorker,* 70:324 (March 11, 1911).

74. *The Iowa State Register and Farmer* (Des Moines), March 15, 1911, p. 6; *Northwestern Agriculturist,* 26:668 (June 24, 1911).

75. *The Dakota Farmer* (Aberdeen, S.D.), 31:766 (June 1, 1911); *Northwestern Agriculturist,* 26:513 (April 22, 1911).

76. This opinion-analysis is based upon a scrutiny of the files of thirty-two farm journals distributed geographically as follows: East, 8; South, 4; Middle West, 9; Northwest, 9; Far West, 2. Of this total eleven paid practically no attention to the issue.

publication that offers aid to our farming population only at a time when it is evident that its own interest may be jeopardized."[77] Others were not so puristic. *The Northwestern Agriculturist*, for example, furnished numerous editorials, to be reprinted in the *Economist*; it carried dispatches from Washington over the signature of Wilbur F. Wakeman, secretary of the League; and its editor addressed a meeting in Brooklyn to which he was presented by Wakeman.[78] The League sent out floods of telegrams, according to a press report, urging businessmen to bring pressure to bear upon their Congressmen at the crisis of the House debate.[79] It was reported to have invested a considerable sum in postal cards which were distributed with the request that they be mailed to members of Congress. The resolutions printed on the cards touchingly evidenced the League's concern for the farmer: "Whereas the manufacturer cannot hope to retain protection for his industry when protection shall have been denied the farmer, therefore, be it resolved, that the American Protective Tariff League is unalterably opposed to the adoption of the Canadian tariff agreement, and urges that all friends of protection bring to bear every proper influence upon the congress of the United States against the adoption of said agreement."[80] The League self-righteously denied any connection with Allen and Graham, asserting that it had "only employed its own machinery in the work of educating public sentiment as to the wrong and the mischief involved in the proposition to withdraw Protection from the farmer while retaining Protection for the manufacturer."[81]

The lumber interest remained divided. The principal opposition argument was that free rough lumber would prevent American producers from competing with Canada in the cheaper grades. This, it was alleged, would make it profitable to produce only the higher grades, with the result that a large proportion of the timber (one journal states from 70 to 80 per cent) would be left to rot or burn. This of course would violate all the canons of conservation. Involved,

77. *American Economist*, 47:185 (March 31, 1911).

78. *Ibid.* p. 171; *Northwestern Agriculturist*, 26:620, 652–653 (June 3, 17, 1911).

79. Burlington *Free Press*, April 20, 1911.

80. *Nebraska State Journal*, April 10; Indianapolis *Star*, April 20, 1911.

81. *American Economist*, 47:340 (June 9, 1911).

too, was the question of transportation costs which had been to the fore earlier in the discussion.[82] This was the only argument commanding any considerable support on the part of the seven trade journals examined. *The New York Lumber Trade Journal* admitted very early in the game that it had "never felt it advisable to take part in any controversy concerning the tariff for the reason that whichever [side] we took would not be representing a part of our constituency whose claims in either case are absolutely legitimate."[83] It seems likely that the lumber interest was largely unconcerned, and that the rather considerable opposition was kept alive by a determined group.

The wheat question, which caused so much discussion in Congress and the press, excited the millers but little, judging by the space devoted to it. From the scanty evidence available it appears that the industry continued divided, but the tendency was rather favorable than hostile toward the end of the discussion. The *Modern Miller*, opposed to reciprocity, reported in June that an inquiry into reasons for the shift disclosed that after an attempted corner in the market in May many millers saw in reciprocity a stabilizing factor which would lessen the likelihood of such manipulations.[84] One principal point of difference was that between the powerful millers near the Canadian border, who would profit by enlarged supplies of spring wheat, and the smaller millers of the East and Middle West, who would be unable to partake because of transportation costs. This would in the long run, it was asserted, be the end of the small miller, whose trade would be battered down by the large producers.[85]

Journals representative of the paper manufacturers again complained bitterly that the publishers were fomenting class legislation which would slaughter the industry in the States and drive manufac-

82. *The St. Louis Lumberman,* July 15, 1911, p. 59; *Miss. Valley Lumberman,* June 23, 1911, p. 31; *American Lumberman,* June 10, 1911, p. 27; *Paper,* 2:23 (March 15, 1911).

83. New York, February 15, 1911, p. 19.

84. *The Roller Mill* (Buffalo), 29:337 (March, 1911); *Northwestern Miller,* 85:643 (March 15, 1911); *Modern Miller,* April 15, 1911, pp. 11–12; April 22, p. 12; June 3, p. 11.

85. *The American Miller* (Chicago), 39:210, 546–547, 814 (March, July, October, 1911).

turers to Canada without benefitting newspaper readers.[86] Little
effort had been wasted by the papermakers in influencing the House,
where the issue was foregone; their concentrated attack upon the
Senate also went for nought and, after the bill passed, the *Paper
Trade Journal* remarked sadly: "The Senate . . . has handed the
newsprint industry of the United States to Canada. The victory for
the moment belongs not to the President and his Democratic allies,
nor to the Secretary of State, but to the American newspapers."[87]
The *Paper Mill* asserted that "no President of the United States
since Washington's time ever received the support from the press
that Mr. Taft did in behalf of this measure. Every daily, evening,
weekly and Sunday paper published in the United States; every
publisher, editor, reporter and cartoonist in the United States has
backed every movement that Taft made in behalf of this reciprocity
agreement."[88] Attention was also called to the fact that the paper
section went into effect immediately upon the passage of the act in
the United States and irrespective of Canadian action.[89]

Examination of editorial and news comment indicates that the
A.N.P.A. propaganda continued to find outlet, but the Association
confined its formal pressure to a circular of March 20 asking editors
to urge passage of the agreement as introduced, since danger lurked
"in amendments, or changes, or delay," and to resolutions of May 5,
again urging passage of the House bill without amendment.[90]

Press opinion manifested essentially the same tendencies as during the regular session: the farmer was the principal object of solicitude, annexation received considerable attention, and the newsprint
matter was aired once more.[91] As earlier, the newspaper friends of
the farmer had first to prove that reciprocity would not hurt him,
and then proceed to argue its positive benefits; as before, they de-

86. *Paper Makers' Journal* (Albany), March, 1911, pp. 2–3; *Paper Trade
Journal* (New York and Chicago), June 15, 1911, p. 34; *Paper*, 3:14 (April
5, 1911); *Paper Mill*, June 3, 1911, p. 1; June 10, p. 20.

87. July 27, 1911, p. 34.

88. July 29, 1911, p. 1.

89. *Paper*, 4:15 (August 2, 1911); *Paper Mill*, August 5, 1911, p. 20.

90. Circular quoted in Grand Forks *Evening Times*, June 6, 1911; resolutions in *Sen. Doc.* 56, 62d Cong., 1st Sess., p. 1225.

91. Forty files of daily newspapers form the basis of this section, with
footnote references sampling opinion geographically where possible.

voted more time to the former.[92] Again major attention was given to divesting the Canadian mind of the belief in an American desire to annex the Dominion; Champ Clark's speech had, in fact, by this time fathered one of the strongest of Canadian nationalist arguments.[93] Efforts were made to offset the earlier argument that reciprocity would help the consumer by cutting living costs.[94] Press interest in free newsprint was aired again with the few antireciprocity dailies exposing their mercenary compatriots, and the latter openly avowing their selfishness. Very little attention was paid to this factor save in the South and Middle West.[95]

Surprisingly few new arguments appeared. Chief among them were three. Several sheets were at pains to expose the extortions of the paper trust.[96] Others enlarged the scope of the indictment to include the lumber trust and the protected interests generally, asserting that these were in league with the farmer to the latter's hurt and their own profit.[97] Finally, much fun was poked at the Insurgents who, having clamored for tariff revision in 1909, were now so embarrassed at Taft's unpalatable serving of their own dish.[98]

The foregoing discussion has indicated that the daily press, as examined by the author, leaned heavily toward reciprocity. That its attitude was not entirely disinterested should be clear from the narrative, which has exhibited metropolitan journals wandering in the dells of agrarian economics rather than admitting their own imme-

92. Lewiston *Evening Journal*, July 7; *The New York Evening Journal*, June 26; Chicago *Tribune*, May 24, June 2; Portland *Oregonian*, March 31; Charleston *News and Courier*, April 25, 1911.

93. Boston *Daily Advertiser*, March 8; New York *American*, June 2; Anaconda *Standard*, April 13; Seattle *Post-Intelligencer*, May 5, June 22; Atlanta *Constitution*, May 1, 1911.

94. Burlington *Free Press*, May 13; Grand Forks *Evening Times*, March 22; Houston *Post*, April 12, 1911.

95. Lewiston *Evening Journal*, May 18; Fargo *Forum*, July 5; Grand Forks *Evening Times*, March 6, 13, 17; *Nebraska State Journal*, May 19, 1911.

96. *The Indianapolis News*, May 12, 24; Salt Lake *Tribune*, May 28, 1911.

97. Lewiston *Evening Journal*, May 23; *The Birmingham* (Ala.) *Age-Herald*, April 18, June 21; Minneapolis *Tribune*, March 8, 1911.

98. Atlanta *Constitution*, June 12, 28; Buffalo *Evening News*, late June and early July, *passim;* Minneapolis *Tribune*, March 22, 28, 1911.

diate pecuniary interest in tariff-free newsprint. That the author's sampling of the press has been representative is indicated by the results of a poll published by the Chicago *Tribune*, June 3, the day of Taft's visit to the city. This pictures the answers to a question sent to ten thousand newspapers in twenty-two States of the Central and Far West: "Are you in favor of the approval by Congress of the reciprocity agreement with Canada negotiated by President Taft?" Of 4,303 replies 63 were noncommittal, leaving a total of 4,240 definite answers. The division was 3,113 ayes and 1,127 nays, a ratio of about three to one. The papers were divided as to politics as follows: Republican, 1,393; Democrat, 628; Independent, 1,065; not given, 1,212. (It will be noticed that the totals do not check exactly.) The proportion between weekly and daily papers was eight to one. This poll was of course attacked in details, but there seems no good reason to suspect its general findings.[99] A poll of Vermont's nine dailies and fifty-one weeklies gave eight dailies pro and one neutral, the weeklies being thirty-eight pro, seven anti, and three neutral. The Burlington *Free Press*, which conducted the poll, admitted frankly that public opinion, as expressed outside the editorial columns, was hostile to the agreement, and explained the discrepancy in part by the fact that a greater effort had been made to secure such expressions.[100] This information, incomplete though it is, points clearly to the conclusion that the enemies of reciprocity received relatively slight comfort from the newspapers, daily or weekly, urban or rural.

One other matter deserves mention in this chronicle of the registry of public opinion: the work of William Randolph Hearst's *New York American*. The Hearst press, then comprising seven papers, used in 1910 approximately four hundred tons of newsprint per day —a tenth of the entire country's consumption.[101] When, late in May, reciprocity's chances looked none too bright and the President was working tooth and nail to sway public sentiment, the *American* launched a campaign combining support of the agreement and vitu-

99. The *American Economist* commented upon a poll conducted by *The Des Moines Capital* showing inaccuracies in the *Tribune* count in Iowa. 47: 376 (June 30, 1911).

100. May 1, June 8, 1911. Three dailies failed to reply.

101. A.N.P.A. Bulletin, No. 2338, p. 1101 (December 24, 1910).

peration of its enemies which was paralleled by no other American paper. Its most powerful tirades blasted the trust elements supposedly backing opposition to reciprocity, particularly the lumber and paper combines, and their Senatorial servants who, together with the Insurgents, endangered the act's passage. The campaign was carried on unremittingly after May 22, reached a shrill crescendo at the time of Senate action on the Root amendment (June 19), and thereafter was quickly dropped, evidently on the assumption that the bill would pass. In its editorial of July 19 the *American* boasted that at the psychological moment the Hearst papers entered the fray and by concentrating "their entire news and editorial strength upon the advocacy of this measure" earned the meed of presidential praise which was blazoned full across the front page: "I wish to express my high appreciation of the energetic work of the seven Hearst papers and of the members of your staff for their earnest and useful effort to spread the gospel of reciprocity, and I congratulate them on the success that has attended the Evangel."[102] The whole Hearst play and Taft's apparent sanction of its excesses of language made considerable antireciprocity capital in Canada, where Hearst became the whipping boy of the agreement.

Several figures had emerged from the total American discussion of reciprocity. As noted in the previous chapter the first debate brought forward Taft and the American farmer. These actors had to share the stage during the second debate with another, the Insurgent, whose somewhat clumsy antics Taft rather enjoyed, writing to Myron Herrick, "It also is most gratifying and not a little amusing to know that our advocacy of the measure served to unmask some whose good faith we were inclined to question but whom we found it somewhat difficult to 'show up.' "[103] The Insurgents' antics, clumsy though they were, served as a rehearsal for other and later acts which were not to give the President so much amusement. The American

102. New York *American,* July 25, 1911. The original of this telegram in the *Taft Papers* has the words "In answer to your telegram" prefaced to the above quotation, indicating that the presidential testimonial was a solicited one.

103. July 25, 1911. *Taft Papers.* He had written Charles P. Taft three days earlier that he was rather surprised at Insurgent tactics, as he had expected them "not only to support the bill but to claim that I was only trailing after them." *Ibid.*

drama was played out, though the lines that had been recited were to echo for some weeks across the border. There other actors were preparing to tread the boards of another stage, for the scheme which had led Taft to initial defeat, an extra session, and ultimate victory, had by this time forced the Laurier government to the country in an election which was to be the tragic opposite of the American victory.

CHAPTER X

THE CANADIAN ISSUE JOINED

AT some risk of assuming wisdom after the event, it has seemed desirable to preface detailed discussion of the Canadian situation by casting a trial balance between the interested parties in the Dominion. This may emphasize certain factors which the succeeding months of argument either ignored or deliberately beclouded, and indicate that the smoke of battle hid flames which, though not often apparent in the actual fray, were nonetheless hot. It should hint too that a violent reaction between powerful interests and forces threatening their existence may give off by-products unlike either reagent.

The problem involved may be stated, if not explained, quite simply. It is the Canadian rejection of the Taft-Fielding agreement. This pact had been deliberately applied mainly to agricultural products. Within this limitation its wide scope had left a stammering opposition momentarily demoralized. It achieved a goal which bipartisan efforts had sought vainly for years. It opened to an essentially agricultural country a vast new sales outlet. It carried the backing of a party long entrenched in all the recesses of political power, led by a man whom one of his own greatest enemies in the forthcoming fight termed "perhaps the most striking and brilliant personality in the British Empire."[1] And yet the agreement, backed by all these resources of timeliness, power, and personality, was rejected by an overwhelming verdict. Why?

The ensuing chapters are designed to show the process by which this verdict was rendered. Here an attempt is made to indicate some less obvious factors which made the verdict possible—factors which the author believes were not less important because they were not screamed from streamer headlines nor shouted from the Commons rostrum or the campaign platform. The National Policy, born as has been seen out of reciprocity's failure, fattened Canadian capital while excluding American manufactures. Industrial beneficiaries of

1. Sifton, Clifford, "Reciprocity," *The Annals of the American Academy of Political and Social Science*, 45:26 (January, 1913). This article well portrays the Canadian capitalist antireciprocity viewpoint.

protection were no more likely than their American contemporaries to welcome any breach in the tariff wall, even though they themselves were not immediately involved. Transportation interests, managing long lines of railroad built with government subsidies in defiance of natural trade routes, might likewise feel qualms at prospective changes which would allow commerce to seek its own level. And bankers have not been noted for their indifference to the wants of industry and commerce. These interests, though powerful, were concentrated in a relatively small area of the Dominion and counted relatively few of its total franchises. Their aims must needs be gained, therefore, by organizing themselves in such a way as to influence wide areas and convince many voters that reciprocity was bad on grounds that would move the majority to hostility or fear.

Several factors predisposed to favor these designs. The proposition involved the United States, and despite pious platitudes about the undefended frontier, not all Canadians viewed the Southern neighbor with undying affection. Again, it involved Anglo-Canadian relations and the possibility, easily exaggerated, of loosening the Imperial tie; under such circumstances the Union Jack could become an extremely useful emblem. The time element also aided reciprocity's opponents. Contemporary opinion, as surveyed by the author, agrees almost unanimously that an early verdict would have been a favorable one. An early verdict, however, was not easy to secure. Lack of closure and natural unwillingness to act too precipitately, lest American rejection make the Government look ridiculous, postponed immediate decision. Then the failure of the American Congress to take action at the regular session gave the growing opposition time to gather headway for continued obstruction until the approaching Coronation ceremonies and the accompanying Imperial Conference forced the Government to a recess of Parliament. During Laurier's absence the summer sun warmed Canadian opposition to rugged growth. Finally, the tactical position of reciprocity's opponents was a good one. Possessed of a great hunger after office, they could satisfy their craving by appealing to national and Imperial patriotism and by saying "No" to the Government's program. Thus backed by strong moneyed interests, sheltered beneath the Union Jack, and so placed as to be able to wage a negative campaign, the Conservative party entered a fight to defeat an agreement evidently advantageous

to Canada's greatest single economic interest, the farmer, who alone
was directly affected by it.[2]

February 9 beheld Parliament entering upon a long debate. It
witnessed the loss of the Liberal advantage of surprise, the development of stout opposition in Parliament and country, the passage of
the Liberals to a definitely defensive position, and an adjournment
for the Imperial Conference with at least a strong possibility that
reassembly would find the Government faced with an early appeal to
the country. The recess found Laurier in London and Borden on the
Prairies, facing the same determined farmers who a year before had
helped to turn the Premier toward reciprocity. Against this background of legislative argument developed a tide of adroitly fanned
public sentiment which rose rapidly to overmatch defensive propaganda. To these two stories the narrative now turns.

Debate opened two weeks to the day from the announcement of
the agreement, and two days before the McCall bill was reported to
the House of Representatives. The first move was F. D. Monk's motion to take the matter to the people before proceeding to debate.
This was defeated and Borden and Paterson took up the cudgels for
prosecution and defense. Borden's argument, essentially a let-well-
enough-alone plea, called attention to the uncertain duration of the
agreement, the danger of commercial union with the United States,
and the threat to Canadian transportation interests. Its tone, while
hostile, still carried a note of cautious reserve, perhaps the aftermath of recent hot caucus fights over party policy. The Minister of
Customs opened the Government's case with more than a hint of the
defensive in his argument, which was largely devoted to refuting
Conservative contentions. There would be, he asserted, no danger of
foreign entanglements, nor would the British preference be jeopard-

2. Contemporary statements confirming parts of the above analysis are as
follows: New York *Tribune,* August 24; *The Minneapolis* (Minn.) *Journal,*
February 11, 1911; Laut, Agnes C., "Robert Laird Borden, the New Premier
of Canada, Who Heads the First Conservative Ministry in Canada for Fifteen
Years," *Review of Reviews* 44:558–560 (November, 1911); Porritt, E.,
"Laurier's Defeat," *Independent,* 71:678 (September 28, 1911); Hammond,
M. O., "The Tragedy of Reciprocity," *The Canadian Magazine,* 38:84–91
(November, 1911); Skelton, O. D., "Reciprocity," *Queen's Quarterly,* 18:
330–336 (April–June, 1911). The two last, though both favorably biased,
are among the calmest of contemporary analyses.

ized. If Hill and others could carry Canadian grain more cheaply, Canadian roads must prepare to compete; furthermore, if rates dropped, business would increase. On the positive side his argument cited advantages that would accrue through the development of Canada's natural resources.[3]

George E. Foster, following, called up what the *Globe* termed "a more formidable spectre" than that presented by Borden. His remarks, while addressing themselves to the economic disadvantages of reciprocity, emphasized the national and Imperial aspects of the agreement. The people and the interests involved, he charged, had been given no hearing, nor had they any inkling of what was going on during negotiations; the resulting deal would cut interprovincial trade, make Canada dependent upon the United States, destroy Canadian fiscal freedom and the Imperial preference.[4]

These opening guns launched a duel which occupied all or part of twenty-five legislative days during February, March, April, and early May. All of the most-discussed arguments on both sides appeared in February, but the April debate marked the emergence of a number of arguments more strictly political, as distinguished from the economic, national, and Imperial topics which were to the fore earlier.[5] On the whole, the Opposition arguments exceeded those of the Government in number and variety and forced the latter, despite an occasional note of amused tolerance, to spend an inordinate amount of time refuting the Opposition instead of supporting its own affirmative contentions. Both sides took a leaf out of the American book in making their most numerous appeals to the producer, who was variously told that the "Ninety-Million Market" opened by the agreement was, or was not, to his advantage.

Against this oratorical background a series of episodes strengthened the Conservative arm after a flurry of intraparty squabbling, and launched the party on a program of opposition merging into

3. *Hansard,* II, 3284–3324.

4. Toronto *Globe,* February 15, 1911; *Hansard,* II, 3327–3343, 3532–3556. His remarks were continued on the fourteenth.

5. The term "political" as used here refers to arguments less directly applicable to the merits of the agreement than to efforts to develop public sentiment concerning it. Several such had appeared in February and were still under discussion in April; it is intended here to call attention to a shift in the emphasis and direction of the discussion.

nicely calculated obstruction, which held the floor until too late for
Laurier to appeal to the country with a chance of success. Held the
floor, too, until time for the Coronation recess, during which the
party was able, during Laurier's absence, to make considerable capital for the dissolution and election which it was becoming increasingly evident was to be forced upon the Government.

The February debate reached the high-water mark of Parliamentary discussion; the floods of bombast and obstruction, to character-
ize the later stages, had not yet been turned loose. Both sides argued
economic merits and demerits and both canvassed reciprocity's implications for national autonomy and Imperial relationships, while
quoting copiously from the Fathers, from George Brown through
Sir John A. Macdonald, to prove respectively that reciprocity was,
or was not, these worthies' most cherished ambition. A number of
Conservatives followed Borden's lead in asking, "Why not let well
enough alone?" and this exhortation became one of the main February arguments.[6] Frequent attacks were leveled at the Ministry because of the technique of negotiations. Martin Burrell (Yale-Cari-
boo), as in duty bound, voiced the plaint of the unconsulted in
echoing Foster's "no mandate" argument, asserting that "there is
something inherently and radically wrong in the working out of our
constitutional theories when it is possible for a small group of men
to bind the country hand and foot to so gigantic a proposition as
this without the opportunity to anybody of saying yea or nay or of
offering a single word of protest or advice."[7] Again, the uncertain
duration of the proposed arrangement was viewed as a danger to
Canadian unity should proposed future alterations appeal more
strongly to one section of the country than to another.[8]

6. *Hansard,* II, 3685, 3750. The remarks of T. S. Sproule (E. Grey) may
be taken as a fair sample of this argument, *ibid.,* III, 4003: "Canada is now
enjoying a prosperity she has not had for years. Her products are abundant,
her granaries are overflowing, she has profitable markets for all she has to
sell at home as well as outside. Canada produces nothing which she cannot
now dispose of readily at remunerative prices, her people are happily employed, and are being paid good wages and what more can she want? . . .
Why then should the government carry on this flirtation with Miss Jona-
than?"

7. *Ibid.,* II, 3581. *Cf.* also *ibid.,* p. 3738; III, 4072, 4085, 4389.

8. *Ibid.,* II, 3582, 3754.

On the Imperial front it was asserted that letting down the bars to the United States was a threat to the preference.[9] National integrity was also threatened by the forfeiture of fiscal freedom entailed by reciprocity.[10] The danger of annexation—to become the manna called down for the scaremongers by Champ Clark, the Missouri Moses—had less emphasis than later; perhaps its potentialities were not yet realized.[11]

On the more purely economic side several points were made. H. B. Ames (St. Antoine) claimed that under the operation of the most-favored-nation clause the advantages extended to the United States would automatically accrue to all British possessions and to at least a dozen foreign countries.[12] The frequently noted danger to Canada's established east-west lines of transport was called up.[13] As a sort of thread upon which the whole discussion might be hung were recurring allusions, some general and many worded with reference to particular interests, to the dangers of reciprocity to the producer—on whose behalf, indeed, the Government asserted the agreement had been made. Farmer, cattleman, fruit raiser, all would suffer direst consequences if the pact were ratified.[14] These arguments, and many more which lack of space precludes detailing, were put into the record for Liberals to refute—and to serve as grist for the propaganda mills soon to be put into operation.[15]

9. *Ibid.*, II, 3742; III, 4091. This argument was much used in the press in the later stages of the fight, and Liberals were not slow to point out that the same Conservatives now so intent on maintaining the preference had opposed it when first established. It might be noted, too, that only once was the logical conclusion of the weakening of the Imperial preference, a danger to the Imperial connection itself, mentioned in the Commons. *Ibid.*, II, 3700 ff.

10. *Ibid.*, II, 3744; III, 4064, 4089.

11. *Ibid.*, II, 3586, 3742–3743; III, 4069–4070.

12. *Ibid.*, III, 4096–4097.   13. *Ibid.*, II, 3693; III, 3991.

14. *Ibid.*, II, 3586 ff., 3741; III, 4094–4095, 4172–4182, 4394, 4401–4402.

15. Some other arguments which appeared but infrequently in the Parliamentary debate, but which may have had some influence upon newspaper propaganda, were the following: reciprocity would cut interprovincial trade, endanger manufactures, injure labor, destroy Canadian credit in Great Britain, stop the influx of capital for investment, halt the establishment of

Liberal debaters concerned themselves largely with answering Conservative attacks. Most prominently displayed was the confidence, on the part of the Liberals, that Canadian transportation interests would not suffer. Western farming, asserted D. B. Neely (Humboldt), would become so much more prosperous as to induce an influx of immigrants who would jump production until it would be necessary to call Hill to the rescue to carry some of the surplus southward.[16] Some time was devoted to combating the annexation argument,[17] and more to decrying Conservative fears for the safety of the British connection.[18] Manufacturers, it was again asserted, would profit by the larger Northwestern market resulting from reciprocity-induced immigration.[19] The central effort was directed toward demonstrating the agreement's benefits to producers of all classes by providing larger markets for Canadian natural products. Instead of two markets now available, argued Hugh S. Guthrie (Wellington), Canadian farmers under reciprocity could sell in three—the British, the Canadian, and the American.[20] Thus a month of oratory had elicited the essential Parliamentary points of view, launched the principal arguments, and drawn tight the lines of battle. The close of the month was to witness the first jolting blow to Liberal complacency in the formal defection of Clifford Sifton (Brandon) from Liberal ranks—a departure which Laurier himself was later to say cost the Liberals their hold on government.[21]

Sifton, one of the ablest figures in Canadian public life, a power in the settlement and development of the Prairie Provinces, a wheel horse in Liberal ranks for over twenty years, formerly Laurier's Minister of the Interior, and at the time of the reciprocity episode

branches of American factories, and endanger the program of conserving Canada's natural resources; also the aftermath of possible annexation would be disastrous to French-Canadian religious and linguistic privileges.

16. *Ibid.*, II, 3574–3575. *Cf.* also *ibid.*, pp. 3712–3713; III, 3966, 4025, 4191.

17. *Ibid.*, II, 3713, 3721–3722; III, 3965–3966, 4037.

18. *Ibid.*, II, 3719; III, 3977, 4036, 4193.

19. *Ibid.*, II, 3659–3660.

20. *Ibid.*, II, 3648. Other arguments along this line: *ibid.*, pp. 3566, 3578, 3727 ff.; III, 4020, 4185, 4432.

21. Dafoe, *Sifton*, p. 377; Winnipeg *Free Press*, September 21, 1929.

Chairman of the Dominion Conservation Commission, had not been active in party management for some time, but had nevertheless retained his party connections. More percipient than most Canadians, or perhaps better informed, he had expected reciprocity since the Taft-Fielding meeting of March, 1910, and had promptly made up his mind against the idea.[22] During the January negotiations he had twice made public statements, and some days before he rose in the Commons to make his confession of disbelief it had been known that he was about to desert the Liberal bark which he had helped to guide so long.[23] The question of his motive is still a mooted one. Some contemporaries in a fair position to know the facts have intimated to the author that he desired revenge upon Laurier and the party for being ousted from his Cabinet portfolio.[24] His January addresses based his opposition on the threat to Canada's natural resources. A logical explanation, but one difficult of demonstration, would be that increasing wealth had so changed his point of view that he feared letting down the protective bars. Whatever the explanation, the effect was electrical. His speech of February 28 contributed no more than some new twists to oft-repeated arguments, but the prospect of his adherence to their cause, following the Manifesto of the Eighteen Toronto Liberals, to be noted presently, must have given considerable heart to Conservative strategists, as well as misgivings to his erstwhile confreres.[25] He was presently followed into the opposition by William German (Welland), another prominent Liberal.[26]

To offset the Sifton defection and to rally his ranks to the attack, the Prime Minister himself entered the arena on March 7, the day after the Conservative whip had threatened obstruction by serving notice of a motion to postpone consideration of reciprocity until after

22. Dafoe, *Sifton,* pp. 361–362.

23. In speeches to the Canadian Clubs of London (Ont.), January 6, and of Montreal, January 9, he had stated his personal opposition. Montreal *Star,* January 6; Toronto *Globe,* January 10, 1911. Foster reported the approaching break as early as February 24.

24. The rupture had occurred over the Laurier policy of granting separate schools to Roman Catholics in the newly admitted Provinces of Alberta and Saskatchewan, a policy which he had helped to defeat in Manitoba some years previously.

25. *Hansard,* III, 4385–4409.

26. *Ibid.,* pp. 4484–4487. March 2, 1911.

the United States had acted.[27] Adopting a now well-worn historical approach, he intimated that the Conservatives had told everything possible about the National Policy except the pertinent fact that it had been adopted to force reciprocity. On the whole a moderate statement of the usual arguments, the Premier's speech included a sarcastic and fairly personal attack on Foster and on those who feared the loss of Canadian autonomy. Most of his time was spent in answering rather than affirming, save for the effort to demonstrate the advantages of the ninety-million market. He made a bow to the West by saying that he would have preferred to go farther in opening the Canadian market to American agricultural implements. The next day Borden introduced the threatened motion to delay, which was defeated.[28]

Debate continued during several days of March, but nothing essential was added and the most important developments were outside of Parliament. The middle of the month brought a legislative deadlock in which the *Globe* accused the Opposition of attempting to block the passage of supply bills, thus leaving the Government without funds, in order to force modification of the proposal or a dissolution.[29] Neither result was attained. The supply bills were voted at the last minute, the while an important crisis in Conservative party affairs was taking place behind the scenes.

This crisis had to do with Borden's position as leader and, once passed successfully, cleared the way for the application of the obstructionist tactics of the coming weeks. The inner story of this uprising (for such it undoubtedly was) against Borden's leadership has not been fully told, and the writer has not the facts to tell it. It is important here simply as an element in the developing of Conservative opposition to reciprocity, and in that connection the following outline must suffice. Late in March opposition to Borden—nothing new in the party—came to a head in a near revolution seemingly led by Montreal and Quebec capitalist elements which objected to his too gentlemanly conduct of the antireciprocity campaign. It reached the point where his resignation was at least threatened, with the result that a round-robin expressing confidence was circulated and signed by most of the party membership, tiding over the immediate

27. *Ibid.,* pp. 4741–4771; Toronto *Globe,* March 7, 8, 1911.
28. *Hansard,* III, 4844–4877. 29. March 20, 1911.

crisis and leaving Borden free to go ahead with party plans.[30] The significance of the episode lies in what might have happened had Borden resigned under the existing pressure. So wily a leader as Laurier might well have seized upon the confusion resulting from changing leadership to go to the country upon the reciprocity issue, in which case the Government would doubtless have been returned. As it was, Borden stayed in, the debate continued, and out of doors the rapidly organizing antireciprocity machine gathered funds and headway for a determined assault.

In mid-April Fielding tried to comfort the endangered industrial interests by stating that the only changes contemplated in the domestic tariff were those which might be made necessary by the reciprocity agreement, and that there would be no increase in the preference to Great Britain and no effort to put agricultural implements on the free list. "We hope," he said, "to persuade the people of Canada that they should not press for these changes now. . . . We desire to see all classes of the community prosper." This statement coördinated nicely with a rumor that the Canadian Manufacturers Association was about to withdraw opposition to reciprocity.[31] At about the same time the Easter recess gave members of Parliament an opportunity to receive impressions from home, with the result, as a careful observer put it, that "each side seemed to have heard what it wanted to hear"[32] and came back prepared for the increasingly inevitable dissolution. Parliamentary arguments in April and early May, which will not be surveyed in detail, continued February's Conservative emphasis on the danger to producers, the lack of ministerial mandate, the loss of fiscal freedom, the unrequited benefits granted the most-favored nations, and the danger of annexation,

---

30. The press was full of wild rumors, from which the above story has been sifted as the closest approximation of pertinent information. Toronto *Globe*, March 28; Montreal *Daily Witness*, March 28, 31; Halifax *Chronicle*, March 28–30, April 5; Toronto *Star*, March 28, 29, 1911. The writer was told in confidence by one close to the situation at the time that the effort to oust Borden resulted from the fact that he was negotiating with Sifton and other Liberals—a coöperation of which this element disapproved. If this suggestion be accepted, it still leaves room for the credibility of the explanation in the text above.

31. Toronto *Globe*, Montreal *Daily Witness*, April 13, 1911.

32. Hammond, M. O., "The Tragedy of Reciprocity," p. 88.

and added a new note—why not wait and let the United States act by herself? This was doubtless prompted by the tariff-revision sentiments manifested by the Democratic majority in the newly convened House. The Liberals, now definitely on the defensive save for their continued efforts to develop the advantages of reciprocity to producers, devoted themselves mainly to answering these arguments. The important thing was that time was passing and the Coronation–Imperial Conference season approaching; the Premier would soon have to decide his policy relative to these events. When, late in April, Conservative tactics became definitely obstructive, the Montreal *Star* began vociferating that Laurier must go to England, and the party caucus decided to carry reciprocity to a bitter-end fight, the success of Conservative strategy began to loom large.[33] It appeared increasingly unlikely that reciprocity could be passed before the Coronation and increasingly evident that the Conservatives wanted ultimately to force the issue to the country.

On April 28 Borden asked Laurier point-blank whether he intended to go to England. The latter replied that he had taken passage on a boat sailing May 12, but would remain in Canada if necessary. Borden then laid down three possible alternatives on the basis of which the Opposition would permit him to leave the country.[34] A compromise was finally worked out whereby an adjournment of approximately two months was to end on July 18. Thus the Parliament was not prorogued, reciprocity was not passed, the Premier had to carry the issue in his baggage to Britain, and the Conservatives had gained a considerable victory in the jockeying which had been in progress since February. While Laurier was in England they could build stronger their offenses, already powerful, and could come back to Parliament in July to take up the work of obstruction where it had left off in early May. The Conservative strategy—to force Laurier to the country, but not too soon—was working.[35] That Lau-

33. The Conservative caucus was held the twenty-sixth. Toronto *Globe,* April 27. *Cf.* also Montreal *Star,* April 27.

34. Toronto *Globe,* April 29, 1911.

35. It is interesting to speculate upon just how much the situation in the United States had to do with the development of Conservative plans. The House passed the bill April 22, after which it became very evident that the Senate would follow the long course of delay already described. This delay certainly worked in neatly with Conservative desires, since it made more

rier was not unaware of what was happening was evidenced by the fact that he wished to remain at home and fight out the issue to a conclusion, whether in Parliament or before the country, but was overborne by a majority of his Cabinet colleagues and gave in.[36]

Leaving Laurier on his way to the Coronation festivities and Borden preparing to invade the Prairies, it is now time to turn back the narrative and survey the development of sentiment in the country at large, as reflected by various interests and organizations and by the daily press. The Canadian farm press, with the exception of the noisily proreciprocity *Grain Growers' Guide*, said relatively little. A number of factors may have contributed to this attitude of reserve. Canadian farm sentiment seems to have been sharply and honestly divided. Such interests as the Niagara Peninsula and British Columbia fruitgrowers distrusted their ability to compete with the earlier-maturing crops below the border. The Ontario dairymen were keen for an agreement which would let them into such markets as Buffalo and Detroit. Thus a paper with wide circulation might well wish to avoid offending powerful groups in its clientele. The Canadian journals, too, seem to have been more scrupulous than those below the border in keeping political matters out of their columns. As a whole the farm press undoubtedly favored the agreement, however little was actually said.[37]

The manufacturers were for the most part opposed. Their Association memorialized the Prime Minister in February urging, with a solicitude only matched by their American brothers, that the farmers were prospering and that reciprocity would endanger the national investment in agriculture (to say nothing, of course, of the country's industries). Examination of the files of the Association's

plausible Canadian demands to wait until the United States had acted; conversely, it hamstrung any possible Government efforts to push affirmative action in Parliament.

36. Based on letters to the writer by George P. Graham, Minister of Railways, and W. L. Mackenzie King, Minister of Labor in the Laurier Cabinet.

37. A survey of the periodical files in the Library of the Dominion Department of Agriculture forms the basis of the above paragraph. Of the papers available two ignored the matter entirely, one closed its columns to further correspondence shortly after the election campaign opened, and the rest dropped the matter after simple statements of proreciprocity sentiments. There was none of the heated propaganda found in the American journals.

organ, *Industrial Canada*, from October, 1910, to September, 1911, yields fruitful grist of antireciprocity arguments, many of them directed to the farm interest and many others openly deprecating any breach in the protective wall. In addition, individual members did yeoman service in the cause. Boards of Trade, representing also the industrial and commercial interests, were well-nigh unanimous in opposing the agreement, though in several isolated instances a bitter fight preceded the passage of hostile resolutions.

Railroad sentiment was divided. Sir William Whyte, Sir William Mackenzie, Sir Thomas Shaughnessy, and E. J. Chamberlin have been quoted as reflecting the early executive attitude. Shortly afterward Sir Donald Mann, Mackenzie's associate in the Great Northern enterprise, was quoted as believing that "no harm can come to our Canadian railways from this reciprocity agreement."[38] Sir William Van Horne, former President of the Canadian Pacific, and, like Shaughnessy, of American birth, announced on February 22 that he "was out to bust the damned thing," came out of his retirement to oppose it, and stumped the Maritimes during the election campaign.[39] In March he wrote Charles Chaput that in reciprocity Canada was "making a bed to lie in and die in."[40] As the campaign progressed it became increasingly apparent that the railroads as such for the most part kept out of the limelight, permitting their undoubtedly great influence to be exercised behind the scenes by individuals in their personnel. On the eve of the election the New York *Tribune's* Ottawa correspondent reported that the Grand Trunk was "quiescent" and the Canadian Northern "apparently neutral."[41]

Provincial sentiment, as expressed in legislative action, was divided largely along party lines. Of the five Liberal legislatures those of Nova Scotia, Prince Edward Island, and Saskatchewan recorded themselves in favor of the agreement. Four Conservative bodies, in Manitoba, Ontario, New Brunswick, and British Columbia took the opposite stand.[42]

The parties busied themselves out of doors as well as in Parliament. Members of Government, leaders of Opposition, and party

38. Edmonton *Bulletin*, February 9, 1911.
39. Quoted in Dafoe, *Sifton*, p. 364.
40. Halifax *Herald*, March 8, 1911.   41. September 18, 1911.
42. *Can. Ann. Rev.*, 1911, pp. 96–110.

spellbinders, in meetings carefully organized to serve as sounding boards for partisan oratory, vied in argument and invective. First invading the important centers of population, they spread their respective gospels farther and farther into the back ridings until the stock arguments had seeped thoroughly through the land. Sifton played an important role in this campaign, as did one of the most important of the nonpolitical campaigners, Professor Stephen Leacock of McGill University, whose articles, written from the standpoint of a strong imperialism, were widely copied.

An extremely well-publicized Opposition asset was the highly dramatized "Revolt of the Eighteen Toronto Liberals." Any party suffers from the defection of its members, and particularly its highly connected members, even though these are not personally wealthy and not previously active in party affairs. The group in question was probably organized by Z. A. Lash, a Toronto corporation lawyer, and its manifesto appeared in the Conservative press, February 20, opposing reciprocity on grounds of maintaining Canadian nationality and the British connection. According to the Toronto *News* the members represented interests employing 110,000 men. Though highly touted as a group, it is doubtful if there was much united action beyond signing the manifesto and the meeting of March 9. As far as can be ascertained its influence was largely exerted through Lash and the Canadian National League. If the facts could be learned in detail they would probably show that the Eighteen made substantial financial contributions, either personally or through their business connections, to the Conservative war chest.[43]

The first and only openly coöperative effort was the sponsoring

---

43. Preston, W. T. R., *My Generation of Politics and Politicians,* Toronto, 1927, pp. 323–327, a gossipy account, associates the Eighteen closely with the Mackenzie and Mann railroad interests, and asserts that Mackenzie wrote a blank check, later filled in for two million dollars, and handed it to one of the Eighteen. The group counted the following members:
Sir Edmund Walker, President, Canadian Bank of Commerce.
J. L. Blaikie, investments and utilities.
W. D. Mathews, grain dealer and director, C.P.R.
W. K. George, head of Standard Silver Co.
Z. A. Lash, corporation lawyer, Vice President, C.N.R.
W. T. White, Managing Director, National Trust Co.
G. T. Somers, President, Sterling Bank, Vice President, Board of Trade.

of a large meeting at Massey Hall, Toronto, arranged by Lash and presided over and addressed by Sir Mortimer Clark, who asserted that Canada "must either choose the way to Washington or the way to the great Empire beyond the sea. We do not want our trade going south of the line to the American nation, which has always been hostile."[44] This meeting actively launched the Canadian National League, which was headed by Lash with Arthur Hawkes as secretary and Clifford Sifton as *sub rosa* adviser, at least to the secretary.[45] A meeting of its leaders at Montreal, including Lash, Sifton, and Sir Hugh Graham of the Montreal *Star*, divided the country for propaganda purposes, and a campaign was started in which, with the *Star* and its owner playing a large part, educational and emotional matter was spread far and wide. A telling pamphlet, *The Road to Washington*, assembled evidence on the intention of the United States to absorb Canada economically and politically. Another, *Home Market and Farm*, attempted to show the identical interest of farmer and manufacturer in the maintenance of protection. *Reciprocity with the United States—Canadian Nationality, British Connection and Fiscal Independence* covered the ground indicated in its title. The bills of the League, according to Hawkes, were met

R. S. Gourlay, piano manufacturer, President, Board of Trade.
Sir Mortimer Clark, former Lieutenant Governor of Ontario.
R. J. Christie, Managing Director, Christie, Brown Biscuit Co.
H. Blain, Director, Toronto *Globe*, Eby, Blain & Co., wholesale grocers.
H. S. Strathy, Director, Traders' Bank.
L. Goldman, Managing Director, North American Life Assurance Co.
G. A. Somerville, Managing Director, Manufacturers' Life Assurance Co.
W. Francis, Director, Standard Bank, Consumers' Gas.
J. D. Allen, Vice President, A. A. Allen, Wholesale Hats and Furs.
E. R. Wood, Managing Director, Central Canadian Loan & Savings Co.
J. C. Eaton, President, T. E. Eaton Co.

44. Toronto *Globe*, March 10, 1911.
45. Hawkes tells of his relations with Sifton, the League, and the campaign in an interesting article in the Winnipeg *Free Press*, September 21, 1929. The League's work and propaganda are outlined in a collection of bound pamphlets in the Dominion Archives, presented by Lash and supplied with an introduction written after the election. It is No. 3849 in the Archives' pamphlet collection and is entitled *Canadian National League Campaign of 1911 Against Reciprocity with the United States of America*, n.p., n.d. (cited subsequently as *Can. Nat. League*).

by Lash personally; he infers that the latter collected in turn from the Eighteen.

On Sifton's advice Hawkes launched another campaign during the summer which was to call down upon him many Liberal maledictions. This was the "Appeal to the British Born." Hawkes had estimated that British immigrants numbered about a quarter-million, half of whom had come in since the 1908 election. To appeal to this group he wrote in February a newspaper article based upon a statement of Sir John A. Macdonald, "A British subject I was born, a British subject I will die." This was reprinted as a pamphlet and its contents tried out on the platform without conspicuous success.[46] In July, Sifton advised Hawkes to start a campaign among the old-country men apart from the regular Conservative propaganda, which he did with vigor. It is improbable that the appeal turned the tide in any Province, but it created considerable annoyance, since Hawkes's work was widely copied in the Conservative press.

By early March a third antireciprocity organization, the Anti-Reciprocity League, was at work in Montreal. It carried on a petition campaign, and attempted, by enlisting Liberals, to acquire the color of a nonpartisan organization. Many of Sifton's speeches were made under its sponsorship.[47]

The press campaign gathered headway during February and March, a period which saw most of the important arguments of the Parliamentary discussion canvassed. It then settled down to reiteration, with an occasional new tack being discovered by the Conservatives, forcing Liberal journals to build new defenses. As in Parliament, Conservative opinion took the initiative. The journals of Quebec and Ontario furnished most of the ammunition, particularly the Montreal *Star* and the *News* of Toronto, while the Toronto *Star* was the stoutest fighter for the agreement, with the *Globe* active but somewhat less inclined to a shirt-sleeve campaign. Reciprocity tended to decline in news value during the Coronation season, but July saw the forces rallying for renewal of the Parliamentary battle and the likely appeal to the country.[48]

46. *An Appeal to the British-Born,* n.p., 1911.

47. Toronto *Star,* March 6; Toronto *Globe,* June 7, 1911; Dafoe, *Sifton,* p. 371.

48. The following observations are based on careful reading of four On-

Each side developed special devices to spread its gospel. Liberals, somewhat less affluent than their opponents, had at least three outlets: the frank, which was of course available to both sides; the rural postmasters, who were supplied with literature to be purveyed with the mails; and the census enumerators who were similarly equipped.[49] To offset these advantages the Opposition dug into its war chest to pay for dissemination of selected matter. A Montreal advertising firm was soon retained to buy space indiscriminately in papers of both parties for material originally appearing in the *Star*. Somewhat later a like arrangement placed a series of articles singing protection's praises, originating in the *Canadian Century*, in over four hundred rural weeklies. The firm's circular agreed to furnish weekly instalments, which it was hoped would find room on the editorial page. The letter went on: "If you do not agree with the views expressed you will, of course, be at liberty to criticize them in a fair and courteous way, and on the other hand, if they meet with your approval your editorial endorsation from time to time will be appreciated."[50]

The *Star* launched its formal attack February 4 with a full-page spread under the title: "An Appeal to Sir Wilfrid Laurier, The One Man Who Can Save Canada." This widely copied appeal called the tune for the early Conservative press campaign. It noted the danger to Canadian national unity inherent in a reciprocity which would break the transportation bridge north of Lake Superior by turning Western trade south to Chicago and the Twin Cities, destroying both railroads and Eastern industries. "Nothing but a high national spirit and a tariff which makes the American frontier a reality," it argued, "can keep trade flowing across the empty country from Manitoba to Ontario and from Ontario to Manitoba."

tario files, three from Quebec, and two each from Manitoba, British Columbia, Prince Edward Island, and Nova Scotia. The Ottawa Libraries had available but one file each (all proreciprocity) from Alberta, Saskatchewan, and New Brunswick. Except for some matters of local importance, it is not believed that these gaps seriously affect the validity of the conclusions offered. General tendencies of press opinion will be noted without definite footnote citations.

49. *Toronto Saturday Night*, June 3, 1911.

50. Edmonton *Bulletin*, February 17; St. John *Telegraph-Sun*, April 26; *Grain Growers' Guide*, March 15, May 3, 1911.

Again, the Imperial connection was greatly endangered, with annexation likely to result from closer commercial relations with the States. Thus the three arguments used most tellingly during the early days were put into the record—the danger to transportation interests, with consequent perils to Imperial connection and national integrity. Only one of these arguments, incidentally, was directly related to the economic merits and demerits of reciprocity. A companion plea characteristic of the early days was to let well enough alone, or to wait for the United States to act first.[51]

Liberal efforts were largely directed to meeting these attacks. On the positive side attempts were made to show that the agreement opened a larger market for Canadian farm produce, here as all through the discussion one of the most prominent Liberal arguments.[52] Other efforts were made to prove that both producer and consumer were benefited, an essay which was later to afford Conservatives much ground for caustic criticism.[53] In March, while annexation and Imperial connection continued to receive considerable attention, new matters were injected into the discussion. Most prominent of these was the determined effort to prove the agreement's dangers to the farm interest.[54] The *Star* here launched a series of widely quoted articles showing, with pictures and descriptions, the deserted farms of New England, and drawing the conclusion that if these farmers, so close to the reputedly hungry American market, could not meet the competition of the American West, the Canadians, with their greater distances, certainly could not hope to invade the market successfully. The Toronto *News* took up this appeal to the farmer with a vengeance in April, and the battle was on, with Liberals trying tardily to meet Conservative attacks by harping on the larger market. Two other Conservative arguments appeared. On March 11 the *Star* launched an oft-repeated effort to show that reciprocity would subject Canada to the hard times recurrent in the States. Two days later the *News* added that it would open Canadian gates to the activities of the American trusts.

51. Montreal *Gazette, Star,* February 7, 1911.
52. Toronto *Star,* February 27; St. John *Telegraph-Sun,* February 24, 1911.
53. Toronto *Star,* February 10, 27, 1911.
54. Montreal *Star,* March 14, 22, 25; Halifax *Herald,* March 10, 17, 1911.

April saw both sides recurring to annexation and the farm interest, and in May there was a new flurry of charge and countercharge on annexation and Imperial relationships, growing out of Taft's unfortunate utterance of April 27. These months also witnessed the appearance of Conservative emphasis on a series of scandals which were supposed to blacken the Liberal record and which received more and more attention during the election campaign.[55] Three of these were pressed at the moment. One concerned Frank Oliver, Minister of the Interior, who was accused of having certain mysterious bank deposits made to his credit shortly after issuance of an Order in Council (1907) allowing the Canadian Northern to select 600,000 acres of land in Saskatchewan. The Farmers' Bank case also received considerable attention. In this connection Fielding's department was charged, as early as February, 1911, with having allowed a bank in dangerous financial condition to remain in business, with the inference that the action was taken because the manager had contributed heavily to the Fielding Memorial. Finally, Adélard Lanctôt, Liberal Member of Parliament, was accused of using government labor and supplies on his private dwelling.

The foregoing discussion covers the principal general tendencies of press opinion. It should of course be noted that particular local interests received occasional attention, such as the paper manufacturers in Quebec, the millers in Ontario, miners and fishermen in Nova Scotia, and fruit and lumber producers in British Columbia. The slight emphasis upon matters of immediate economic concern, aside from the agricultural interest, is a rather remarkable feature of Canadian discussion. Perhaps, however, it is not so remarkable when one realizes that one of the principal aims of Conservative policy was to distract attention from the economic aspects of the agreement and direct it to those national, Imperial, and political phases which were more easily capitalized. That this was possible was largely due to the fact that the opposition press had assumed and retained the initiative in the discussion; the Liberal journals, left at the post, were forced to the heartbreaking task of coming from

55. Toronto *News,* May 4, 18, 26; Montreal *Gazette,* April 19, 27, 29, May 3, 5, 6; Edmonton *Bulletin,* May 2; *The Daily Colonist* (Victoria, B.C.), May 11, 1911; *Hansard,* III, 4645–4656; *Can. Ann. Rev.,* 1911, pp. 273–274.

behind to overtake a strong front runner. Finally, the emphasis on the farming interest, though less prominent than in the States, was of some importance. Above the border, as below, the tiller of the soil was an important lay figure. The opposition, led by capitalist groups anxious to avoid any breach in the protective system, was not loath to distract attention from itself by claiming damage to some interest other than its own; the defense, largely dependent on Western votes and anxious also to retain any possible remnants of capitalist support, was likewise willing to pay considerable attention to the farmer. Thus, North and South, the farmer had his day.

While the propagandists gathered momentum the Prime Minister was in London and the Opposition leader toured the Prairies; neither made for himself much capital for the forthcoming contest. The Premier's statements furnished his detractors with much ammunition; Borden faced the Grain Growers with fearless mien but his promises along other lines left them cold in the face of his determined antireciprocity stand. When Laurier took ship for England on May 12 he removed himself from one embarrassing position only to place himself in another upon arrival. By deciding to go he had absolved himself for the moment from the charges, levied by the Conservative press, of belittling the Empire and the Crown by absenting himself. By adjourning Parliament instead of allowing the discussion of reciprocity to continue in his absence, he permitted the same press to insinuate a quarrel between himself and Fielding, who was allegedly piqued because the Premier did not trust him to manage his own measure on the floor of the Commons.[56]

The other embarrassment concerned his policy at London—should he represent Canada as Imperialist or Autonomist? He was vulnerable either way: a too strongly Imperialist course would alienate friends of closer American trade ties and French-Canadians who cared little for reciprocity but much for nationalism; advocacy of autonomy would play into the hands of those who had for weeks been accusing him of trying to take Canada out of the Empire. Whatever his motives, he chose the path of autonomy and urged that Canada be permitted to shape her own commercial policy without British interference. This gave Conservative and Protestant ground

56. Victoria *Colonist*, May 5; Montreal *Gazette*, May 10, 11, 1911.

for charging that he was trying to wreck the Empire and that his London policy was guided by the principles of Monk, Bourassa, and Quebec separatism.[57]

The leader of the Opposition invaded the Prairies at a good time. Laurier was in England, Parliament out of session, and the farmers were at a slack season. His problem was a delicate one. His one long chance to wean the West from reciprocity was to make promises in other directions, but these must not be too sweeping, lest they reëcho in the East, where a surer support must not be alienated. Circumstances soon made it apparent that promises were not enough.[58] Making his first address at Winnipeg, June 19, he showed his wares, agreeing to sponsor government operation and ownership of the Hudson Bay Railroad, government operation of terminal elevators, surrender to the Prairie Provinces of public lands and resources then under control of the federal government, encouragement of the chilled-meat industry, and that hoary chestnut, tariff revision by a permanent, nonpartisan tariff commission which would keep the protective system within bounds.[59]

The next day's meeting at Brandon was probably the most important of the tour, for here the Grain Growers called a halt on the promising campaign, brought reciprocity out into the open and, nettling Mr. Borden, called forth the first of a series of straight-from-the-shoulder avowals which, if not influential in the West, served a useful purpose in the East. Met by the Grain Growers at the City Hall before the main address, Borden listened to a sharp lecture by several of their leaders. Stung by their tactics, he struck back full force: "All I have to say about that agreement is that I am absolutely opposed to it and that if you gentlemen in the West were prepared to make me Prime Minister of Canada tomorrow if I would support that agreement, I would not do it and I would not be fit to be Prime Minister of this country if I said anything else to you than that, having the convictions upon it that I have."[60] This

57. Toronto *News*, June 3, 8, 9, 10, 19; Montreal *Gazette*, May 13; Toronto *Saturday Night*, June 17; *Sentinel*, June 15, July 27, 1911.

58. Winnipeg *Free Press*, June 6; Toronto *Star*, May 8; *Sentinel*, May 18, 1911.

59. Winnipeg *Free Press*, June 20, 1911.

60. *Ibid.*, June 21; *Grain Growers' Guide*, June 28, 1911.

pronouncement left no doubt whatever as to his position; it gave him, and the Grain Growers as well, a text from which to preach at each other on subsequent meetings. From Brandon the tour worked its way through eighteen days and more than a hundred speeches, past the delivery of thirty-five bouquets for each of which a damsel levied toll of a kiss, and, almost unprecedentedly, only one banquet.[61]

Again and again the Grain Growers urged him to talk reciprocity, and again and again he discussed the Imperial connection which must be preserved against American encroachments.[62] Another thorn with which the farmers pricked him was his attitude toward increasing the tariff preference granted imports of British goods—another means to the West's goal of tariff reductions unlikely to be palatable to Borden's Eastern supporters. He several times side-stepped the issue but he left the distinct impression that no relief could be looked for in that quarter. On one occasion, pressed for a statement, he said: "I stand for reciprocity within the Empire and within the Empire I stand for Canada first."[63]

The tour cleared the air. It showed the West what could be expected from Mr. Borden, and what could not. What was probably more important, it also showed the East what to look for from him. It is unlikely that it gained him many Prairie votes, but it gained him considerable Prairie respect for his forthrightness and candor. The experience in trying out his arguments in an unfavorable atmosphere stood him in good stead for the future. His emphasis upon the national and Imperial aspects of reciprocity and his minimizing of its economic aspects were at once reflections of the past discussions and keynotes of those ahead.[64]

When Parliament reassembled July 18, the prevailing winds were blowing strong. Within ten minutes after the session opened Con-

61. Statistics vouched for by *Grain Growers' Guide*, July 26, 1911.

62. *Ibid.*, June 21, July 12; Victoria *Colonist*, July 6; Toronto *Globe*, June 21, 1911. "The real issue which now presents itself," he was once quoted as saying, "is British connection versus American dominance. Let us preserve our fiscal freedom and the control of our destinies."

63. Edmonton *Bulletin*, June 22, 29; Toronto *Globe*, June 30; Winnipeg *Free Press*, July 14, 1911.

64. Contemporary estimates of the expedition may be found in Toronto *News*, July 6; *The Victoria* (B.C.) *Daily Times*, July 7; Winnipeg *Free Press*, July 8; Toronto *Star*, July 10, 1911.

servative obstruction had begun. All the tricks of parliamentary opposition which years of practice had perfected were brought into
play. In response the Government resorted to morning sessions, but
the floods of oratory went unchecked and all the old arguments were
reiterated. In addition a good deal of attention was devoted to placing the Government in the wrong on the question of redistribution.
If the prospective election were held before the census returns were
in, the West stood to be deprived of twenty seats. Conservatives took
delight in condemning this base injustice, washing their own hands
righteously of all responsibility. The climax was reached with dramatic suddenness on the twenty-ninth, when the Government decided
upon an immediate dissolution, with an election on September 21.[65]

Thus the issue was joined, with the initiative having passed from
Government to Opposition. Since January 26, when Fielding
brought down his agreement, which he firmly believed beneficial to
the country (a belief shared at the time by many of his opponents),
a complex of circumstances had conspired to despoil his party of
many of the advantages of surprise, economic benefit, and entrenched power. A staggered Opposition, uncertain and disunited,
had received stiffening from powerful quarters; it had ironed out its
domestic difficulties, profiting, moreover, from American delay, and
had taken the Parliamentary offensive; and, in a country-wide campaign, it had built up sufficient momentum to enforce its demands
for a popular verdict. Laurier was to have the finish fight he had
desired in May. It was now to be waged, however, on ground chosen
by his adversaries.

65. *Hansard,* V, 9646–10590; Toronto *Globe,* July 19–31, 1911.

CHAPTER XI

CONSERVATIVE STRATEGY WINS

"Not since 1896 has there been such confusion of opinion, such disturbance of party relationship, and such uncertainty concerning the ultimate result of an election." So wrote the Toronto correspondent of *The Times*, August 23, just as the Canadian campaign was gathering headway.[1] To such a pass had the Dominion come since the January day when Fielding faced the Commons and drew gasps of astonishment from friend and foe alike at the scope of his agreement. The events chronicled in the preceding chapters have accounted in part for the situation. Reciprocity had blown breath into antipathies whose fires had been banked or smoldering, had aroused sectional and racial feelings, had called in question national and Imperial relationships, had encouraged or alarmed vastly powerful economic interests, and had set in train momentous political consequences.

From the day when Mr. Monk, to prevent quick acceptance of the American offer, had proposed a plebiscite on the agreement, only to be voted down, Opposition strategy had developed slowly but steadily from Parliamentary argument and out-of-doors propaganda back to Parliamentary obstruction carried just far enough to prevent a Liberal appeal to the people when such an appeal could still have succeeded. The Conservative party, reinforced by the defection of individual Liberals and, more important, by the adherence of notable economic interests which had supported the Liberals in 1908 but were frightened by Liberal policy in 1911, gathered momentum during the early summer until it could force the Government to a trial of strength knowing that its own war chest would be full and its leadership powerful. During these developments a figure had been emerging—that of Mr. Borden. Still by no means the leader who was to take Canada through a World War and who later was to assume the mantle of her Elder Statesman, recent events had given him strength and confidence. The handling of the intraparty crisis of March, the adherence of the powerful Sifton to the ranks of party counselors, the stout if unsuccessful invasion of the Prairies had all

1. *The Times* (London), September 2, 1911.

contributed to this end; the campaign to come was to disclose marked advances in forensic skill and crowd appeal.

While Conservative party and leader were adding strength to strength the Liberals were being forced into a more and more dubious position. At first confident that Parliament would accept reciprocity at command, discussion had been tolerantly permitted to proceed pending action by the United States. American action delayed, discussion passed to well-calculated obstruction which finally forced Liberal strategists to a choice between a continued fight on reciprocity and an adjournment to permit the Premier to attend to his Imperial obligations; that choice, and its consequences, have been detailed. The result was that when obstruction finally brought dissolution in July the Liberals found themselves minus powerful figures and important interests previously on their side. They still had, however, Sir Wilfrid Laurier, whose leadership had carried them through many another campaign, and they had reciprocity, which they hoped would help him, and them, through this one.

Reciprocity itself, as has been seen, had been the focal point of many interests and the cause of many disturbances. The election witnessed the playing of its last role, for which preceding events had been rehearsals. On the Liberal side it was to be pushed toward the footlights as the principal character of the drama; Conservatives were to try to hiss it off the stage by stirring up national and Imperial issues allegedly more important; and their left-handed allies, the French Nationalists, were to give it an approving if somewhat preoccupied hand and ease it out in favor of their mass attack upon Laurier's ultra-imperialism as expressed in his naval policy. In the shuffle reciprocity was crowded more and more backstage despite valiant Liberal efforts, and on September 21 elbowed decisively into the wings.

Manifestoes by the two leaders sought to fix reciprocity's status.[2] Laurier reviewed historically the bipartisan support accorded the policy, charged Conservatives with obstructing a vote in Parliament,

2. Toronto *Globe*, July 31, August 1, 15, 1911. Laurier's was dated July 29. Borden issued a preliminary statement at the time of dissolution and on August 14, after consultation with Montreal and Toronto leaders, an "Address to the People of Canada." The itineraries of Laurier, Borden, and others, with excerpts from speeches, are covered in *Can. Ann. Rev.*, 1911, pp. 158–203.

and handed the issue to the people, dismissing as beneath contempt alleged dangers to national and Imperial integrity, and nailing to the mast the British preference. It was plainly his intent to make the issue, as Taft had done, "the bill, the whole bill, and nothing but the bill." Borden's preliminary statement called a different tune. It emphasized Taft's "parting-of-the-ways" pronouncement, chided the Government for adjourning while charges were still pending against one of its members, and took exception to Laurier's policy at the Imperial Conference. His considered pronouncement of August 14 elaborated on the old themes of threatened national integrity, Imperial solidarity, commercial independence, and fiscal freedom, and passed thence to specific economic disadvantages, concluding that "it is at the best a rash and perilous experiment, inconsiderately and unwarrantably undertaken in a period of unequalled development and prosperity, after Canada had long since outgrown the conditions under which such a policy was once thought desirable."

Passing from reciprocity itself to attack the Prime Minister's manifesto in detail, he put into the record a number of prospective issues centering around uninvestigated charges of governmental corruption and inefficiency. He charged that the naval policy was expensive and ineffective and would in time of war probably result "in the useless sacrifice of many valuable lives." For himself and his party, if elected, he promised closer supervision of expenditures, the fulfilment of Western demands, except reciprocity, highway subsidies, civil-service reform, agricultural education, and rural mail delivery. Essentially it was a plea to the agricultural elements to take something else, and to all elements to behold the evils of Laurierism and to hold fast to endangered Canadian nationality and Imperial integrity by giving the conduct of government to their true defenders. "In the past," he concluded, "we have made great sacrifices to further our national ideals. We are now face to face with a misguided attempt to throw away the result of these sacrifices. The true issue is this: Shall we continue in the course which has led us to our present enviable position of great prosperity and national development, or shall we, at the moment of greatest success and achievement, lose heart and abandon the fight for national existence?" Thus it was early made evident that reciprocity must share the stage with other and alien issues.

Party strategy called for the leaders to use the eastern Provinces as sounding boards for their oratory, leaving the local campaigns in the hands of lieutenants. After two weeks devoted by the party press to placing opponents in the wrong, Laurier and Borden swung into action in Ontario on August 15, the former at Simcoe and the latter at London. Thence the Premier toured his native Province from August 17 to 27, spent the days from the twenty-eighth through September 2 in the Maritimes, carried the gospel to the Ontario heathen from the third through the ninth, and swung back to Quebec from the eleventh to the conclusion of his campaign on the twentieth.[3] For the first few days he valiantly insisted that reciprocity was the sole issue, but shortly gave over this contention and addressed himself to other matters. Particularly he tried to lay the annexation bogey once and for all. This, together with prolonged scoffing at the "Unholy Alliance" between Borden and Bourassa, formed the burden of his plea, though he did make a fairly consistent effort to keep some of the economic phases of reciprocity to the fore. Toward the end of the campaign he addressed himself pointedly to assertions that the manufacturers had been treated kindly in the negotiation and that the farmers had been vastly aided by the agreement. The trend of discussion makes it obvious that despite his stout front he was forced into a program of justifying himself against attack, and of discussing matters only remotely connected with the immediate issue. In each Province he was accompanied by a Minister—in Ontario by George P. Graham, in Nova Scotia by Fielding, and in Quebec at various times by Rodolphe Lemieux and H. S. Beland.

As far as can be gathered from study of his speeches and of the sympathetic press, he was alert, vigorous, and optimistic as to the final outcome to the very end, coining new epigrams and refurbishing old ones to further service. An occasional reference to his gray hairs and his desire to retire if defeated were magnified in the hostile press into confessions of weariness and defeatism; they were more likely pleas to his followers to give him one more term in power before accepting well-earned repose. Privately he had begun to have his doubts as early as three weeks before election, when his usual

3. The following summary of the Laurier campaign is based upon a careful reading of his speeches as reported in the Toronto *Globe* and the account in the *Can. Ann. Rev.*, 1911, pp. 161–169.

barometer, commercial travelers' reports, brought rumblings of defections in the East.[4]

Following the London meeting Borden continued his tour of Ontario through August 28, devoting over a third of his speaking en-
gagements to this area which it was superlatively necessary for him
to capture if he were to win, and to which he was largely directing
his campaign. He spent four speaking days in Quebec, then turned
back home to spend from September 2 till the election was over
in the Maritimes.[5] At London he urged Canada to let well enough
alone, asserted that the farmer was victimized, quoted, as in most of
his subsequent addresses, Taft's unfortunate parting-of-the-ways
remark, opened Canada's gates to the favored nations, commented
unfavorably upon the uncertain duration of the agreement, and appealed to Canadians to tighten the Imperial tie rather than loosen it
at Taft's behest. Like Laurier, he paid considerable attention to the
economic aspects of reciprocity, but these remarks were generally
connected with the national aspects and an effort was made to show
that the economic consequences of the pact would endanger Canadian commercial, fiscal, or political independence. Taft became Borden's lay figure, to be stood up and knocked down for the edification
of Canadian audiences. As a variant, the dangers to Imperial connection appeared in many guises. Some attention was paid to the
Liberal record; names were named and chapter and verse cited to
make clear the story of extravagance and corruption. Occasionally
time was taken to make the promises necessary to the out-of-office
campaigner. From Halifax he directed his final "Message to the
People of Canada" just before the election. In this he reiterated his
fears for the national and Imperial destinies of the Dominion should
the agreement be consummated, entreating Canadians "not to swerve
from the straight path that leads to the making of a great nation; I
beg them to cast a soberly considered and serious vote for the pres-
ervation of our heritage, for the maintenance of our commercial and
political freedom, for the permanence of Canada as an autonomous
nation within the British Empire."[6] Thus the campaign closed as it

4. As reported by Arthur Hawkes from a conversation with Laurier. Winnipeg *Free Press*, September 21, 1929.

5. *Can. Ann. Rev.*, 1911, pp. 169–179, describes and analyzes the tour.

6. *Ibid.*, p. 179.

had opened, on a note of national and Imperial defiance of American encroachment.

Aside from the two leaders, perhaps the most important personal influence was that of Clifford Sifton.[7] Some mention has already been made of his work as counselor of the Conservative forces. In addition to this quiet effort he attacked the agreement in a letter to his former constituents—he declined to stand again—three days before the dissolution which he had predicted since early July. Beginning August 23 he spoke in Ontario, New Brunswick, Nova Scotia, and again in Ontario, addressing himself to the economic and fiscal aspects of the problem in a series of trenchant criticisms. Since many of his speeches were made in industrial centers, they undoubtedly carried great weight.

Two racial factors deserve mention. The launching of the Arthur Hawkes "Appeal to the British Born" has already been noted. This was directed largely to Ontario, where Hawkes thought it might turn enough votes to swing the election. No sooner had the campaign begun to move than the Toronto *Globe* printed what purported to be a facsimile letter sent to editors of Ontario Conservative journals by Frank Cochrane, Minister of Lands, Forests, and Mines of the Province, announcing Hawkes's plan of campaign and offering his journalistic services to the party press. These consisted of ten long and twenty-six short articles, the last under the pseudonym "John V. Borne." In addition Hawkes proposed to make at least one address a day until election and to write, as a by-product of his pilgrimage, a series of articles, "Through Ontario with the British-Born."[8] Though it is improbable that Hawkes's work was more than an irritant, it is interesting as a sample of Conservative tactics.

The Nationalist campaign in Quebec was much more formidable —so formidable as to cause Laurier to spend over half of his campaigning time in that Province and, whatever its ultimate influence, sufficiently important to alarm a large segment of the Liberal press, particularly the Toronto *Globe*, to the point of hysteria. Enough has been said to indicate that the principal platform of the Quebec Nationalists was bitter hostility to the Laurier navy. Led by Henri Bourassa and his ably staffed and fiery journal of opinion, *Le Devoir*,

7. *Ibid.,* pp. 196–199.   8. August 19, 1911.

the group had frequently attacked the Premier on this issue. When reciprocity was broached, therefore, the Nationalist stand was a matter of moment to both sides. *Le Devoir* first struck a note of mild approval, on the ground that it aided the farmer without hurting Canadian industries, and, as an obstacle to the commercial federation of the British Empire, also hindered its political federation.[9] Some fun was poked at Conservative scaremongering and the matter was accorded an imprimatur, subject to conviction of change by developments in the Parliamentary debate. When the American Congress failed to act in March, Bourassa announced himself still favorable to American reciprocity as against Imperial reciprocity, but believed that the agreement ought to be renegotiated, in view of the changed complexion of Congress.[10]

With the looming of a Dominion election the Nationalist position became more complicated. Quebec Conservatives, led by F. D. Monk, opposed Laurier and his reciprocity. Quebec Nationalism opposed Laurier and his navy, but not his reciprocity. Thus instead of a united opposition there emerged the possibility of several three-cornered provincial contests, which might well allow the Laurier candidates to win. Since this would profit neither anti-Laurier group, the result was a Bourassa-Monk alliance.[11] Some months later Bourassa explained the grounds of this *rapprochement* in a series of articles in *Le Devoir*, asserting that at an unspecified date during the Parliamentary session two Conservative leaders approached him and, suggesting that two sets of candidates might prove mutually embarrassing, intimated that Conservative and Nationalist positions on the navy were not poles apart. Bourassa, by his own account, averred that the only common ground between himself and Monk's followers was their mutual insistence upon a plebiscite prior to action upon the navy. Borden, he said, had been edging toward this position. The arrangement seems to have been that, on the tacit understanding that a plebiscite on the navy would follow a Borden victory,

9. A series of articles from the paper, covering dates January 31–February 7, 1911, were collected and edited by Bourassa under the title *The Reciprocity Agreement and Its Consequences as Viewed from the Nationalist Standpoint* (pamphlet), Montreal, 1911.

10. *Le Devoir* (Montreal), March 6, 1911.

11. Toronto *Globe*, June 23, July 8, 1911.

the Nationalists agreed not to put forward candidates, but to back any who would stand on a platform of no participation in Imperial wars outside of Canada without a referendum. The result was that in most of the French-speaking ridings the Conservative candidates were acceptable to the Nationalists.[12]

This Monk-Bourassa working arrangement soon gave the Liberals an excuse to assert that there was a third party involved—no less than Borden himself—and rumors arose of a Borden-Bourassa alliance appealing to racial antipathies to make political capital. The fact that Borden never formally repudiated Bourassa, and that his manifesto of August 14 contained language which might be interpreted to condone the Nationalist position, gave color to the rumors. The true inwardness of the Borden-Bourassa relationship is not essential to the purpose of the present study; suffice it to say here that there was sufficient appearance of coöperation to furnish the Liberal press, particularly the *Globe*, with much headline material.

Bourassa's manifesto of August 2 set forth the official Nationalist position and condemned both party leaders for dodging the main issue of the day. Laurier, he charged, tried to make reciprocity paramount, neglecting important economic and political matters; Borden was not much better. Neither took a clear stand on the fundamental problem of Imperial relationships as manifested in the naval matter. Reciprocity, he asserted, could be looked at either way— there was much to be said on both sides. What, under the circumstances, was the Nationalist cue? It was to put up candidates of independence, Liberal, Nationalist, Conservative, who would rally round Monk in Parliament and assert the principles of autonomy in the face of whatever government was returned to power.[13] Throughout August and September his paper attacked Laurier bitterly, emphasizing the scandals of his administration, mentioning reciprocity occasionally and less and less favorably, referring to Borden but seldom, and harping on the navy in season and out of season. As a counterirritant, other papers were accused of appealing to race prejudice, particularly the *Globe* and *La Presse*, Laurier's French

12. Bourassa, H., *The Story of the Nationalist-Conservative Alliance Told by Henri Bourassa, the Nationalist Leader* (pamphlet), Ottawa, 1914, pp. 2–6.

13. *Le Devoir*, August 2, 1911.

organ.[14] Bourassa himself spent much time on the stump, holding
notable meetings at Ste. Hyacinthe, at Hull, and at Sudbury, at
each of which he thumped Laurier and his navy most soundly.

This course of action encouraged the *Globe* to appeal to race
prejudice on its own account, and accusations were made that the
Bourassa campaign was encouraged by Ontario Conservatives.[15] It
was further charged that a double game was being played, with Borden in Ontario making loud protestations of loyalty to the Empire
while his Quebec allies were "doing their treasonable utmost to in-
flame the minds of the French-Canadians against that very Imperial
idea which Mr. Borden extols."[16] The matter was given more and
more space until by mid-September the "Unholy Alliance" over-
shadowed everything else in the news columns. Laurier himself on
several occasions noticed and attacked the unnatural union.[17] Thus
what was, in Stephen Leacock's words, probably nothing more than
hunting in couples was magnified into a powerful propaganda factor
and forced Laurier to spend much valuable time on an issue far removed from the reciprocity question.

Turning to the press, the reader is bewildered by the welter of old
arguments reiterated to the point of utter monotony, and struck by
the poverty of new approaches to the problem, which now became
definitely a political one. In fact, after studying the press campaign
one is tempted to agree with the editorial writer of the Toronto
Sentinel, who greeted his readers on election day with the following
diagnosis of the situation:

A careful reading of the party papers leads to the conclusion that
Mr. Borden will be returned to power with a majority of thirty for Sir
Wilfrid Laurier and the Nationalists holding the balance of power.
This, of course, involves the defeat of the reciprocity pact, which will be
put into effect as soon as Parliament meets, the United States already
having adopted it.

This paradoxical situation will make Canada an ideal place to live,
as the producer will get higher prices than before, while the consumer

14. *Ibid.*, August 14–September 20, *passim*.
15. Toronto *Globe*, August 15, 1911.   16. *Ibid.*, August 19, 1911.
17. *Ibid.*, September, *passim*. Examples of Laurier's pronouncements are
found in his remarks at New Glasgow, N.S., August 31, and at Quebec, September 14, 1911. *Ibid.*, September 1, 15, 1911.

will get his goods for less money. Seeing that almost everybody in Canada is a producer of something, and seeing, too, that they are all consumers, it follows that everything a man has to sell will be higher and everything he has to buy will be cheaper.

The national song will be, "Yankee Doodle's Maple Leaf," to be sung as a solo by your Uncle Samuel and Britannia, who rules the waves.[18]

If arguments were ancient and phrases familiar, variety was given by all the typographical pyrotechnics available to the trade. Red ink, streamer headlines, important messages from important personages, cartoons, pictures of the Union Jack, of leading Conservatives who supported reciprocity, and of those who did not, were sprinkled liberally over front pages until ordinary news had to be content with a minor place—all rising to a shrill crescendo of epithet and counterblast which made the last days a bedlam which all but drowned out Liberal efforts to keep the economic phases of reciprocity to the fore.[19]

The press campaign gathered headway during the first half of August while the parties laid their plans. Liberal newspapers followed the lead in Laurier's manifesto and at first tried to insist that reciprocity was the sole issue at stake.[20] Conservative strategy soon spiked this contention, however, and the battle was on in earnest. Speaking generally, the Liberal side tried valiantly to emphasize the economic side of the agreement and to confine discussion to the merits of the case. Again the plan was unsuccessful, and as before a great deal of time had to be spent refuting the more dangerous Conservative thrusts, particularly those directed toward national and Imperial safety. Some factors of which the Conservative press made much were seemingly deliberately ignored or played down by the Liberal sheets. Among these were the annexation bogey, the navy question (outside of Quebec and Ontario), the uncertain duration of the agreement and the status of the British preference under reci-

18. September 21, 1911.

19. The following survey of press opinion covers from August 1 through the election, and is based upon the same files used in the previous chapter. Footnote references will sample editorial opinion on the more important points.

20. Halifax *Chronicle*, August 1; Regina *Leader*, August 10; Montreal *Witness*, August 2, 1911.

procity. On the other hand, certain factors received much space. The net result was that the press campaign tended to become one of mere assertion and counterassertion rather than a discussion of the actual issues.

Two points received the greatest Liberal emphasis in the early stages of the campaign and continued to the fore during the last hectic days. These were the appeal of the larger market to the producing class, couched in widely variant language aimed at differing local interests, and condemnation of the alleged alliance between Borden and Bourassa. Two markets instead of one were held out to the farmer, from Prince Edward Island to the Rockies, and he was encouraged to think that better prices for his products would prevail with the increased business. Prince Edward Island potatoes, Ontario livestock, Saskatchewan barley, and Manitoba wheat would all benefit by freer exchange with the United States, and the result would be prosperity for the Dominion's predominant producing group.[21] An unfortunate effort was made to link this benefit to the producer with a corresponding benefit to the consumer in lowered living costs. Reciprocity's lowering of the tariff wall, it was argued, would lengthen the season for many agricultural products by allowing the earlier-maturing United States crops to supply the Canadian table. Thus the producer would get higher prices for his crops and the consumer pay less for his foodstuffs.[22] When this last aspect of consumer benefit received more attention late in the campaign Opposition papers gleefully called attention to the apparent inconsistency between higher prices for producers and lower costs for consumers.[23]

The dire consequences of the "Unholy Alliance" between Borden and the Bourassa Nationalists were widely heralded. This union, it was alleged, would result in the surrender of Borden's control over the party, the dictatorship of Bourassa, and the passing of affairs into the hands of French-Canadian separatists. Since this argument afforded Liberals one of their best chances to put their opponents in

21. Charlottetown *Patriot,* August 3, 5; Toronto *Star,* August 3; Regina *Leader,* August 17; Winnipeg *Free Press,* August 30, 1911.

22. Toronto *Star,* August 11, 17, 1911.

23. Montreal *Gazette,* September 14; Toronto *News,* September 9, 1911.

the wrong, much was made of it, and the racial antagonisms involved were not lost sight of. The Toronto *Globe*, in an unusually bitter outburst, asked on July 31:

Who are the Nationalists whose alliance is so keenly desired by the former Grand Sovereign of the Orange Order? What are their ideals? They are the most anti-British, the most frankly ultramontane propagandists that French Canada has ever seen. There is no concealment about their methods. They hate Sir Wilfrid Laurier and seek to destroy him for exactly the opposite reason put forward by their allies in Ontario. In this province Laurier is to be destroyed because he is not British enough, because he does not safeguard Protestant rights. The Nationalists wish to destroy him because they assert that he has betrayed his race and his religion at the behest of the Orangemen of Ontario.

Much space was given in this and other papers to Bourassa's campaign against the navy, to his decrying of Laurier's ultraimperialism, and to the danger to the Dominion should Borden secure office dependent upon a Quebec delegation composed of anti-British Nationalists. British-born in the Maritimes and on the Prairies were volubly urged to note the inconsistency with which Borden, stalwart defender of the British connection, compromised his principles by accepting such support. The fact that he chose to remain silent under these thrusts was perhaps the part of wisdom in the circumstances, but his attitude furnished his opponents with still further opportunities to belabor him for his failure to repudiate his disreputable allies.[24]

Toward the end of the campaign, when it became evident that the appeal to the farmer would not turn the tide, efforts were made to reassure industry and win the worker to favor reciprocity. Fielding's broadside took the lead in assuring industry that it would not be harmed.[25] Still later the worker, both as laborer and as consumer,

24. The following set forth the principal points of view: Toronto *Globe*, August 9, 15, 19; September 1, 11; Charlottetown *Patriot*, September 13, 14; Halifax *Chronicle*, September 8; Winnipeg *Free Press*, August 24, 28; Edmonton *Bulletin*, August 17, September 8; Regina *Leader*, August 22, September 1, 1911.

25. Halifax *Chronicle*, August 22; Charlottetown *Patriot*, August 31; Edmonton *Bulletin*, August 16, 1911.

was told that his job was safe, his wages would be higher, and his food was sure to be cheaper under the agreement. Thus the high-cost-of-living argument, which had been much used below the border, was borrowed in Canada in a last-minute effort to gain new recruits.[26] Liberals doubtless intended this approach not as a substitute for the farmer appeal but as a parallel argument to win other groups; Conservatives, however, saw in it a desertion of the much-courted farmer and attacked such a dastardly abandonment.

One last Liberal plea was seized on by the enemy as a counsel of despair. This was the argument, which found space in many Liberal papers, to give the agreement a trial until it had a chance to prove itself in operation. Such a stand was, indeed, a far cry from the confidence with which reciprocity had been supported at first, and furnished further grounds for merriment on the part of the Conservative headline writers.[27]

The usual campaign promises indulged in by the Liberals offered the usual opportunity for the Opposition to poke fun, despite its resort to identical tactics. Prince Edward Island and New Brunswick seem to have been the principal object of Liberal affection in this regard, with some attention being paid the Prairie Provinces and British Columbia. In New Brunswick one section of the electorate was given to believe that Government success would mean the acquisition of branch railway lines feeding the Intercolonial, as a preliminary to putting the whole system on a paying basis. At St. John the subject of an improved harbor terminal was broached and the site for a new post office chosen. By August 11 tenders were completed and contracts let for the building of the first section of the Hudson Bay Railroad, thus stealing some small share of Borden's thunder in the Prairie Provinces. Hedged about by numerous precautions, promises were made to turn over to these Provinces control of their natural resources in lieu of existing cash grants. William Templeman, Minister of Mines, advocated making Victoria, British Columbia, a national port by the expenditure of some millions of

26. Halifax *Chronicle,* September 8; St. John *Telegraph-Sun,* August 28; Charlottetown *Patriot,* September 7; Regina *Leader,* September 18; Victoria *Times,* September 7, 1911.

27. Regina *Leader,* September 20; Winnipeg *Free Press,* September 13, 1911.

dollars on breakwaters. Borden himself promised the Prince Edward Islanders to have surveys made in the matter of a tunnel connecting the island with the mainland, long a cherished local dream.[28]

Thus high Liberal hopes of keeping the contest on the elevated plane of tariff discussion had been swept aside by the weight of Opposition argument directed to national, Imperial, and emotional factors. Still trying valiantly to keep to the main issue, Liberal press opinion had had to veer more and more into channels dug by its opponents, and had in turn adopted some of their racial and emotional appeals, the while more solid economic arguments were reiterated with less and less effect. To this deluge of Conservative argument we now turn.

The Conservative press tended as before to obscure the reciprocity issue with a multitude of extraneous factors, many of them imported from south of the border especially for the occasion. Many stock arguments reappeared, sometimes with refinements; among these were the loyalty-to-Empire plea and Liberal scandals; others were perhaps less emphasized. One long-familiar story was that of annexation, a hardy bogey begot by Conservative suspicion and nurtured by Champ Clark's and Taft's indiscretions.[29] The producer was the other chief object of solicitude. The farmer, the fisherman, the raiser of cattle and hogs were told over and over, with variations and statistics too numerous to detail, how disastrous the agreement would be to their respective interests.

A third imminent danger, according to the Montreal *Star* and its satellites, was that American hard times, along with other things, would be put on the free list by reciprocity. A correspondent toured several leading industrial cities, sending from each doleful reports of depression conditions, of factories closing or going on part time, of men being laid off. In Pittsburgh, still feeling the panic of 1907, the United States Steel Company was operating at about 50 per cent capacity. Places as widely separated as Lowell, Massachusetts, Detroit, and Chicago were found in dire straits. A Boston financial

28. Toronto *Saturday Night*, August 26; St. John *Telegraph-Sun*, August 14, 23, September 1, 7, 18; Toronto *Globe*, August 1, 11; Edmonton *Bulletin*, August 1, 11; Victoria *Times*, September 19; Charlottetown *Patriot*, September 8, 1911.

29. Since no new light was shed on this matter it will not be noted in detail; it was one of the two points most consistently pushed.

sheet was quoted as placing the number of unemployed in the States at 2,500,000. The tariff wall was represented as the dike which kept this wave of disaster from overwhelming the Dominion.[30] Other journals took up the burden and the tale was spread far and wide.[31] As the campaign got fairly under way insinuations began to appear that American money was coming in to influence the election. At first this was expressed as a discreet fear or rumor; later chapter and verse were cited, and definite amounts were named in the record.[32]

Two developments marked the late stages: the first a counter to the Liberal drive to enlist the worker and the consumer under the reciprocity banner, the second an attack on the alleged efforts of William Randolph Hearst to influence the election. Workers were in danger of losing their employment, branches of American factories would no longer be established, and the cost of the laboring man's living would not be reduced, were the arguments used. On September 18 the Montreal *Star* devoted nearly a full page to showing the worker that his job was precarious unless he obeyed the adjuration to "vote against Reciprocity, keep the price of Labor up and the 'cost of living' down." Liberals accused Conservative employers of intimidating their workers into voting against the agreement on pain of dismissal because of the curtailment of available work.[33]

Numerous accusations were afloat to the effect that Hearst was trying to influence the Canadian situation as he had done the American. These came to a sensational head in a "revelation" linking him with Taft as coplotters to deliver Canada to the United States—announced simultaneously in widely separated parts of the Dominion on September 18, too late for successful contradiction before the election, but early enough for wide reprinting. The story as presented in the Toronto *News* on the basis of a "pre-print" from the Ottawa *Evening Journal* was to the effect that an unnamed "promi-

30. Montreal *Star*, August 3, 8, 9, September 8, 1911. The above is merely a sample of the argument; the files are filled with similar examples.

31. The Toronto *News* and Halifax *Herald* followed this lead extensively.

32. Montreal *Gazette*, August 24; Montreal *Star*, August 24; Victoria *Colonist*, August 24; Halifax *Herald*, September 16, 1911.

33. Montreal *Star*, September 7, 18; Halifax *Herald*, September 2; Toronto *News*, September 11; Toronto *Star*, September 5; Winnipeg *Free Press*, August 24; Toronto *Globe*, September 11, 1911.

nent citizen" of Montreal had become intimate with William Hoster, long a Hearst correspondent at Washington, who told of being sent to Canada by his employer at Taft's instigation and against his own wishes. This alleged effort of the American Chief Executive to meddle in Canadian affairs with such an obnoxious confederate brought the nationalist indignation of the Ottawa paper to the boiling point.[34]

Before turning to a few features of some interest but of minor importance, some observations in a summary of the press campaign present themselves. The Conservative press, somewhat the more fertile in argument, kept a jump ahead of the Liberal journals and

34. Montreal *Star,* September 7, 9, 18; Toronto *News,* September 18; Victoria *Colonist,* September 2; Halifax *Herald,* September 19, 1911. As quoted in the Toronto *News* the blast was as follows:

"Here in boldest outline is the story of a plot against Canadian independence which for consummate impudence has no parallel in history. Hearst has been freely denounced and righteously execrated of late for his unblishing campaign for annexation, towards which goal reciprocity is a long step. But we now see [him] and Taft as the prime mover the crafty originator of the agitation.

"What do Canadians think of this foreign interference in our elections? Are we a pack of ignoramuses that we need the guidance of a despicable brigand like Hearst or the council of a scheming politician like Taft, who under cover of the smile of friendship, snatched our birthright from us? What business have the rapacious trusts of the United States or their confederate Taft to meddle with our elections?

"With impious hand Taft would snatch away the right of the suffrage. By debauching the electorate with his tons of imported sheets flaring forth the praises of Laurier and his commercial pact with Washington, by dispatching highly paid propagandists to Canada, by publicly bestowing his blessing on Hearst for his annexation creeds, and most of all, by himself instituting and abetting this shameless agitation, President Taft stands before the world convicted of the grossest intermeddling in the intimate concerns of a friendly nation.

"Was it for this that the illustrous heroes of our British history fought their age-long battles, and freely gave their lives? Was the soil of England empurpled by a hundred wars to vouchsafe to succeeding generations the right of the subject to the untrammelled ballot, only to have this priceless heritage torn from our grasp by the greedy magnates and the designing demagogues of the United States?"

It is only fair to say that the printer's errors in the above were probably due to the pressure of some early or special edition.

forced them to be continually on the defensive. This burden of answering attacks, many of them wide of the mark, handicapped the Liberal papers in their faithful efforts to keep reciprocity to the fore, and the very nature of the attacks perhaps prompted the Liberals to reply in kind. Both sides courted the producer, as had been done on the other side of the border. Both saw toward the close of the campaign that the consumer also had a vote—a point which had been capitalized much earlier in the American campaign—and sought to secure it. Both made much of matters not strictly connected with reciprocity at all—the Conservatives in Mr. Hearst and the American depression, the Liberals in the Borden-Bourassa combine. Both tried to ignore or soft-pedal matters which were considered dangerous—Liberals in annexation and the preference; Conservatives in the Nationalist alliance in Quebec, which was given very little attention in other Provinces. Finally, it must be noted that this survey, in its effort to portray trends rather than incidents, has failed to picture adequately either the intensity or the picturesqueness of the battle—a story which is well worth the telling in more detail than is possible here.

To the student of political mores the election offers many interesting examples of campaign technique in addition to some which have already appeared in the narrative. Each side was devoted to the practice of publicizing the pictures and opinions of adherents of the opposite political faith whom the virtues or vices of reciprocity had compelled to desert the political allegiances of a lifetime. These renegades for principle found themselves and their opinions spread liberally upon the front pages until it would appear as if the whole political fabric were about to disintegrate. From the length of the lists, however, it would appear that defections from one side about balanced those from the other.[35] All sorts of underhanded dodges were credited to the Conservatives, of which the following samples are illustrative. According to the Victoria *Times*, as reported in the Toronto *Globe*, a western railway passenger agent was queried as to rates for sending large numbers of people into Canada ten days or

35. Examples in Halifax *Herald,* September 4; Toronto *News,* September 6; Montreal *Gazette,* August 25 ff.; Halifax *Chronicle,* August 24, 25; Regina *Leader,* August 16, September 7, 1911.

so before the election. It was planned, according to the report, to have these men, poorly dressed, go to the industrial centers and paint dark pictures of conditions in the United States. In one Ontario riding it was reported that the Conservatives were circulating a printed report that the agreement was terminable only after twenty-one years. The country districts in Quebec were reported to have been canvassed by Conservative agents in military uniform who asked the number of young men in each household, saying that they were wanted as Laurier's contribution to Imperial demands. The canners were reported as urging wholesalers to lay in large supplies of beans and peas, since the effectuation of the agreement would raise prices of these vegetables fifty cents per bushel. The women were appealed to on the ground that reciprocity would reduce the price of eggs by three cents per dozen, which would deprive women in the farm homes of "former comforts and bright adornments."[36] Further indications that the Conservatives were willing to pay for press propaganda might be mentioned. Bourassa asserted that *Le Devoir* received from a prominent Conservative paid-up subscriptions for "thousands and thousands of electors" based upon the voters' lists of the eastern Quebec ridings. The Montreal *Star* prepared and offered, at Borden's expense, according to a letter signed by the editor and widely reprinted in the Liberal press, a supplement to be circulated with regular issues of Conservative papers. It contained on one page a patriotic article entitled "Under Which Flag?"; on another evidence to show that the farmer was being fooled and the industrial worker menaced in wages and employment; on a third extracts from American papers and speeches showing that reciprocity meant annexation; and on the last a paean to Canada's great future, if worked out by Canadians.[37]

Both sides resorted to the theatrical in their speaking tours. Laurier was reported before starting as preparing the properties for his appearances. These included a car which preceded him to each town

36. Toronto *Globe*, August 22, September 14; Winnipeg *Free Press*, August 18; Preston, *My Generation*, p. 348; *Egg Money, the Rightful Perquisite of the Women on the Canadian Farms* (pamphlet), n.p., n.d.

37. Bourassa, *Story of the Nationalist-Conservative Alliance*, pp. 6–7; Toronto *Globe*, September 13, 1911.

to decorate and bemotto in advance—with one set of mottoes for Quebec and another for Ontario. Among the decorations the Union Jack was prominently displayed. Borden improved upon this, however. It was reported that at one of his meetings "nearly all the stalwarts in the theatre were supplied with small flags, which they cheerfully waved when the cue came from the platform."[38] The literary genius of Rudyard Kipling was enlisted in the Conservative cause. Replying to the Montreal *Star's* request for his opinion, he announced:

It is her own soul that Canada risks today. Once that soul is pawned for any consideration Canada must inevitably conform to the commercial, legal, financial, social and ethical standards which will be imposed upon her by the sheer admitted weight of the United States.

Why, when Canada has made herself what she is, should she throw the enormous gifts of her inheritance and her future into the hands of a people who, by their haste and waste, have so dissipated their own resources that even before national middle age they are driven to seek virgin fields for cheaper food and living?

Whatever the United States may gain, and I presume that the United States proposals are not wholly altruistic, I see nothing for Canada in reciprocity except a little ready money, which she does not need, and a very long repentance.[39]

One proreciprocity paper was so unkind as to suggest that Kipling once caught pneumonia while waiting for the customs officers, which had caused him to dislike the American tariff, even in the process of being lowered.[40]

At the very close of the campaign the roorback, which the Halifax *Chronicle* defined as "a well-known political device in the United States for stampeding public opinion when sprung on the eve of election," made its appearance. In some instances these had been placed in the record earlier, only to reappear in new quarters just before election; in others they appeared almost simultaneously in widely separated areas too close to the election for successful denial.

38. Toronto *Globe,* August 25; Montreal *Gazette,* August 10, September 5, 1911.

39. Montreal *Star,* September 7, 1911. This was widely quoted.

40. Montreal *Witness,* September 8, 1911.

A few samples may be listed. On September 12 the Montreal *Star* printed accusations that American bills of large denominations were being brought to banks in St. John, New Brunswick, to be changed into smaller figures for use in the campaign. This report was widely circulated during the remaining days.[41] On September 14 the Toronto *News* reported that "the movement upon Ontario constituencies of American election workers, primed with American money and skilled in ballot-switching, personation and the other devices for frustrating the will of the people has begun." Papers of the nineteenth reported a situation which reputedly arose in the Prime Minister's riding of Quebec East where his Conservative opponent, René Leduc, was said to have been drugged and forced by Liberal henchmen to sign an agreement whereby he received five thousand dollars in cash and a civil-service position worth fifteen hundred dollars a year in return for withdrawing his candidacy.[42] On September 15 the Toronto *News* carried an undated excerpt from the *Southern Lumber Journal* (Wilmington, North Carolina): "Give us Cuba, Mexico and Canada and the balance of the world can have the rest. Indeed, if coming events cast their shadows before then it is only a question of time till OLD GLORY—THE STARS AND STRIPES—will triumphantly float from the masthead at Washington, D.C., Havana, Cuba, Mexico City and Ottawa, Canada."[43] The Victoria *Colonist* used the Hearst-Taft-Hoster story.[44]

Not the least-interested spectator at this parade of propaganda was President Taft, whose hopes and future were by now so closely wrapped up in the Canadian campaign. When the annexation furor waxed powerful several suggestions were made that he once and for all disavow American designs.[45] The pressure became so great that

41. Montreal *Star,* September 12, 19; Halifax *Herald,* September 16, 1911.

42. Montreal *Gazette,* Halifax *Herald,* Toronto *Globe,* September 19, 1911.

43. Reprinted in Halifax *Herald,* September 18, 1911.

44. September 19, 1911.

45. For example, by Consul-General Jones of Winnipeg, at some time before August 23, as indicated by a letter of Pepper to Hilles of that date; by S. R. L. Richardson, August 23, 1911. Hilles to Pepper, August 25, 1911. *Taft Papers.*

Hilles suggested that Pepper sound out the Canadian authorities, indicating Taft's willingness "to make his position very emphatic," provided he could do so with propriety. Pepper had communicated with Fielding about the matter by August 29. Meantime Taft approached Bryce (August 26) and asked him to get in touch with Laurier. No reply was forthcoming from this move until September 6, when Bryce informed the President that Laurier deemed it inadvisable for him to say anything at the moment, due to conditions in Canada.[46] By September 7, however, the Prime Minister had changed his mind and sought to convey to Taft his desire for a pronouncement, to be delivered at Sault Ste. Marie, where a speaking tour was scheduled to take the President on September 19.[47] Warned by a telegram from Consul-General Foster that "Conservatives . . . will undoubtedly misconstrue if possible any utterance upon this subject," the President held his peace.[48]

When the returns began to come in on the night of election it became apparent that Conservative predictions would be borne out, but few realized, or had guessed, to what extent. Preëlection estimates varied from a Liberal majority of forty-nine to a Conservative one of twenty-nine.[49] When the votes were finally counted (elections were delayed in a few constituencies) the results showed that the figures of the previous session (Conservatives 85, Liberals 133, Independents 3) had almost been reversed, and that the new Parliament would assemble with Borden in the Prime Minister's place, backed by 133 votes to 86 Liberals (2 Independents)—a sufficient majority to make him independent of the Quebec Nationalists. Conservative victory, while evidently expected by many observers close to the scene, surprised the most ardent partisans by its proportions. The turning of the tide during the closing days of the campaign

46. Hilles to Pepper, August 25; Pepper to Hilles, August 29; Taft to Bryce, August 26; Bryce to Taft, September 6, 1911. *Ibid.*

47. Chase S. Osborn to Taft, September 12, enclosing letter from H. Appleton to himself, September 11, 1911, purporting to report an interview between Appleton and Laurier at Sudbury, September 7. *Ibid.*

48. Foster to Knox, September 15, 1911. *Ibid.*

49. *Can. Ann. Rev.,* 1911, p. 260. John A. Stewart reported to Hilles that a canvass by the Liberal campaign manager indicated a majority of 49 for the Government. September 14, 1911. *Taft Papers.*

was tremendous. Canada had spoken a most emphatic "Nay" to the American proposal.[50]

September 22 found commentators for both sides seeking explanations of the previous day's phenomenon. Reserving personal observations for a concluding chapter, the press has been surveyed by the author with a view to ascertaining the prevailing notes of contemporary opinion. The most obvious and oft-repeated points were suggested by the preëlection discussion—the desire to preserve Canadian nationality and Imperial loyalty against the encroachments of American annexationists occupied most space in the assignment of reasons. A number of papers called attention to the fact, but slightly emphasized during the campaign, that Canadian capital was tooth and nail against the agreement as a danger to its entrenched position in Canada's economic life. Relatively little attempt was made to show any relationship between this fear and the annexation-imperial loyalty cry which was to the fore in the public prints and on the platform.[51] Some admitted that Canadians did not like the United States, and had allowed this antipathy free rein when approaching the ballot box. A few editors mentioned the navy, racial and religious prejudices, and the weaknesses and corruptions of the Liberal administration. Few mentioned the Bourassa campaign as an important factor. And reciprocity itself, as a matter of intrinsic

50. The writer's files contain numerous statements by newspapermen and politicians who went through the campaign, to the effect that the outcome was evident from two to three weeks before the balloting. On the other hand, some have written that the result was as great a surprise to them as to the casual observer.

51. The Montreal *Witness* drew a number of these threads together in one of the best contemporary summaries, September 22:

"An ounce of scare is more potent than a pound of common sense or a ton of reasoned argument. . . . Mr. Bourassa appealed to race prejudice and fear that Canadian lads would be forced from their homes to fight in Britain's wars. The scare was effective. Mr. Borden appealed to race prejudice and the fear that reciprocity would bring about annexation. The scare was effective. . . .

"The Canadian people have been of late in conditions of great progress and are a little high strung. It was, we believe, a scared people that voted yesterday, and the manufacturing monopolies who paid out large sums for inculcating such fears are to-day congratulating themselves that they will have a period of still greater profits at the expense of a fearful nation."

merit, received almost no consideration. Seldom, it is safe to say, has a national campaign been assessed by its late participants with so little attention to the issue by which the whole struggle was precipitated. Here, it almost seemed, was *Hamlet* minus the Melancholy Dane.[52]

52. Most of the papers were content to drop the discussion quickly, as if tired of the whole business. The Montreal *Witness,* however, invited expressions of opinion from its readers, which it published in considerable volume between September 28 and October 14. Upon these in part is based a series of illuminating editorials running into October. The letters, most of which came from Ontario and Quebec, present cumulative evidence to show that religious sentiment was an important factor in these Provinces. In Ontario, Laurier was represented as a Papal tool; in Quebec his loyalty to Britain was used to question his devotion to Rome. Little of this showed itself in the metropolitan papers; perusal of the files of the Toronto *Sentinel,* organ of the ultra-Protestant Orange Order, offers some support to the theory of the importance of the part played by religion. It is probable that further research in the local press would indicate that the present study errs in underestimating the importance of this factor.

CHAPTER XII

SUMMARY AND CONCLUSIONS

THE preceding chapters have unfolded a narrative of mingled forces impinging upon the economic and political life of two nations and their elected leaders. Opening in an effort on the part of these leaders to solve personal and party problems through a mutually advantageous economic bargain, the story broadened gradually through the intervention of interested groups to include the whole scope of national politics and international relations. On each side of the border this enlarging scene involved the alteration of long-standing political relationships, loosed a flood of propaganda intended to obscure the real issue involved, and exerted important influences upon immediate political destinies. To the south it helped to complete a party disintegration already under way and thus contributed to the overturn of 1912. To the north it reaped a more immediate harvest in the defeat of the Liberal government. And behind the scenes on both sides were protected interests anxiously trying to influence political results for private advantage—interests which, defeated by the passage of reciprocity in the American Congress, ultimately triumphed through its defeat by the Canadian people.

The story opened with reciprocity seemingly a dead issue, American indifference to repeated Canadian overtures having turned discouragement into channels of retaliatory high tariffs and Imperial preference. In each nation, however, a tide was setting against continued tariff restrictions as evidenced by the revolt of the Prairies and the hullabaloo created by the failure of the Payne-Aldrich Act to meet advance expectations. These tariff dissatisfactions seemed to fit into a pattern spelling release to President Taft and Premier Laurier from a complex of problems endangering the political future of each. Each chief of state headed a government old in power and hence vulnerable upon its record. Each was plagued by persistent sniping from within his party or without. Each needed means to restore personal and party prestige. Taft's need was the more urgent. Faced with charges of ineffective leadership, with the press hounding him because the Payne-Aldrich Act had not provided duty-free newsprint, and with a Congressional election in the autumn of 1910, his position was becoming more and more precarious. In March, both he and his agents had suggested reciprocity as one way out of this mutual emergency, in connection with the settlement of immediate difficulties raised by the Payne-Aldrich Act. Laurier replied favorably and facilitated a solution of the immediate problem acceptable to the United States on the understanding that in return an opportunity would be offered for reciprocity negotiations. Thus Canada eagerly swallowed the bait offered by the United States, despite previous protestations of indifference.

Crowded by newspaper pressure and the imminent November elections, Taft tried during the later spring to capitalize upon Canadian promises, only to be put off for the time being. Returning to the charge in the early autumn, an unsuccessful attempt was made to score some progress prior to election. Canada evinced an increasing coyness in the November negotiations, possibly because of alarms registered during the summer by domestic business interests. Finally, after considerable jockeying, agreement was reached to the effect that further negotiations should be undertaken with the express understanding that any adjustments on manufactures would be at the expense of the smaller industries. Thus the January agreement, sweeping though it was, applied principally to natural products. A loophole was left whereby the press appetite for free newsprint could be appeased without disturbing the balance of Dominion relations with the Provinces.

Publication of the agreement transferred reciprocity from the realm of diplomacy to that of politics, and subjected it to all the pressures of propaganda whose practitioners were immediately enlisted on both sides of the border. These forces at first tended to cancel each other. Canadian opposition arguments had been more thoroughly canvassed during the period of negotiation and the issue was more clearly before the Canadian people, who as a whole were more likely to be interested in such an arrangement. On the other hand, in the United States all the forces of an aroused newspaper press were enlisted in support of the agreement. This support was assured by an adroit move whereby the bill implementing the agreement contained a provision assuring free newsprint as soon as the United States had acted, regardless of Canada's ultimate decision.

The immediate problem was a legislative one. In the States, Taft, too late to use reciprocity as a makeweight in the election, now stood committed to it as one of the major objectives of his administration. In the short session of Congress, despite his insistence, registered on a hitherto unprecedented scale, the measure was defeated by a combination of other pressing matters, shortness of time, Insurgent opposition, and Republican indifference. This failure was of great moment to both parties to the agreement. In the States it forced the President to call a special session of Congress, where his objective could be gained only by alliance with the Democrats and a final breach in Republican solidarity. Furthermore, it afforded tariff reformers an opportunity, months earlier than otherwise possible, to drag the whole tariff question into the open and still further embarrass the President and his party. Thus reciprocity precipitated the tariff into the background of the 1912 presidential campaign. American inaction prevented Canadian friends of the agreement from applying the pressure which might have resulted either in a favorable Parliamentary decision or a successful appeal to the country, and gave the gathering opposition a chance to solidify. Congressional and press discussion indicated the principal line of approach. The farmer was to be made the main object of pressure and the agreement was to be attacked or defended because of its alleged benefits or injuries to his interest.

The special session found reciprocity inevitably involved with other issues. Taft's task became one of keeping his program ahead of Insurgent efforts at general tariff revision. With Democratic assistance he broke down an Insurgent filibuster and forced his measure through unamended, after which Democrats and Insurgents allied to attack the larger tariff problem. All of this was accomplished to the accompaniment of intraparty bickerings which completed the Republican-Insurgent breach. Again Congressional and press comment centered around the farmer's prospective woes under reciprocity, but various phases of the discussion showed forth, more clearly than before, the real protagonists in the struggle. The press was proreciprocity. The protected interests, threatened by the least breach in the tariff wall, headed the opposition. But they cloaked their own fears behind an earnest solicitude for the son of the soil.

In Canada circumstances conspired against the Government. Proud of its agreement and confident it would win when the time came, the Government, minus the machinery of closure, permitted discussion to proceed unhindered. By the end of February the principal arguments were in the record and Conservative opposition was gathering headway. By April, aided by failure of the United States to act in March, and by stiffening applied to the somewhat shaken Opposition ranks, Conservative policy assumed a tone of obstruction which increasingly betokened developing party strategy. This emerged as an effort to place the Government as fully in the wrong as possible through Parliamentary and press discussion, and then force the issue to the country—a scheme which succeeded late in July when Parliament was dissolved and an election was set for September 21.

Parliamentary debate and press propaganda had meantime been adroitly used to further Conservative ends. Taking what on the face of it was an economic proposition advantageous to Canada's greatest producing interest, the Opposition brought to bear all sorts of arguments to show that instead of economic benefit Canada faced a menace to her national existence and her cherished position as a member of the British Commonwealth. Thus the basis of discussion was shifted from economics to emotion, a much more fruitful area for partisan exploitation. The shift was facilitated to no small degree by the unfortunate utterances of American leaders, too intent upon winning their own part of the battle to see the possible implications of their remarks in another sector. In the process the initiative in argument passed from Liberal hands and that party and its press were presently spending most of their time refuting Conservative attacks rather than launching affirmative thrusts. So, when the date of the election was finally set, the Opposition had improved its position to the point where the September campaign was by no means the hopeless one it would have been in May.

The campaign witnessed a repetition of preceding tactics on an enlarged scale. Despite valiant Liberal efforts to confine the issue to its economic aspects, the Conservative orators and press appealed again to emotional and patriotic factors, together with judicious emphasis upon the shortcomings of their opponents and appeals to racial and religious differences. Thus attacked, the Liberals perforce fought fire with fire and the campaign became a mixture of patriotism, emotion, charges and countercharges, until reciprocity was put to it to keep in the running at all. In this campaign the Conservatives were again aided by American indiscretions and by the fact that, the American campaign being over, all the proreciprocity arguments used in the States were available to its opponents above the border. In the net result Canada assured herself that she was a nation, that the Union Jack would be her flag rather than the Stars and Stripes, and, incidentally, that protection against imports from the United States would continue to be her tariff motto.

The reader who has followed this intensive discussion of a limited period in the neighborly and domestic history of Canada and the United States has doubtless observed certain trends which should be gathered together in conclusion. These may be grouped under three heads—factors affecting the United States primarily, those affecting Canada, and finally those with a common interest. Taking the United States first as the initiator of the movement, the most obvious beneficiary was the American newspaper. Sufficient information has been put in the record to show that the President entered upon reciprocity, if not at the direct behest of the American Newspaper Publishers Association, at least in close harmony with that group's desires. The exchange of letters at the conclusion of the agreement devoted more time to the pulp and paper provisions than to any other single matter. The negotiators, while unable to guarantee free newsprint because of Provincial restrictions, inserted in the agreement a loophole whereby the matter could be arranged by legislative action in the United States, and the bill implementing the agreement contained the necessary provision. The result was that print paper and wood pulp from private lands entered the United States free of duty from July 26, 1911, to October 3, 1913—the only legislative result of the months of negotiation and agitation here described.[1] The *Taft Papers* indicate that Pepper, the chief agent of the State Department, was in close touch with John Norris

1. That this made less difference in the import figures than might have been expected may be inferred from the fact that during the first year the section was in operation imports of pulp decreased 20 per cent and imports of print paper increased less than 5 per cent. U.S. Tar. Comm., *Rec. with Can.*, p. 49.

of the A.N.P.A. all through the negotiation and passage of the proposal and that the Department furnished propaganda material which Norris disseminated through his Association. The well-nigh universal press support of the agreement has been commented upon. The President himself made one of his stoutest (and incidentally one of his most unfortunate) pleas for the agreement before the joint meeting of the Publishers Association and the closely affiliated Associated Press. Thus the power of the press and of the executive office were closely linked to secure an end important to both.

Inaugurated as a means of propitiating the press and of starting a backfire against the tariff-reform sentiment rife in the land, reciprocity rapidly came to be one of the major objectives of Taft's administration, upon the success of which he staked his present and much of his future. As far as the President personally was concerned, the whole episode marked a milestone in his evolution as an executive leader. It showed him capable of assuming the initiative, of dragooning unwilling support, and of pushing an important matter to a successful conclusion. This was done, however, at a considerable cost, as it widened the already perceptible breach in Republican ranks and hurried the Insurgent exodus, on the way before reciprocity was an issue. It also hastened the inevitable by allowing Congressional discussion of the tariff in the summer of 1911, instead of postponing this divisive factor until the winter. The episode therefore played an appreciable part in the background of the turmoil of 1912. What part it would have played had the Canadian decision been different offers an interesting field for speculation.

In Canada the agreement caught one party on the upgrade and the other on the downward slope and offered a dramatic setting for a change which would in the nature of things have occurred before long, but which might have been temporarily averted except for the fact that important interests, which in 1908 had supported Laurier, transferred their allegiance to his opponent.[2] It found a Government confident of its strength and incautious in its strategy, which

2. The following Canadian analyses of the agreement, some contemporary and some of later vintage, will be of assistance in evaluating that side of the episode: Canadian, A, "Why Canada Rejected Reciprocity," *Yale Review,* N.S., 1:173–188 (January, 1912); Dafoe, *Sifton,* pp. 363–369; Keenleyside, *Canada and the U.S.,* chapter on the "Reciprocity Episode of 1911";

allowed itself to be gradually maneuvered into a position where strength was of no avail and strategic control passed to the Opposition. The time element, whereby Canadian action was postponed at first because of American inaction and later because of Conservative obstruction, was an important factor in this transfer of the whip hand from Liberal to Conservative. Once an election was inevitable the Conservative position became more and more advantageous. An issue, originally economic and of considerable intrinsic appeal, was precipitated into a political campaign where its merits could be easily slurred over and soft-pedaled in favor of other matters more likely to arouse patriotic fear or fervor. Conservative tactics took essentially the form of saying "No" to reciprocity, and "Yes" to the British connection, which relieved the party of the necessity of saying too much about its affirmative program and brought it into office with a clean slate upon which to write. At the same time the whole episode left Canada, by inference at least, committed to another period of high protection, whereas the net result in the States had been in the opposite direction. From the standpoint of the Dominion's growth the affair marked Canada's coming of age through her emphatic assertion of nationhood.

Looking at the matter from both sides of the border, the similarity of the burden of reciprocity's defenders is apparent. On each side they had to assume the double task of proving that reciprocity would not result in injury, and that it would be a positive aid. In Canada this task proved too heavy. Furthermore, it so happened that almost every proreciprocity argument suggested at least one stronger antireciprocity argument, once the safe ground of economic advantage was left behind. Again, the fact that the American campaign had been successfully concluded before the agreement was submitted to the arbitrament of the Canadian people afforded powerful ammunition for its opponents. If it was so good for the United States, it was at least arguable that there must be an Ethiopian lurking in the woodpile from the standpoint of Canada. Moreover, all the arguments used to put the proposal across in the American Congress and

Laut, "Robert Laird Borden," pp. 555–560; Patton, "Reciprocity with Canada," pp. 574–596; Pepper, C. M., *American Foreign Trade*, New York, 1919, pp. 261–262; Skelton, O. D., "Canada's Rejection of Reciprocity," *Journal of Political Economy*, 19:726–731 (November, 1911).

press were available to the Canadian Opposition. Thus reciprocity's friends always carried a double burden and its Canadian supporters an added weight in the election campaign.

So far no attempt has been made to assess the economic pros and cons of the agreement. The student of the matter is at once faced with the fact that relatively little statistical preparation was made by the negotiators. There was some effort to present statistics during the campaign, but hardly enough information was brought out upon which to base an accurate judgment. Decision must be based, therefore, upon such information as may be gathered from the welter of claim and counterclaim which characterized the contemporary scene, and upon the probabilities inherent in the case. It seems to the writer unlikely that any vast change in prices, wages, or the cost of living would have resulted on either side of the border. Doubtless local areas on both sides of the line would have suffered at times, as would producers of particular commodities: Maine potatoes might have invaded markets hitherto sacred to the Maritimes, and Canadian dairy products might have competed in northern New York cities. The Northwestern wheatgrower would probably have faced dangerous competition from the Canadian product in the Minneapolis market. Loudly as these interests and their representatives might shout, however (and few could shout more loudly), the likelihood is that over such a long frontier and with so many commodities involved, the net result would have been moderating rather than revolutionary. It is doubtful whether the "larger market" would have proven other than mildly advantageous to the Canadian producer, whereas the American consumer would probably have reaped little reward by the time Canadian products reached him through the American middleman. The most important effects of reciprocity, had the agreement been put into operation, would not have been what it actually accomplished, but what it presaged.

One of the most interesting phases of the study is that of the propaganda methods used by the contestants. The farmer in the States rapidly became a symbol around which rallied interests that in normal times would have been hard put to it to recognize, much less wax lachrymose, over his sad plight. The inalienable right of the American agriculturist to the bounties of the protective system had been proclaimed since the days of William McKinley's tariff, but seldom or never had this right been so adroitly forwarded by such well-paid agents whose boots had never been soiled by prairie mud. On the other hand, seldom had the press, from metropolitan journal down through country weekly, displayed such unalloyed affection for the farmer and been so unselfishly willing to assure him that his interests would be safe under an agreement which incidentally allowed the press to secure more cheaply the raw materials of its trade. Seldom have organized pressure groups waged a more intensive campaign to influence Congress and public opinion in the United States. In Canada a like attempt was made to stress the farmer's position under reciprocity and to prove that economically it was good or bad for him. Here, however, the principal objective of the opponents of the agreement was to distract attention from its economic side; hence a substitute was sought and soon found in the waving of the flag and the proclamation from the housetops and from blood-red headlines that Canada was British and would so remain until the last drop of ink had been spilled to prevent her annexation by the hungry ogre to the south. North as well as south of the line organized propaganda had its heyday, and north as well as south it reaped its reward.

But propaganda is not self-starting. It is obvious that the newspapers which backed the President and the lobbyists who opposed his reciprocity before the committee, Congress, and country were not interested in the farmer for himself alone. It is equally apparent that in Canada the Conservative high command and the journals which voiced its pleas wrote their words and their headlines with tongue in cheek; whatever the man in the rural riding may have been taught to think by cries of annexation and loss of the British connection, no Canadian in a position of real authority believed that either fate faced the Dominion in the predictable future. The key to the propaganda, and with it of course to the opposition to reciprocity on both sides of the border, is to be found in the fact that beneficiaries of the protective system in both countries feared the breaching of the wall behind which they had flourished for so many years. Solicitude for the farmer, loyalty, imperialism, all meant one thing to the groups which used all these pleas to avert a danger which knows no national boundaries—the danger to a self-interest well developed and long entrenched. Any analysis of the reciprocity episode which stops with the explanation that the American farmer opposed reciprocity, and that it was defeated in Canada because of the annexation-loyalty cries, misses the fundamental factor involved; the farmer may have been opposed, and the average Canadian may have feared the United States, but this opposition and these fears were assiduously cultivated, if not implanted, by interests motivated by a common fear of the consequences of lower tariffs.

One last observation might be made to the effect that the 1911 episode marks a stage in the evolution of reciprocity procedure. The reciprocity of 1854 was effectuated by treaty; it ran for a definite period and was then subject to denunciation. At the earliest possible opportunity it was abandoned. The reciprocity of 1911 was of indefinite duration and was to be effectuated by legislative enactment; the lessons of the story just told would argue the dangers of such procedure in countries so closely situated and subject to the play of propagandist factors. The reciprocity of 1936, no matter what its duration or the circumstances under which it is abrogated, was placed in operation with an efficiency and lack of fanfare which at least argues the possibility that nations may learn by experience.

BIBLIOGRAPHY

COLLECTED SOURCES

Canadian Tariff Negotiations: EXCEPTIONALLY CONFIDENTIAL. TO BE FILED AS A CONFIDENTIAL DOCUMENT AND ISSUED ONLY UPON THE WRITTEN ORDER OF THE SECRETARY OF STATE. Printed pamphlet in the *Philander C. Knox Papers,* Library of Congress, covering negotiations up to November 18, 1910.

Eugene G. Hay Papers. Library of Congress.

Philander C. Knox Papers. Library of Congress.

Newfoundland Tariff Negotiations: EXCEPTIONALLY CONFIDENTIAL. TO BE FILED AS A CONFIDENTIAL DOCUMENT AND ISSUED ONLY UPON THE WRITTEN ORDER OF THE SECRETARY OF STATE. Printed pamphlet in the *Philander C. Knox Papers,* Library of Congress, covering negotiations up to November 26, 1910.

United States Department of State: Reciprocity. Bundle of miscellaneous correspondence and memoranda in the Archives of the Department; much of the material is reproduced in *Canadian Tariff Negotiations,* above, which is cited wherever possible because of greater accessibility. This item is cited as *State Department Archives,* with identification of individual document.

William Howard Taft Papers. Library of Congress.

GOVERNMENT DOCUMENTS

The Congressional Record. Washington, D.C., 1874 ff.

Daily Consular and Trade Reports: Department of Commerce, Bureau of Manufactures. Washington, D.C., 1910.

Documents Relating to Reciprocity with Canada. Washington, D.C., 1911. Senate Documents, 61st Congress, 3d Session, Vol. 84, particularly the following:

> No. 828: *Letter of Nahum J. Bachelder Relating to Reciprocity with Canada.*
>
> No. 862: *Papers Relating to Reciprocity with Canada.*

Official Report of the Debates of the House of Commons of the Dominion of Canada. Third Session, Eleventh Parliament, 1–2 George V, 1910–1911. 5 vols., Ottawa, 1910–1911.

Pulp and News-Print Industry: Report by the Tariff Board Relative to Pulp and News-Print Industry. Washington, D.C., 1911. Senate Document 31, 62d Congress, 1st Session.

Reciprocity with Canada: Hearings before the Committee on Finance of the United States Senate on H.R. 32216 An Act to Promote Reciprocal Trade

Relations with the Dominion of Canada and for Other Purposes. Washington, D.C., 1911. *Senate Document 834, 61st Congress, 3d Session.*

Reciprocity with Canada: Hearings before the Committee on Finance of the United States Senate Sixty-Second Congress on H.R. 4412 An Act to Promote Reciprocal Trade Relations with the Dominion of Canada and for Other Purposes. Washington, D.C., 1911. *Senate Document 56, 62d Congress, 1st Session.*

Reciprocity with Canada: Hearings before the Committee on Ways and Means of the House of Representatives 61st Congress, 3d Session on H.R. 32216. Washington, D.C., 1911. (No document number assigned.)

Reciprocity with Canada. Washington, D.C., 1911. *House Report 2150, 61st Congress, 3d Session.*

Reciprocity with Canada. Washington, D.C., 1911. *House Report 3, 62d Congress, 1st Session.*

Reciprocity with Canada: Papers in the Consideration of Bill (H.R. 32216) Relating to Reciprocity with Canada. Washington, D.C., 1911. *Senate Document 862, 61st Congress, 3d Session.*

Report of Proceedings in the Hearing by Members of the Government of the Farmers' Delegation, December 16, 1910, With Correspondence Preliminary to the Hearing. Ottawa, 1911. 1 George V. Sessional Papers No. 113. A. 1911.

Report on Pulp and Paper Investigation. Washington, D.C., 1909. *House Report 2206, 60th Congress, 2d Session.*

Reports from His Majesty's Ambassador at Washington respecting a Reciprocal Tariff Arrangement between Canada and the United States. London, 1911. Commercial Dispatch No. 1, 1911.

RUTTER, F. R., *Tariff Relations of Canada.* Washington, D.C., 1911. Department of Commerce and Labor; Bureau of Manufactures, Tariff Series, No. 26.

Statutes of the United States of America, Passed at the First Session of the Fifty-first Congress, 1889–1890, and Recent Treaties and Executive Proclamations. Washington, D.C., 1890.

Tariff Relations between the United States and the Dominion of Canada: Correspondence Concerning Negotiations 1910. Ottawa, 1910.

To Promote Reciprocal Relations with Canada. Washington, D.C., 1911. *Senate Report 3, 62d Congress, 1st Session.*

United States Tariff Commission, *Reciprocity with Canada: A Study of the Arrangement of 1911.* Washington, D.C., 1920.

OTHER PRINTED SOURCES

BEMIS, S. F. (ed.), *The American Secretaries of State and Their Diplomacy.* New York, 1927 ff. 10 vols.

BORDEN, HENRY (ed.), *Robert Laird Borden: His Memoirs.* New York, 1938. 2 vols.

BUTT, ARCHIE, *Taft and Roosevelt: The Intimate Letters of Archie Butt, Military Aide.* Garden City, New York, 1930. 2 vols.

DAFOE, JOHN W., *Clifford Sifton in Relation to His Times.* Toronto, 1931.

DAFOE, JOHN W., *Laurier: A Study in Canadian Politics.* Toronto, 1922.

HACKER, L. M., and KENDRICK, B. B., *The United States Since 1865.* New York, 1932.

HARPELL, JAMES J., *Canadian National Economy: The Cause of High Prices and Their Effect upon the Country.* Toronto, 1911.

HOPKINS, J. CASTELL (comp.), *The Canadian Annual Review of Public Affairs.* Toronto, 1901 ff.

KEENLEYSIDE, HUGH L., *Canada and the United States: Some Aspects of the History of the Republic and the Dominion.* New York, 1929.

PEPPER, CHARLES M., *American Foreign Trade: The United States as a World Power in the New Era of International Commerce.* New York, 1919.

PORRITT, EDWARD, *Sixty Years of Protection in Canada, 1846–1907: Where Industry Leans on the Politicians.* London, 1908.

PRESTON, W. T. R., *My Generation of Politics and Politicians.* Toronto, 1927.

PYLE, JOSEPH GILPIN, *The Life of James J. Hill.* Garden City, New York, 1917. 2 vols.

PAMPHLETS

Numbers refer to files of the Dominion Archives, Ottawa.

BOURASSA, HENRI, *The Reciprocity Agreement and its Consequences as viewed from the Nationalist standpoint.* Montreal, 1911. 3844.

BOURASSA, HENRI, *The Story of the Nationalist-Conservative Alliance Told by Henri Bourassa, the Nationalist Leader.* Ottawa, 1914. In volume numbered 4628 ff.

Bulletin of the National Association of Wool Manufacturers. Boston, 1911.

Canadian National League Campaign of 1911 Against Reciprocity with the United States of America. n.p., n.d. 3849.

Circular of Information of the National Association of Manufacturers of the United States of America. Number 43. Philadelphia, 1911.

Egg Money, the Rightful Perquisite of the Women on the Canadian Farms. n.p., n.d. In volume containing Nos. 3824–3827.

HAWKES, ARTHUR, *An Appeal to the British-Born.* n.p., 1911. 3821.

HAY, EUGENE G., *Reciprocity with Canada: Report of Eugene G. Hay, to the Advisory Board of the Minnesota Branch of the National Reciprocity League, upon the Present Attitude of United States and Canada and the Prospects for Reciprocity between the two Countries.* Minneapolis, n.d. (probably 1903).

PALMER, LINCOLN B., *Light on the Print Paper Situation: Being an address delivered by Lincoln B. Palmer . . . before the New York Associated Dailies at Albany, New York.* New York, 1917.

Reciprocity: A Retrospect. Ottawa, 1915. In volume numbered 4628 ff.

Reciprocity with Canada: Address of President Taft before the Western Economic Society at Orchestra Hall, Chicago, June 3, 1911. Washington, 1911. 3852.

Ross, SIR GEORGE W., *Reciprocity.* n.p., n.d. 3609.

Sixty-Eighth Annual Report of the Council of the Montreal Board of Trade: Being for the Year 1910. Montreal, 1911.

PERIODICALS: ARTICLES

Canadian, A, "Why Canada Rejected Reciprocity." *Yale Review,* N.S., 1: 173–188 (January, 1912).

FOSTER, GEORGE E., "Canadian Autonomy and American Reciprocity." *The Nineteenth Century and After,* 69:961–975 (June, 1911).

FOSTER, GEORGE E., "Reciprocity with the United States." *University Magazine* (Toronto), 9:550–563 (December, 1910).

HAMMOND, M. O., "The Tragedy of Reciprocity." *The Canadian Magazine of Politics, Science, Art and Literature,* 38:84–91 (November, 1911).

HOPKINS, J. CASTELL, "Canada's Conservative Policies." *The North American Review,* 194:818–825 (December, 1911).

LAUT, AGNES C., "Robert Laird Borden, the New Premier of Canada, Who Heads the First Conservative Ministry in Canada for Fifteen Years." *The American Review of Reviews: An International Magazine,* 44:555–560 (November, 1911).

OSBORNE, JOHN BALL, "Commercial Relations of the United States with Canada." *The Annals of the American Academy of Political and Social Science,* 32:330–342 (September, 1908).

PATTON, H. S., "Reciprocity with Canada. The Canadian Viewpoint." *The Quarterly Journal of Economics,* 35:574–596 (August, 1921).

PORRITT, E., "Canada's Tariff Mood Towards the United States." *The North American Review,* 182:565–578 (April, 1906).

PORRITT, E., "Laurier's Defeat." *The Independent,* 71:676–678 (September 28, 1911).

PORRITT, E., "The Value of Political Editorials." *The Atlantic Monthly,* 105:62–68 (January, 1910).

SIFTON, CLIFFORD, "Reciprocity." *The Annals of the American Academy of Political and Social Science,* 45:20–29 (January, 1913).

SKELTON, O. D., "Canada's Rejection of Reciprocity." *The Journal of Political Economy,* 19:726–731 (November, 1911).

SKELTON, O. D., "Reciprocity." *Queen's Quarterly,* 18:329–337 (April–June, 1911).

SWARTZ, WILLIS G., "The Proposed Canadian-American Reciprocity Agreement of 1911." *Journal of Economic and Business History,* 3:118–148 (November, 1930).

INDEX

DATE DUE

41956

RECIPROCITY, 1911

A STUDY IN CANADIAN-AMERICAN RELATIONS